HOMICIDE IN FACT AND FICTION

An Analytical Study of the Statistical Reality and Its Literary Portrayal

Alvin Rudoff
and
T. C. Esselstyn

HOMICIDE IN FACT AND FICTION
An Analytical Study of the Statistical Reality and Its Literary Portrayal

The Rhodes-Fulbright Library

by Alvin Rudoff and T. C. Esselstyn

ProdCode: CSS/250/4.65/221/32

Library of Congress
Catalog in Publication

00-106795

International Standard Book Number

1-55605-310-X

Printed in the United States of America

Wyndham Hall Press
Bristol, IN 46507-9460

For Belle and Norma

TABLE OF CONTENTS

LIST OF TABLES

PREFACE

Violence and its lethal outcome remains a public concern whether it is increasing or decreasing. Conceivably this is because it is recognized that it has always been with us and is likely to remain a part of social life. The media too are a part of social life. They influence the public for good or evil while they inform and entertain. Does this influence extend to behavior of a violent and lethal nature? This work endeavors to scrutinize this question. Homicide in fact and in fiction is explored and compared using the FBI Uniform Crime Reports for the fact and the American mystery/detective genre for the fiction. Both deal with the process of killing – the reasons, the weapons, the chase, the capture, and the outcome. Homicide is traced in history and America while the best of the genre is the form of the literature. Additionally, myth, the bible, and immigration are assessed for their contribution to the kind of attitudes, values, and behavior that effect the American psyche with consequences for the process of killing. The major target of the endeavor is those students of, or those interested in, and/or involved in the Administration of Justice System.

The genre encompassed 115 novels. The authors wish to express their appreciation to Belle Rudoff for her part in the reading and the structured summarizing of the particular novels. Helen Boesser was also helpful in that capacity. The authors maintain the full responsibility for the contents of the book.

CHAPTER ONE

INTRODUCTION

It is often said that America is a violent country. The outcome of the violence is, too often, homicide. Riesman once observed that to understand America one should go to south Bend on a Saturday afternoon for a football game. With all the violence, America emphasizes gentleness and kindness and is well-known for generosity and sentimentality. Is this hypocrisy? Probably not! Violence and homicide, gentility and sentimentality are world-wide phenomena (perhaps even universal if there is extraterrestrial intelligence). It even predates civilization and includes most life forms. Its presence is ubiquitous, but its extent and form varies – a variation that is not infinite. Football may be one example of violence and its impact, the media is a more significant other.

Football may be an example of violence in play with its consequences debatable. For some it teaches positive behavior like sportsmanship. For others it encourages violence as a way to get ahead. The media too are well-known examples of potential influences on violence. Most people are influenced one way or another by a book they read, a movie they see, or a song they hear. The consequences could be for good or evil – or perhaps both for the same person. But the connection is complex and the attempts to assess the connection are manifold. The results are far from decisive with some consensus on aggression as an outcome. However, aggression is not necessarily violence but could be part of play, work, or everyday interactions. Will a book focusing on murder so influence the reader as to lead to a real homicide? It is highly unlikely that someone will read a mystery and be so effected as to commit a homicide. Perhaps the best possibility for a connection is with a copycat. But even in this case, the impact would be to copy a common motive or technique and not generate an impulse to kill. If a killer claims he got the idea to kill from a book, it would be a specific book. Why then condemn the whole medium or just the genre? What about the vast majority of such books that do not lead to a homicide? And what of such books that may turn someone away from a homicide? If a killer claims another killer as his idol and reproduces the idol's crimes, we call it a copy-cat crime. We do not condemn all people. If we extrapolate a killing from a person to the people and a book to the medium, it should be extrapolated further to history because it must have happened before – and history is part fact and part fiction.

This book examines the facts and fictions about homicide in America plus much else. For instance, Chapter II presents a history of homicide in broad general terms from early man through Western civilization. A list of well-known killers is included. Chapter III presents a lengthy review of scholarly efforts to describe homicide in America. It summarizes the work of a national commission and one professional workshop on violence. The question: is America a violent nation? Is addressed. The frequency of violent acts recorded in the Uniform Crime Reports is shown for selected years. Kinds of homicide are discussed, including murder as one of its forms. The several efforts to develop a typology of murders are included. The concept of a subculture of violence is reviewed as analyzed by Wolfgang, Ferracuti, and others, and still other kinds of murders.

Fiction is usually uncommon and even bizarre. If there is a link, it is more likely to evoke a feeling or attitude and the act occur from a predisposition and then the motive and method would be different from the source. We do know that some writers produce such books mimicking or reporting on a homicide – a case in fiction or fact. The question is do they reflect each other? Real homicide is rarely a creative act; fictional homicide is rarely an impulsive one. In both fact and fiction the carnage is ancient and wide-spread. How can one person kill another? Notwithstanding the motive, perhaps one way is to redefine the victim emotionally as pre-human (animal), non-human (property), or quasi-human (primitive). This book examines both the fact and the fiction of homicide to see how close they come to each other – whether they are linked in any way. This is not a search for causal relationships, just how close they image each other.

The genre – the distinctive novels – of crime, mystery, and murder are reviewed in Chapter IV. Here one meets pioneers in crime and detective fiction, such as Poe in *Murders in the Rue Morgue*, Wilkie Collins with *The Moonstone*, Dickens with *The Mystery of Edwin Drood*, and of course Conan Doyle with the many tales of Sherlock Holmes. There are dozens of others. Agatha Christie is known world wide. Prominent too are Dorothy Sayers, Dashiell Hammet, Mickey Spillane, Ellery Queen, Naigo Marsh and many well-known authors who have contributed to the development of the crime novel. All of these raise questions: Do crime novels increase crime rates?

American crime fiction dates from James Fenimore Cooper, Nathaniel Hawthorne, Mark Twain, to name just three. How the ethos controlled the plot of the genre and reflected the era when written have been of interest to literary critics, some of whom have traced changes in the scope of mystery tales as times changed. These issues are explored in Chapter V. Also in that section there is discussion of the method in this book to study what, if any, differences there may be between the facts of crime and the fictions adopted by crime writers.

There is considerable evidence that violence and homicide are pristine impelling forces traceable to animals and the earliest of humans. Did homicides occur among the Neanderthals? It probably did if we impose our rules upon an anthropoid interaction. One chapter reports on the likelihood that homicide began millions of years ago with prehistoric man. Using some anthropological data such an incident is considered.

In fact, the search is for some of the potential influences that served as a legacy for the violence in America. Some are overt (perhaps our Revolution), others less so. Other considerations deal with homicide and murder in ancient myths and legends which are familiar to many of us even now, and which raise anew our bafflement over the persistence of violent behavior regardless of all efforts to dampen it down. The bible is not only a guide to justice and morality. It is also a chronicle of war, betrayal, murder, and violent death from the time of Cain, through the life of David, and crucifixion, and the martydom of saints. Immigration has kept the so-called melting pot hot enough to pour out great quantities of art, material goods, scientific marvels, and a staggering number of technologies. Has it also affected the incidence of its crime, and if so, how? Have its crime rates increased or decreased, and in either case, what is the causal link, if any? These are the issues treated in several chapters.

Hellenistic Greece and Imperial Rome had a profound impact upon the modern Western world. Greece flourished in the first millennium BC – a Golden Age of civilization. Indirectly America too was affected by that archaic time. The 5th century BC witnessed the emergence of Classical Greek Art and Architecture. The oracles were conceived as the intermediaries between gods and men. Consultations were ritualized and response cryptic. The most famous of the oracles was located at Delphi. The Greek anthropomorphic imagination created an Olympian pantheon in the image of man with all his faults and virtues. Art and Architecture in the style of ancient Greece and Rome influenced the Italian Renaissance and the neoclassical style in England and America in the early 19th century. The Hippocratic Oath of physicians today is based upon the ideas and principles of the ancient Greek physician Hippocrates. The Romans gave us law. The Olympic Games have survived and grown into a periodic extravaganza. Greek democracy is (more or less) mimicked in many places around the world. The principle of inalienable rights has been linked to the idea of higher or natural law. That idea appeared in the works of Greek dramatists and Greek and Roman stoics. Ancient Athens prospered under people like Cimon and Pericles with the genius of men like Aeschylus, Euripides, Sophocles, Socrates, and Plato. The Romans adopted and modified a good deal of the Greek creations and equally prosperous under Caesar Augustus and genius the like of Virgil, Julius Caesar, and Cicero. Europe and subsequently the United States were fertile areas for the influence of Greco-Roman civilization. The legacy covers a large part of our culture. The mythology of Greece and Rome could be a distinct part of this legacy. There are moments where myth spills over into the bible. According to the bible two hostile forces will appear on earth before the end of the world – Gog and Magog. In Celtic mythology gogmagog was a chieftain in England slain by one Corineus.

George Santayana suggested that to ignore history is to repeat its failures. The past offers a legacy – a bequest from the past to the future. America is a nation that has been effected by a number of such influences. The bible is one of them. It is considered the sacred scriptures of Judaism and Christianity. It is a source of divine revelation and a blueprint for moral living. The Old Testament is accepted by Christians and Jews as sacred, except for Apocrypha. The Roman Catholic Church and Eastern Orthodox Church accept parts of the Apocrypha, but the Jews and Protestants do not. The New Testament is accepted as sacred only by the Christians. The earliest books of the Old Testament were collected from older sources dating long before 1000 BC. The Hebrew text was adopted c. AD 100. The New Testament was written in Greek during the early part of the Christian era. Puritanism was the reform movement that developed in the Church of England during the latter part of the 16th century. It's origin was in the writings and reasoning of early reformers like Thomas Cranmer and later ones like John Calvin. They sought to purify the church of any remaining influence of Roman Catholicism. They were faithful to the bible. They influenced all aspects of life and were responsible for the founding of the North American colonies. Our Protestant Ethic came from this ascetic branch of Protestantism offering a religious and historical account with a biblical source as a benefit. The source is rife with violence. In Genesis Cain murdered Abel. Though the Commandments tell us not to kill, there are enough killing incidents to permit readers to interpret or misinterpret them to commit such acts.

America is known as a country of immigrants. Those who came brought with them patterns of the culture of their home country. This would be exposed to a process of accommodation in the host country. In this process there is an exchange – an uneven one – where the immigrant's culture passes something off to the new one and takes on the bulk of the new culture. Immigrants are not always met with open arms and many were victims of discrimination and had difficulty accommodating to the new culture. The earliest immigrants did not arrive to an unpopulated land. There was a native population which was cruelly treated but still survives today. Called Indians they are the Native-Americans. The Puritans were followed by a host of others from almost every country in the world. The Africans came as slaves and some from Great Britain came as prisoners or indentured servants. In the 19th and 20th century about 70 million people came to the United States. Upheavals of different kinds and at different times generated a multitude of immigrants to the "Promised Land." Each generation became "American," a definition that changed over the years as it embraced the legacy offered by the immigrants. This legacy covered many facets of culture such as language, food, life styles, personality characteristics, and ways and reasons for loving, and ways and reasons for hating. They came and most assimilated a national characteristic that included their own legacy.

The data source for the fact and fiction of homicide was identified. Fact came from the Uniform Crime Reports of two periods, an early and later one to coincide with the fiction source of the mystery genre of two periods, an early and later one. The analysis covered a description of the fact data, fiction data, and then a comparison of fact and fiction data. The essential method was Content Analysis and the comparisons utilized the chi square statistic.

Written and antediluvian history offers a legacy from various sources that help define and construct our culture. Relative to violence and homicide it makes one wonder why there is so little rather than so much. The answer lies in the manifold ways in which the strain towards it is controlled, modified, or eliminated, through the mechanisms to offset the pressure.

Emile Durkheim, the French sociologist, insisted that crime was both functional and normal. He wrote, "there is, then, no phenomenon that presents more indisputably all the symptoms of normality, since it appears closely connected with the conditions of all collective life," (Durkheim 1964: 66). He argued that there would always be some individuals who differ from the collective type and some were bound to be criminal in character. Their criminality is not an intrinsic quality of their acts, but is so defined by the collectivity (This notion is important for labeling theorists). Crime then is "bound up with the fundamental conditions of all social life, and by the very fact, is useful, because these conditions of which it is a part are themselves indispensable to the normal evolution of morality and law," (Durkheim 1964: 70).

Tanay (1976: 25) supports the assumption that crime is normal as he states, "Prevention requires, in my opinion, first the acceptance of homicide as a natural phenomenon. People will always kill people. The issue is not whether homicide will occur, but how many."

Crime is functional because it can lead to social change. Without deviations, a society can become stagnant. This does not mean that the more the violence and killing, the better the society. Though crime may be normal, it becomes pathological when it is morbid. "No doubt it is possible that crime itself will have abnormal forms, as, for example, when its rate is unusually high," (Durkheim 1964: 66). In short, the presence of crime is normal and becomes morbid when excessive for a given social system.

Rudoff (1971) examined this idea with a morbidity ratio which compared a community's crime rate over two periods of time to see if the changes in the crime rates were morbid or what could be expected with the changes in demographics. The crime rate remained normal for that community at that time.

Homicide in fact and fiction surveys the realities in homicide and the imagination in fiction. Where possible, the two aspects are compared and tested for significance. Books sporadically become patterns for reality and reality frequently becomes material for a book, but other than a mystery novel of an actual crime, does it become a pattern for that genre?

Basically there are three major themes in this book. First, there is no single explanation for homicide. Second, homicide occurs everywhere. Third, the facts about homicide differ from the fictions about it.

CHAPTER TWO

A HISTORY OF HOMICIDE

A Lethal Legacy?

Hunting and gathering dominated human life for at least two million years (Leakey & Lewin 1978). This episode lasting through the late Pliocene and Pleistocene epochs helped form the mind, body, and social demeanor of our inchoate ancestors and translated into what we are today. The seeds of homicide along with those of compassion, and cooperation had their roots that long ago. And then there was what was learned from the other animals – what to eat, how to eat, where to go and how to go, and how to interact and how to kill. The capacity to kill is not merely a contemporary phenomenon. Animals kill, mostly to survive, but on occasion, perhaps anthropomorphically, the death could be a homicide. The male lion will kill cubs if he can get to them. Researchers have found cases of killing among egret chicks as a result of sibling rivalry. The two eldest chicks in the nest often attack and kill the youngest. This is being recognized in increasing numbers of species. Harry Truman once said, "The only thing new in the world is the history you don't know."

Life was complex; hunting was often less than successful. Gathering included nuts, roots, vegetables, and fruits. Men hunted, women gathered, and they survived. Their needs were finite, there was relative affluence, and ample recreation. Hunting gains were shared as the hunt was shared. Gathering was not shared as it was done individually, though often in the presence of other women. Since gathering was more successful than hunting, the more "wives" one had, the more bountiful the larder. Women developed a keen sense of where to find nutritional food. Men became skillful naturalists with a remarkable understanding of animal behavior. Both hunter and gatherer underutilized the food source in the environment and therefore preserved it in the area for longer periods. Abortions and infanticide (especially females) were common but covert. They practiced exogamy. They belonged to the animal kingdom and evidenced similar behavior, principally before socialization and organization took hold. Therefore the scarcity of important resources like food and females

increased the prospect for disputes. Some of those without either may have seized the opportunity to steal both or either.
The early encounters were individual affairs not group – homicide not war. There were a number of remains of early hominids found with facial and cranial fractures. Speculation has attributed it to the force of a blunt instrument; some suggest it was the result of damage by the pressure of sediment, rocks, or movement after their burial. As weapons were developed to kill game, they were quickly applied to the killing of each other. Retaliation could follow. A theft or a retaliation could involve homicide. It seems that man, like other animals, has always killed members of his own species.

The development of agriculture, the notion of territory and property, the emergence of organization, culture, and politics led to the proliferation of acts defined as crime, including homicide. Those were the sources of crime and homicide, not biology or evolutionary factors. The idea of man's killing instinct was popularized by Robert Ardrey's (1961) *African Genesis* and Knorad Lorenz's (1966) *On Aggression.* Ardrey referred to man as "Cain's Children." But others (Erich Fromm, Quincy Wright, Louis Leakey) portray man as peaceful and propose that the aggressiveness grew proportionately to civilization. John Calhoun's (1983) experiments with rats indicated that excessive behavior occurred with crowded conditions, as would be found in densely populated areas. Freud strongly suggests that we are born criminals and learn not to be one. Perhaps in modern times violence is romaniticised by the young and reinforced by the media which retards maturity. Why man misbehaves remains recondite and moot. Theories abound; proof is sparse. But whether explained genetically, biologically, psycologically, or environmentally, it occurs. It happened in the inchoate past; it happens in the present. It occurs in animals; it occurs in men.

Some anthropologists comment that feud, bloodshed, rampant killings and *lex talionis* are reported to be widespread among primitive nonliterate peoples, but the facts do not support this. There is limited evidence of feuds in nonliterate societies (Hoebel and Weaver). The very fear of feud is enough to evade it by less violent and more symbolic means. Prior to the establishment of white man's law among the Eskimo, infanticide, invalidicide, suicide, and senilicide were socially justified. Wife stealing was often settled peaceably. However, it sometimes gave rise to vengeance and murder as much as two generations after the incident. Prior to the coming of American and Philippine national law, the Ifugao tried to settle all serious disputes through *monkalum* – a prominent member of an area who served as mediator. If he succeeded, peace followed. If he failed, which was seldom, the result was murder of the accused or any of his relatives, and later feud. Among the Nuer in the African Sudan, a mediator was also used to help settle serious disputes. He was known as the Priest of the Earth. The Nuer tried to avoid feud and sought to maintain peace between villages and family lineages without calling on the Priest of the Earth through payment of fines by the murderer's family to the family of the victim. If this failed, the Priest of the Earth could impose a curse which would doom all litigants, their crops and cattle.

Gluckman (1968) holds that murder, feud, and vendetta rarely occurred among preliterate peoples in Africa. While conflicts and enmities existed between individuals and groups, there was an overall strain toward unity and group harmony. Thus when killing occurred which pitted one family or group against another, there were likely to emerge many other families and groups which then generated pressure to settle the dispute before it erupted into large-scale violence. Killings, feuds, and vendettas were remembered and became embellished in tribal legends. What tended to be forgotten were the many disputes that were settled by compromise, marriage, gifts, and many other measures which succeeded in maintaining peace within and between many African tribes.

In the Trobiands, inter-tribal hostility diminished with the slow rise of trade relations between individuals and tribes which up to that time were murderous head hunters (Oliver 1995). Australian administrators imposed an effective measure of peace between hostile and warring tribes, but this was disturbed by Christian missionaries who unwittingly stimulated ancient rivalries as Catholic and Methodist converts proclaimed their exclusive religious truths as taught to them by mission priests and pastors. Quarrels between individuals occasionally resulted in murder, but this was seen as a minor incident unless a tribal chief decreed otherwise, in which case the killing was a cause for organized war between families, clans, or tribes.

The history of Spanish and American relations with the Indians is bloody in the extreme on both sides. However, within the Indian bands and tribes themselves, murder and feuds were rare. Disputes between individuals were settled chiefly by non-violent means designed to preserve group life. Disputes between tribes frequently led to open warfare, but even here wars were often limited to ritual combat between champions, quick thrusts followed by speedy withdrawal, symbolic raids on crops, horses, or hunting and fishing reserves. Seldom did these result in widespread slaughter of either war party or non-combatants. But there were homicides and wars with blood shed.

Homicide Among The Ancients

The first recorded murder trial occurred in Sumer in ancient Mesopotamia in 1850 B.C. (Wilson 1984:108). Three men were sentenced for slaying a temple servant. Brigands haunted the roads and pirates plagued the seas in Ancient Greece. Piracy probably existed in the 3d millenium B.C. In some areas of ancient Greece a murderer could avoid vengeance if he ate soup on the grave of his victim for nine days. It became a custom in Florence to stand guard over the grave of a victim of murder to see that no one ate soup on it. It has been alleged that the history of Rome manifested more crime and violence than any other city in the world at the time. It embraced assassinations, intrigue, promiscuity, sexual perversions, murders, mayhem, and more. It was a decadent city indeed – the Sodom and Gomorrah of that world. Although the ancient Romans thought human sacrifice was barbaric and suppressed it, they did bury people alive. Vestal Virgins judged to have broken their vows were so buried. It is also believed that at one time in ancient Rome the aged were thrown into the Tiber. The magic age was 60. Even the first Caesar of Rome, Augustus, died mysteriously, probably at the hands of his wife Livia. The fourth Emperor Claudius died in a similar fashion, probably at the hand of his wife. Roman leadership was immersed in homicidal paranoia disguised by political acumen and sophistry. Tiberius was a sadist, Caligula was insane, Nero started out naive, somewhat egotistical, anxious to be liked, a lover of music, and vain. Within one year of becoming Emperor, he murdered his half-brother, committed incest with his mother, tried to assassinate her and succeeded on the second attempt. Tacitus reported on the death of Agrippina, Nero's mother. Nero decided to get rid of her. He considered various methods – poison, dagger, or other violent means. Agrippina was a very experienced killer herself having slain rivals to her ambition. Thus she was vigilant against treachery and guarded herself well. This hampered Nero's intent. He turned to Anicetus, Commander of the fleet at Misenum, who offered a vessel that would break apart and throw Agrippina into the sea. In this way, the blame would fall on nature and not Nero. Unfortunately for Nero the scheme failed as Agrippina escaped with a minor injury. A frightened Nero, fearing Agrippina's revenge, sought advice on deterring her reprisal. Anicitus started the attempt at homicide so accepted the task of completing it. With a body of men he surged into her home and after several blows by club and sword dispatched the fated Agrippina. Eventually Rome rebelled and suicide saved Nero from being flogged to death.

The plotting, conspiracies, intrigue, assassinations, murders, continued to the end of the Roman Empire. Theodosius, angered by a revolt of Thessalonica, invited the whole town to the games in the Circus and the massacre took three hours to kill them all. Even the Church was involved in homicide. The Bishop of Nicomedia murdered the family of Emperor Julian in a struggle for power. The Roman Empire contained a large proportion of the known world. To recount the deeds of the Empire pretty much covers a thousand years of "civilization."

In the 10th and 11th centuries, the Vikings became the scourge of Europe, murdering, raping, and pillaging. Their hit and run raids were motivated by hunger. They lacked land to grow food so turned to others for sustenance. The term assassin comes from the 11th century group of people who adopted that method to achieve political, religious, or social dominance. Assassination remains a tool of dissidents around the world. Some of the targets included Gandhi of India, Sadat of Egypt and Kennedy of America. In early 11th century the Seljuk Turks wrecked havoc upon the Byzantine Empire. The killings by Genghis Khan (1167-1227) were monumental. According to Machiavelli, Florence in the 13th century had more murders and destruction of families than any city in history. The 11th through 13th centuries featured a series of military expeditions launched by Western European Christians to recover the Holy Land from the Muslims. This adventure, the Crusades, often evidenced brutal crimes disguised by religious fervor. The 12th, 13th, and 14th centuries continued to endure the murder of rivals for a crown or intrigue to capture some territory. Frederick II executed those found guilty of treason by first placing them in a leaden shell. Then the shell was placed in a cauldron over a fire and the lead melted around the guilty person. Tamurlane (1336-1405) rivaled Genghis Khan with his bloodshed and destruction. The famous often were infamous and the anonymous were just as likely to be notorious. The bloody chaos of Italian politics in the 13th and 14th century was depicted by Dante thus:

> "O wretched land, search all your coasts, your seas, the bosom of your hills – where will you find a single part that knows the joys of peace?" (Divine Comedy)

In the 15th century it was not unusual for highly placed people to practice assassination. In 1478, the Archbishop of Pisa and two leading bankers of Florence plotted the murder of two members of the infamous Medici family (Wilson 1984: 340). A professional killer named Condottiere was hired for the job.

In the 16th century, the Reformation led by Luther, eventually created religious warfare and consequent slaughter. The Renaissance, from the late 14th to the late 16th centuries, suffered its share of murder and execution along with a more secular spirit and the creations of great artists, poets, scientists, and philosophers. During the reign of the Tudors in England (1485-1603) the common crimes were robbery, perjury, and widespread corruption. Many murders occurred during the commission of a robbery. During the reign of Queen Elizabeth I (1558-1603) crime was widespread but less serious than later periods. London was full of "cony catchers" – thieves and confidence men.

Death was familiar to Olde England. The plague could carry off 30,000 Londoners in one season. There were stabbings and death in taverns and alleys. Men fought duels and some engaged in assassinations. Traitors were hanged, cut down alive, the heart and bowels removed, and the body quartered to be disposed at the King's pleasure.

Between 1688-1815, the English system of criminal law was designated as the Bloody Code (McLynn 1989). In 1688 there were about 50 offenses punishable by the death sentence, including murder, treason, rape, and arson. By 1765 there were 160 such crimes. Sixty-five more were added from 1765-1815 for a grand total of 225. The "benefit of clergy" doctrine was abandoned in 1706. Prior to then, clergy and other literate people could escape a death penalty by so-called ecclesiastical privilege. This was established by reciting a passage from Scripture as a proof of literacy. The problem of crime was exacerbated by the ancient privilege of sanctuary. By 1712, this custom was quashed. The explosion of Tudor severity was part of the supposition that the gallows were the only deterrent to serious crime. The elite supported the system as a means of protecting themselves from the threats to the regime by the feared "mob." It also assured deference from the peasants. This was the outgrowth of a society concerned with protecting the new forms of property and the extensive increase in wealth. Out of the Enlightenment period of the 1700s, marked by humanitarian and egalitarian standards, came theories of crime with concerns that the increased wealth was in itself a cause of crime. Crime and punishment in 18th century England was linked to these changing social and economic circumstances.

Ackroyd (1994) cites an essay by Thomas de Quincey, "On Murder Considered as One of the Fine Arts." De Quincey was associated with the Romantic poets and was a friend of Coleridge and Wordsworth. He is best known for his book *Confessions of an English Opium-Eater*. He describes the spectacular killer as a social and conventional outcast who transcends the filth, poverty, and degradation of 17th to 19th century London by killing not one or two victims secretly and by stealth, but instead wiping out a whole family or group and does so all at once. Or he may kill one person after another over a short period, killing each one in a particularly gruesome way and leaving no clue behind. This terrorized the whole city and gave rise to widespread fears that malevolent supernatural forces were at work. Central to the Romantic movement was the ideal of a single gesture which is so unusual as to lift its maker high above all his contemporaries and elevate him to the symbolic status of what they all want to do or be but fail for lack of courage, ability, and foresight. He lives as they do but suddenly rises to great heights by one extreme murderous spree, and becomes the ideal of the truly gifted artist and Romantic hero.

In spite of the rise of capital offenses, the number of hangings in the 18th century did not follow suit. Executions in the early 1600s were four times as many as those in 1750 (McLynn 1989: 257). Only ten percent of those indicted between 1700-1750 ended up on the gallows. It decreased further into the late 18th century. There were many reasons for this decline. Despite the efforts at control, there was opposition to such savage measures as dictated by the Code. There were intellectual outcries, judges circumventing the laws with discretionary actions, and juries that ignored the evidence to avoid another execution. The severity of the Code was not matched by efficient law enforcement. There was no professional police force to pursue the criminals, apprehend them, and gather evidence. Indictments depended on private prosecutions by victims and the criminal procedures led to many acquittals through the use of loop-holes. Pardons were habitual and reprievals (temporary suspension of sentence) constant and forgotten. The pardon was applied to half of those condemned and a lesser punishment imposed (whippings, fines, detentions, branding, transportation mostly to America). In short, many killers got away with murder. Ironically, the general opinion was that hanging had no deterrent effect.

All homicides were treated as murder. It was up to the defendant to establish the crime as justifiable and thus not murder. The key was malice aforethought; therefore, manslaughter and justifiable homicide were not identified as murder. In spite of the large number of capital crimes, compared to continental Europe, homicides were remarkably low. There was a variety of homicides and motives, not just a few categories. Murder of a husband by a wife, a master by a servant, an ecclesiastical superior by an inferior, were all considered petty treason. The reasoning was that they were related to high treason because they violated the tacit contract between the ruler and ruled.

Although 18th century England had its crimes by the powerful (white collar crimes), the majority of the criminals were young, poor, and male (McLynn 1989: 133). They committed those offenses that did not tempt the wealthier part of the community. High treason was politically directed toward the Jacobites. This was the name given to supporters of the deposed James II and his Stuart descendants who tried to regain the throne. They were found among the Scots (homeland of the Stuarts), Irish Catholics, and perturbed Tories. The many laws relating to high treason eventually were winnowed to include mostly coinage offenses or crimes against the Protestant succession. Smuggling engaged some 20,000 resourceful people full time. The high duties and bureaucratic controls beckoned the hardy into the contraband trade and smuggling effloresced. Poaching tested the new ideas about the rights of property and the old ones about feudal privileges.

In 18th century England, crime was clearly a London phenomenon. Newspaper records indicated criminal activity very reminiscent of contemporary times (McLynn 1989). Casual violence was evident and life was cheap. Women, while serving as prostitutes, were picking pockets of comatose or sleeping clients (rolling the John). Juveniles were very active in felonious behavior.. Alcoholism, fueled by the new panacea gin and financed by petty thefts, was distressing to the authorities. Thefts became unseemly common and the punishment for goods stolen worth more than five shillings, unseemly harsh – hanging. House storming was commonplace as groups forced their way into homes demanding money and torturing victims to discover the hiding places for valuables. This kind of crime has made somewhat of a comeback in the 1990s in such places as Silicon Valley. Organized crime was gradually increasing its range and magnitude of operation; there was a hard core of professional criminals.

Organized crime goes back to ancient Greece and their pirates. During Shakespeare's time (17th century) London and France had their low profile organized crime. It flourished in countries with a history of banditry, hatred of authorities, and/or political unrest. They often maintained a relationship with their surroundings by performing community services. The Chinese Triads started as political opponents of the Dynasty and slid into crime. They moved into Hong Kong where they still flourish today. They have tried to import their system to America. The end of the cold war spawned a Russian Mafia which also came to America. Drugs fed the appetites of other ethnic groups which also organized their criminal activity. The best known such group is the Mafia or Cosa Nostra (our thing), an import from Sicily. The Mafia has developed its own society with rules and initiation rites. Their record, often romanticized, is laden with corruption and death. Murder seems to go hand-in-hand with organized crime.

The change from tribal justice to a metropolitan police force was long and arduous. The development of organized, full-time police agencies was a natural consequence of the increasing heterogeneity and urbanization of cities. As early as the 17th century, continental Europe had developed professional police forces (Blumberg & Niederhoffer 1973: 1-15). England feared the potential for oppression by these forces and did not create police organizations until the 19th century. Law enforcement was left to private citizens who were rewarded for arrests and fined if the pursuit of a criminal ended in failure. The introduction of policing by the legendary Bow Street Runners followed by a Metropolitan police force quickly reduced crime in London. Eventually, the criminal element changed and adapted to the new societal reactions. The Industrial Revolution also effected methods of commission of and reactions to crime.

Compared to Europe, America in the 18th century was relatively law abiding. The Puritan Ethic still dominated the scene. But there still was crime. Samuel Green was believed to be America's first mass murderer (Wilson 1984: 477). He started young as a juvenile delinquent, mostly thefts. When caught he was flogged. He tried to kill one of his punishers and failed. He joined a fellow delinquent and his first murder was of a jewelry salesman. They waylaid, robbed and killed him. Green then began to specialize in burglary, killing when interrupted. The number of victims is unknown but he became the most wanted man in America. Finally caught and imprisoned, he killed another inmate and was hanged.

In 19th century England the ratio of crimes to population was 1 in 822. That was a relatively goodly amount of crime. Prior to the mid-19th century, sex crimes were rare – at least they were not reported. These kinds of acts caused embarrassment. The Puritan Ethic and the prudery of the Victorian era made it easier to closet the event rather than to seek justice. This was altered with such changes as a more open attitude toward sex and later, the Women's Liberation Movement. The late 19th century erupted with the age of anarchy, so coined as the opposite of hierarchy – no government. In the 1870's, the anarchists organized four unsuccessful attempts on crowned heads, two in Germany, one in Spain, and one in Italy. Tsar Alexander II was an early major success for the anarchists. Such attempts at assassination arrived in America in the late 1870s in Chicago in the midst of industrialization and worker unrest. Mob violence included the throwing of a bomb at police and the killing of seven people. In 1901, President McKinley was assassinated by a confused and probably delusional anarchist. Anarchy entered France in the 1890s. The President of France was stabbed to death by an anarchist shouting *vive l' anarchie*. In 1896, Spain became a target and bombs found victims. And so it went in other countries as well.

Hartman (1977) analyzed twelve cases involving thirteen women of respected middle class standing who murdered their husbands, lovers, rivals, children, students, siblings, and grandchildren. The emphasis of the study was upon the ordinary and conventional mode of life in middle class England and France between 1840 and 1890. These thirteen women were typical of their class and not deviant though they committed deviant acts – murders. The author tried to show that the Victorian code of femininity and womanhood came to their rescue. The facts produced at their trials clearly established their guilt. But the courts and public feeling defended them and explained away their crimes. Although most were probably guilty, only six were convicted and none received the death penalty. Five of the six imprisoned did not serve their full terms. Of the other seven, six were acquitted and one was never tried. It seems that middle class women were getting away with murder. In America, Lizzie Borden was acquitted of axing her mother and father to death chiefly because the jury believed her defense attorney that a respectable woman would not and hence could not do such a thing.

Infanticide is included in the terms of homicide and murder and it has a long history. Greek myths abound with tales of gods who killed or devoured the new born. Unwanted children were exposed to the elements and left to die in ancient Greece and Rome. The Bible reports that Moses' mother cast him adrift on a river from which Pharoah's daughter rescued him from certain death. Centuries later, Herod sought to kill all the first born in his realm so as to eliminate all future rivals. Some scholars hold that the story of Abraham and Isaac is a disguise for the end of child sacrifice to Moloch as practiced by proto-Hebrews for many years.

In 18th century France, impoverished women commonly killed the infants whom they could not care for. If the mother was unmarried, she risked the death penalty; if she was married, the courts frequently found her innocent, (Piers 1978: 68). In England throughout the 19th century, children were valued for labor in mines and factories. Infant deaths were part of every day life due to malnutrition, accidents, abuse, and neglect – (causes which in contemporary America could lead to indictments for homicide), (Piers 1978: 80-84). The wet-nurse was an important part of life in Italy and Central Europe as late as the dawn of the 20th century. It was gauche and impolite to inquire what had happened to a child who was never seen and whose fate was never known. The unspoken truth was that it had died because its mother had to sell her milk in order to survive, (Piers 1978: 45-55).

Infanticide, in criminal law, is the killing of a newborn child by its parent or by another with the parent's consent. In most countries, including United States and Great Britain, it is treated as a form of murder. The practice was widespread among many primitive peoples. The principle cause was a shortage of food. In mid-Victorian times, "...the records of coroner's inquests reveal only a fraction of the known cases of infanticide led to an indictment for what is largely a women's crime, and infanticides which were never detected were believed to be numerous." Forty-nine women were executed for murder in England between 1843 and 1890. "Though infanticide may have been employed by lower middle classes when a child threatened to disrupt an achieved standard of living it was largely a crime of the poor," (Hartman 1977: 5-6).

The Kokeshi dolls widely sold in Japan were originally substitutes for children murdered at birth. This practice is said by some writers to be an accepted part of family planning in the 18th and early 19th century (Booth 1995). The result was a precise control over the sex ratio in a family or village since either gender could be eliminated. The act was performed by a midwife who smothered the baby or the mother who bound it in straw mats and crushed it. The dolls represented the murdered children. Similarly japanese whalers set up stone monuments as tributes to the unborn calves discovered when their mothers were harpooned. The practice of infanticide still survives though not as widespread as in feudal times. China, it is alleged, continues to practice infanticide, mostly on females. Deformed infants of both genders were destroyed in ancient Greece and Rome. In later times, the Christian church tried to prevent infanticide by excommunicating women guilty of the practice. Muslims are forbidden this practice by the Koran. The Koran advocates measures that were intended to improve the condition of women. Therefore, the infanticide of girls, formerly prevalent among certain tribes, was forbidden. Polyandry is limited to Central Asia, southern India, and Sri Lanka in communities where the traditional practice of female infanticide resulted in a shortage of women.

Wilson (1984: 14-16) takes Abraham Maslow's "hierarchy of needs" and applies it to the changing patterns of crime throughout history. Though an interesting idea, the accuracy is suspect as it requires scientific confirmation.

1. Physiological needs. By the first part of the nineteenth century most crimes were committed for the need to survive.

2. Security needs. With the Industrial Revolution and wider prosperity, crimes were committed to safeguard security.

3. Belongingness and love needs. By the end of the nineteenth century the sex crime emerged motivated by jealousy or to dispose a spouse for a lover.

4. Esteem needs. Crimes of self-esteem emerge by the 1960s. The murderer feels that society is to blame for not giving him dignity, justice, or recognition. A good example would be the Manson case.

5. Self-actualizing needs. There is the need to know and understand, to create, to solve problems for the fun of it.

One may find a case now and then that may fit one of these patterns but they do not explain all homicides. Wilson and Seaman (1983) build on Maslow's hierarchy. Though very similar, there is some differences. In the self-esteem category they note that in the 1950s there were examples of the motiveless crime. They also suggest a murderer who thinks in magic. He seeks someone or group to blame for his plight. He kills to remedy this plight. Murderers, they claim are under stress. (Of course, so are a lot of non-murderers.)

Gurr (1980: 31-52) asserts that patterns of crime and justice systems surfaced in Western society with modernization. The way crime is defined and dealt with in the West was forged by four basic components of modernization: industrialization, urbanization, expansion of state resources and power, humanization of interpersonal relations.

Industrialization brought masses of rural workers to the city, increased social heterogeneity and material wealth. These factors of industrialization contributed to crime through economic distress and social dislocation. Urbanization established cultural diversity, and introduced people with few ties. Interrelationships were impersonal in contrast to the close associations in the rural areas. The largest cities have the highest homicide rates. Nationalization advances with the growth of the power and resources of the state. This effects the incidence of criminal behavior and impacts the politics of public order and the character of the criminal justice system by organizing social responses like laws, prisons, and courts.

Humanization intruded into the value system. There was greater control of aggression, both internal and external. Violence in medieval times was much greater prior to the humanization period, probably than now as well. There was a marked increase in respect for people regardless of their status. Previously, callous disrespect was rampant. The notion of morally flawed criminals was translated into psychologically flawed ones and slowly replaced by the social environment as responsible for misbehavior. Thus, according to Gurr (1980) the four factors of modernization brought with it changes that increased crime and the social responses to it.

Lane (1980: 91-109) compared homicides in the 19th century with those in the 20th century. In between 1839 and 1900, homicide indictments in Philadelphia declined significantly. Serious crime also declined in Great Britain in the 19th century. Both decreases occurred during periods of rapid urbanization. This decline was in the face of the conventional wisdom that urbanization is positively correlated with crime. Studies have indicated that in 20th century Philadelphia the homicide rate rose significantly (Wolfgang 1966; Lane 1980). However, there is evidence that homicide cases were under-reported in the 19th century. They were likely twice as high as recounted (Lane 1980: 96). Firearms, especially handguns, became more readily available in the 1850s and subsequently there was the increase in homicides in the 19th century. The firearms permitted the inclination to violence to reach a lethal conclusion. This trend, it is argued, continued in the 20th century. The homicide rates dropped through much of the 20th century until about the last generation. Lane (1980: 104-105), argued that a good deal of the increease was related to the increased availability of guns and the unequal opportunites for Afro-Americans. Lane's comparative study concluded that in the 19th century a city and economy could grow while homicides declined. He concluded further: limiting handguns can reduce homicide rates (still a moot point); increased police efficiency alone has little effect on homicide rates; the greater discipline, enforced by schools and other organizations, required in a modern economy, turned aggression inward with an increase in suicide and decrease in homicide (still a moot point); due to the plight of the Afro-American in America, they developed patterns of violence with a rise in their homicide rates, (still a moot point).

Specific Examples of Deadly Acts

The history of man is replete with references to a monstrous appetite for mayhem (Everitt 1993). The annals of murder are often bizarre, bloodthirsty and ancient. In the 15th century one Beane led a Scottish group in waylaying travelers, murdered them, and ate their flesh. Cannibalism, in the 15th century, was not just a cultural event among primitive tribes. When caught, Beane and 26 of his men were dismembered and left to bleed to death. The original Bluebeard was a 15th century French aristocrat named Gilles de Rais. He tortured, mutilated, and killed over 100 children. He was tried and convicted of murder and simultaneously hanged and burned. Two of his servants were convicted as accomplices and were burned alive. Cruel and unusual punishment was an idea whose time had yet to come. The model for Bram Stoker's Dracula was a Romanian called Vlad the Impaler, a member of an aristocratic family. His father was Vlad II with the name of Dracul meaning dragon or devil. Dracula means son of Dracul. Also in the 15th century, Dracul reveled in mas murders, sometimes as many as 500 at one time. He did not drink the blood of his victims but he sure did spill it. His method frequently was by impaling victims upon stakes, sometimes through the heart or navel. He eventually died in a battle against the Turks. Women too contributed to the carnage. Elizabeth Bathory, the "Blood Countess," was a medieval Countess who descended from practicing curses and burning genitals to vampirism. She frolicked in a bathtub full of the blood of her female servants convinced that it was the elixir of youth. After about 40 murders in 10 years, she was placed under house arrest. The Countess died three and a half years later in 1614.

The late 19th century brought us the affair of "Jack the Ripper." Although he was never publicly identified due, it is said, to a royal connection, the killings suddenly stopped. There were many attempts to solve the puzzle. It has been suggested that this was the case of an outraged person alienated and trying to "cleanse" society. This motive is present in contemporary times, occasionally through terroristic tactics. Evans and Gainey (1996) give us an account of the murder and mutilation of the five prostitutes in Whitechapel London in 1888 by "Jack the Ripper". They make a strong and highly detailed case for one Frank (Francis) Tumblety, an American quack doctor who hated women. He was arrested many times, often for homosexuality, a misdemeanor, for which he was "police bailed" and escaped. He was tracked to New York and escaped again. Police could never arrest him for murder for lack of evidence in preforensic times when the only grounds would be an eye-witness or a confession. Tumblety was a striking, colorful, and likeable person. He moved easily through many levels of society. He was stridently pro-Irish and anti-orthodox medical practice. Both were widely popular positions in his day. He was a homeopath and herbalist who peddled numerous cures which killed at least two people. The book gives a detailed account of his life as a teen-ager and on to his death and burial in Rochester, New York on May 28, 1903.

In the early 1920s, the infamous case of Leopold and Loeb was avidly followed by much of America. The story featured two teenagers, from wealthy families, intelligent, university graduates, who decided to accept the supreme challenge to commit the perfect murder. They failed. They selected as the victim a friend of Loeb's younger brother, committed the crime, were caught and defended by the brilliant attorney Clarence Darrow. They were saved from the electric chair and sentenced to life imprisonment. In November of 1966, Robert Smith, an eighteen year old student, shot five women and two children in a beauty parlor. Smith seemed a normal person with no troubled background.. Yet he confessed that he wanted to be known – to get a name for himself. A women walked into a hotel in California and killed a sleeping baseball player in his room. Her motive was that he was famous and she knew that killing him would make her famous too.

The contemporary American crime scene still records these kinds of grisly events. The body parts of a missing 13 year old were found entombed in chunks of fresh concrete. Cement bags, plastic bags, cutting instruments, and blood were found in a shed. One of the blocks weighing 200 pounds was found dripping blood on the lawn of a nearby house. Another chunk was found not too far away. Seven people were arrested for the crime. The determination of a motive and cause of death is still pending.

The record for violence in the 20th century is alarming. There were some 38 million deaths from genocide (Grimshaw 1999). The most recent ones occurred in Cambodia, Rwanda, and Yugoslavia. The next century offers a backlog of unresolved conflicts. The score promises to be close to the previous records.

The history of homicide is replete with repetitions. They not only occur over time but over place as well. Even the rates show repetition by occurring in cycles. The crime seems prolific and endless. But there is some solace in the fact that the vast majority of people do not kill.

CHAPTER THREE

HOMICIDE IN AMERICA

The FBI's Uniform Crime Report (UCR) Index includes two major categories of crime. One is property crime and the other is violent crime. This latter category involves crimes against the person. Although fewer crimes occur against the person than against property, the actual or potential violence and the danger, injury, and death that can occur result in more publicity, greater concern, and a more vigorous public reaction. The UCR violent crime index includes murder, aggravated assault, robbery, and forcible rape. It is sometimes noted, and many times true, that an assault may be a failed homicide while a homicide may be a failed attempt at an assault. There are other crimes against persons as well as those noted. There is kidnapping, child molesting and abuse, bombing, and assassination. Forcible rape is also a sex crime; however, it is a crime in which violence or the threat of violence dominates the victim - criminal interaction. The sex factor may very well be secondary because it can be used as the expedient for the violence. Unlike most crimes against property, person crimes characteistically involve some kind of direct confrontation with the victim, the intent is usually obvious, and the potential for injury of some consequence – sometimes for the criminal as well as for the victim.

Violence

Violence has always been and always will be with us. What does change is our attitude toward it. That is, sometimes it is defined as appropriate and other times as inappropriate. Wars, of course, both require and justify violence while mass murders are invariably condemned and abhorred. Contact sports such as boxing and football may maim, but accompanying violence is not defined as such. In football it is necessary body contact, in assault it is an unnecessary physical attack. For some, capital punishment is violence, for others, it is justice. Revolution is violence at its worst or best, depending on the side one chooses. Perhaps the one kind of violence most abhorred is senseless violence; an interesting concept indeed as it implies that there is useful, rational, and sensible violence. Even the legal system (and moral as well) recognizes the category of justifiable homicide.

There are many different kinds of violence. At times it is impossible to clearly distinguish between violent and nonviolent crimes. Homicides may be clearly violent, but the destruction of property, though devastating and dangerous (such as bombing and arson) may not result in personal injury. Is it therefore nonviolent? Also violence is not limited to crime; it occurs in other contexts as well. Haskell and Yablonsky (1974: 348-365) suggested four patterns of violence: legal violence; socially sanctioned violence; rational violence; ;and illegal, nonsanctioned, irrational violence. Legal violence includes those acts supported by law such as the behavior of the soldier in war, the policeman on the beat, the boxer in the ring, and the football player on the field. Socially sanctioned violence is the kind that may be illegal, but tends to receive wide public approval. This might include the so-called "unwritten law:" the cuckolded husband assaults the adulterer; a Caucasian assaults an Afro-American in a bigoted community where the act receives support from the local population or vica versa; or a crowd assaults an American Nazi Party member. Rational violence may be neither legal nor sanctioned, but appropriate within certain contexts. Examples could include acts of violence in self-defense, or a homicide within the framework of organized crime, or the general act of violence for financial gain such as in a robbery. Illegal, nonsanctioned, irrational violence is the category that best describes senseless violence. Mass murders and killing for "kicks" would be examples of this kind of violence.

Violence may be an individual or a collective act. For some, in the short term, watching a violent act stimulates an appetite for more. The usual crimes of violence are inclined to be individual acts, as are the fist-fight, severe physical disciplining of children, husband-wife altercations (domestic violence), and homicide. Occasionally, violence involves two or three persons such as can occur in a robbery. But also there are instances where larger groups are involved such as in mob violence, lynchings, gang fights, warfare in organized crime, terrorist acts, and some revolutionary groups.

With its various forms and different public reactions, violence is a difficult if not impossible construct to define. One could define it be first adding "crimes of" and thus narrowing the scope of the term (The National Commission on the Causes and Prevention of Violence 1969). Then, the term violent crimes is defined as legally proscribed acts whose primary object is the deliberate use of force to inflict injury. Although this definition does narrow the focus it excludes acts that clearly belong under the violent category. There are crimes that use the threat of force rather than force such as forcible rape. Many violent acts are not deliberate ones. An arsonist may intend no harm but burn a house down and kill its occupants whom he did not know were there. The drunken driver may not even see the victim who he maims or kills. Violence cannot be defined without accounting for both the act and the reaction to it, and even then, the same act will evoke different reactions even within the same context, depending on such things as the gender, age, state of mind, and general background of the perpetrator and victim. Probably an appropriate definition would be elaborate enough to be a theory. Nevertheless, one might suggest that a violent act is one that involves the element of force or its threat, and inflicts or has the potential to inflict some injury or harm upon another person or persons. One thing seems certain, the many attempts to control violence testify to the general societal opposition to it, the historical concern with it, and the many efforts toward its regulation.

The Commission On Violence

The eruption of assassinations that took the lives of President John Kennedy in 1963, then his brother Senator Robert F. Kennedy and Civil Rights leader Dr. Martin Luther King, Jr. in 1968, were largely responsible for the appointment of a National Commission on the Causes and Prevention of Violence. The major assignment of the Commission was to examine the role of violence in American society and to suggest methods of prevention. The subsequent studies were, up to that time, the most extensive ever undertaken on violence in America (National Commission on the Causes and Prevention of Violence. Final Report 1969).

The Commission delineated a profile of violent crime. At the outset it was noted that violent crime was found in all parts of the country and among all groups in the population, though unequally distributed. It further noted:

1. Violent crime in America occurred primarily in large cities.
2. Violent crime in the city was mostly committed by males.
3. Violent crime in the city was concentrated among youths between the ages of 15-24. There was also a disturbing increase in assault and robbery among the 10-14 year age group.
4. The violent offender tended to come from the lower end of the socioeconomic scale.

5. There was a disproportionate rate of violent crime in the Afro-American ghettos. These higher rates were not due to race, but were the result of the life conditions in the ghetto and slums.
6. The victims of violence generally had the same characteristics as the offenders. They tended to be male, young, poor, and Afro-American.
7. Aside from robbery, other violent crimes were inclined to be acts of passion among intimates and acquaintances.
8. The greatest proportion of all serious violence was committed by repeaters.
9. In general, violent crimes were familiar acts to Americans. The data suggested that 600,000 to 1,200,000 Americans committed violent crimes each year. Compared to other nations, America was clearly the leader.

The Commission also listed its assessment of the causes of violent crime. Noting that although it may occur anywhere and among all groups, it is inclined to be concentrated in large cities, especially among the ghetto poor, young, Afro-American males. The roots then are found most often in urban areas characterized by: low income, physical deterioration, dependency, racial and ethnic concentration, broken homes, working mothers, low levels of education and vocational skills, high unemployment, high proportions of single males, overcrowded and substandard housing, high rates of tuberculosis and infant mortality, low rates of home ownership or single family dwellings, mixed land use, and high population density.

The Commission offered several suggestions for the prevention of violent crimes. The basic, long-run solution is nothing less than the reconstruction of urban life–an awesome undertaking. In the short-run, these are some of the actions endorsed:

1. Increased foot patrols in the slum and ghetto areas by inter-racial police teams.
2. Increased police-community relations in the slum and ghetto areas.
3. Further experimentation with controlled drug programs such as the distribution of methadone.
4. Diagnostic machinery to detect violence-prone individuals.
5. Some program to restrict the distribution of the hand gun.

The Commission study on violence in America represented an extensive effort that increased our knowledge of the phenomenon. The long-run solution of a reconstruction of our urban life is monumental in scope and unlikely to be achieved. Further experimentation with controlled drug programs would be useful, but such programs as methadone have proven ineffective. This is unfortunate as there has been an increase in homicides involving drugs. It is interesting that with so many violent crimes emanating from family altercations, little is offered in the way of solutions for this major source. Though the study was outstanding and useful, it was flawed. The notion of "causes" would appear to be only a listing of social problems. Those problems may exist in those areas; however, how does one explain the fact that the majority of the inhabitants are law-abiding citizens?

ASA Workshop On Violence

A workshop was convened by the American Sociolgical Association in 1993 to identify research directions, distinguish existing research on social causes of violence, and address policy issues in crafting a science agenda. The findings were reported by Levine & Rosich (1996). The most vulnerable members of society – poor, female, young, elderly, and minorities were most effected by violence. FBI Director Louis Freeh reported that 37 million people were injured by criminals in a twenty year period (1973-1993), (Levine & Rosich 1996: 2). The cost was 19 billion dollars in 1991-1993 alone. This is possibly somewhat of an exaggeration but certainly not outright hyperbole. A really heavy price is in the consequence – widespread fear – even though it is not persistent and tied to specific places and activities. Chaiken & Chaiken (1982) submit that a small group of individuals commit a great deal of the crimes, they begin early, and then persist in their misbehavior.

Homicide is the leading cause of death among Afro-American youths (Levine & Rosich 1996: 8). Though but twelve percent of the population they represent almost half of the victims and the great majority of the offenders are other Afro-American males. Income and economic capacity is related to the racial impact. Differences between Blacks and Whites disappears in higher income neighborhoods (Loftin et al 1989). Women are more likely to be homicide victims in intimate or familial circumstances. Men are more likely to be killed by friends, acquaintances, or strangers (Roth 1994: 5). Afro-Americans more than Whites are involved in volence as victim and perpetrator. But, poverty, economic inequalities, family disorganization within communities create a spurious relationship between violence and race (see Blau & Blau 1982; Hawkins 1987; Land, *et al* 1990; Crutchfield 1995).

Other factors contributing to violence are population density and location such as concentration of bars, hotspots and convenience stores (Levine & Rosich 1996: 14-16). The list also includes economic viability and *de facto* segregation, residential mobility, fear, and social disorganization.

Traditionally, family and school are cited both as a significant source and control of violence. Some family factors associated with violence include exposure to physical punishment, alcoholism, criminal parents, separation and divorce (Reis & Roth 1993: 368). Other citations involve a lack of nurturance, absence of adult supervision, and parental stress or conflict. The higher the rate of family disorganization, the higher the rate of neighborhood crime and violence (Skogan 1989: 244-45). Family violence is relatively high. The Uniform Crime Report indicates that in 1992, intrafamily homicides happened in about twelve percent of all homicides reported. (The subsequent trend indicated that intrafamily homicides dropped slightly while juvenile gang killings climbed dramatically.) Violence in schools has also increased with the presence of guns there (Levine & Rosich 1996: 28). Incidents of violence in the workplace have followed a similar pattern.

Another major source of violence is from groups of one kind or another. They vary from mob to riot to gang. Since the early studies of gangs (see Thrasher 1927), their numbers have increased and their violence escalated. Klein (1995) estimates over 1000 cities have gang problems. Gangs differ considerably in age, size, and gender. Many are drug related, but probably fewer than commonly proclaimed (Levine & Rosich 1996: 33-34). Their motives for violence also vary. They include territory, status concerns, racial and ethnic conflicts. The homicides have increased as has the use of guns, especially high-caliber automatic or semi-automatic weapons. Forty percent of violent incidents involve guns. The 1994 Uniform Crime Report indicated that 70 percent of all murders involved guns, 12.7% knives or other instruments. Guns, of course, are the more lethal of the weapons. These statistics are not equally distributed over the poulation. There is more involvement with guns by youth and minority groups than other groups. Alcohol and drugs also play a role. The drug traffic involves disagreements in transactions and turf wars. There is some evidence of a link between viewing violence on television and aggression (it should be noted that aggression is not synonymous with violence). In some youth cultures, "dissing" – disrespect of others – is very significant and can lead to violence or death. This could entail an odd look or a simple comment about a girl or mother. Death will have the day.

The ASA Workshop commented on the social responses and programs directed toward violence. Social responses encompass intervention, social control mechanisms, and prevention. The social institution usually charged with the responsibility for violent behavior is the criminal justice system. Its response to ensure public safety includes deterrence, punishment, or rehabilitation. Some programs for conflict resolution show some promise in the control of violence. Lawrence Friedman of the New York Times has mused, "Fluctuations in crime rates are largely independent of changes in the criminal justice system." Scholars have often echoed this sentiment.

The Violent Offender

There have been other attempts to study violent crimes and the violent offender (Sheppard 1971: 12-19). Hans Toch (1969) points out that in violence-prone individuals, though provocation might occur, it plays a minor role in a violent response. The precipitating factor and the victim are often incidental as if the offender is simply a blunt instrument in search of a target. Several studies refer to the offender's experiences with brutality and violence within his own family structure, frequently as the target (Duncan & Duncan 1971: 1498-1502; Mac Donald 1963: 125-130; Peterson, *et al* 1962: 462-470). Wolfgang and Ferracuti (1967) developed the influential theory of a "subculture of violence." They hypothesize an environment in which violent behavior is learned. A theme of violence pervades the cluster of values that contribute to a lifestyle, socialization process, and social interaction of persons living under similar conditions. This subculture accepts and reinforces the use of aggression as a mode of behavior. Growing up in such an environment leads to a predisposition toward violence. In short, if one is brought up in an atmosphere of violence, one will learn to be violent. This may serve as an explanation for some violence, but certainly not all violence. It suggests that certain situations are conducive to the learning of violent responses, a kind of strike or be struck thesis, one that may apply in war. However, it often is defensive in nature rather than offensive. One strikes out because of the threat or the perceived threat of injury. Most violent crimes are not of this character as that type of violence is more apt to occur in the specific environments of some neighborhoods, prisons, or battlefields. And, of course, infinitely more persons from this environment remain nonviolent rather than violent. The experiences are just as likely to cause one to avoid violence as to seek it.

There have been attempts to type violent offenders. Most of these have involved murderers as studies of violence concentrate on these more sensational crimes (Guttmacher 1960; Glaser and O'Leary 1966: 23-32). One study of violent offenders identified seven types (Spencer 1966). These categories were distinguished on the bases of a clinical evaluation using an "aggressive history profile." The differentiation then took place on the basis of a variety of characteristics. Though of some heuristic value, such typologies do more to verify the diversity of violent offenders than to explain its genesis.

The seven types were:

1. The Culturally Violent Offender. This category includes those who were raised in a subculture where violence was an accepted way of life.
2. The Criminally Violent Offender. These offenders use violence to gain some end such as in robbery.
3. the Pathologically Violent Offender. The mentally ill, either functional or organic are included in this category.
4. The Situationally Violent Offender. These offenders commit a rare violent act under extreme provocation.
5. The Accidentally Violent Offender. Any injuries caused by this type are accidental.
6. The Institutionally Violent Offender. These offenders commit violence while incarcerated.
7. The Non-Violent Offender. These miscreants show no record of violent behavior.

Violent America

In the recent past Americans characterized themselves as a peaceful people, especially when they compared themselves to their stereotypes of other nations–the more exotic the people, the less we knew about them, the more peaceful we appeared. In more contemporary times, particularly since the 1960's, Americans have identified themselves as a violent people with a violent history. This view is best characterized by the H. Rap Brown remark in the 1960's that "violence is as American as apple pie." The truth probably lies somewhere in between the two extremes of peace-loving and violent.

Stark and McEvoy (1972: 272-277) make a case for the Americans as a violent people in an article based on material gathered for the National Commission on the Causes and Prevention of Violence. They reported that almost 13 percent of all Americans have, as adults, been slapped or kicked by other persons while 18 percent remember slapping or kicking someone else. About 1 in 8 adults have punched someone or have been punched; for males the statistic is 1 in 5. About 20 percent of all Americans approved of slapping one's spouse. One study indicated that advocacy of violence was associated with age, the younger the person, the more accepting of violence (Brunswick 1970). It was also noted that 1 in 12 adults have been threatened with knives or actually cut; 1 in 17 adults have been threatened by guns or shot at (exclusive of the military experience); 1 in 17 adults admit to using a gun or knife to defend themselves; 41 percent of all adults owned at least one gun at that time. In assessing the data, the authors also challenge several myths about violence. Of particular interest is the finding that Afro-Americans did not constitute an especially violent subculture; the South was probably no more violent than other regions; the poor and less educated were not more likely to resort to physical aggression then the middle class. Similar studies report similar results.

If our present seems violent, some have argued that it is a legacy from our past. America has a violent history. Graham and Gurr (1969: xxv) write in their introduction:

> "Many unique aspects of our society and politics have contributed to the individual and collective violence that troubles contemporary America, among them the psychological residues of slavery, the coexistence of mass consumption with pockets and strata of sullen poverty, the conflict among conflicting ethics that leaves many men

> without clear guides to social action. Other sources of violence in our national life are inheritances of our own past: a celebration of violence in good causes by our revolutionary progenators, frontiersmen, and vigilantes; immigrant expectations of an earthly paradise only partly fulfilled; the unresolved tensions of rapid and unregulated urban and industrial growth."

Brown (1969). Dichotomizes the history of violence in America into positive and negative. The latter refers to violence that does not seem to be directly connected to any socially or historically constructive consequences, while the opposite is true of positive violence. Negative violence includes criminal violence, feuds, lynchings, mobs, violence of racial, ethnic, and religious prejudice, urban riots, mass murders, and political assassinations. Postiive violence includes police violence, revolution (our nation was conceived and born in violence), the civil war, the Indian wars, vigilantes, agrarian uprisings, and labor violence. Inciardi (1975: 85-103) traces the history of American banditry, central to the notion of professional "heavy" crime. These kinds of criminal careers depend on violence for success. Piracy was rampant in the New World; the frontier west spawned outlaws and the robbery of stagecoaches, banks, and trains. Condemned early Americans were treated harshly. Public executions were a ritual response to the evil of murder (Halttumen 1998). The passing of the western bandit was quickly followed by the modern bandits: John Dillinger, Pretty Boy Floyd, Bonnie Parker and Clyde Barrow, Machine Gun Kelly, Ma Barker, Baby Face Nelson, and many others. Contemporary "heavy" crime in the bandit tradition features professional armed robbery and hijacking.

Is America a violent nation? The answer probably is yes. However, this response should be placed in an appropriate context. Yes, violence occurs and always has, but it has not destroyed the fabric of American society nor has it reduced America to a jungle where there are those who prey and those who are preyed upon. Any kind of violence is regrettable and none should be encouraged. Serious concern is always seemly and solutions and preventions should be sought. But there seems to be a concern that may have gone beyond the objective data. The concern, or perhaps more befitting, the inordinate concern highlights the dimorphic attitude toward it – the violence on one hand and its abhorrence on the other. This would seem to testify to a nonviolent bearing rather than to a nation of violent people. It has become prosaic for Americans to be extremely self-critical, sometimes to excess, resulting in breast-beating with self-recriminations and self-denigration, and a tendency to translate historical roots, a slap, a fist-fight, and the presence of a knife as major indicators of uncontrolled violence. More careful consideration of the situation and the process might more readily reveal so many of these acts to be aggressive incidents rather than criminal or negative violence. This kind of behavior exists all over the world, and within its context has structure and control. Violence may be rising, or differently defined, or suddenly more exposed through the media, all with heightened awareness of the consequence. Also, there are many advocacy groups that practice the ploy of data hyperbole to enhance agendas. Thus the size of publics and the number of incidents of interest to them are extrapolated beyond reality.

How much of the focus on violence is there of concern and reaction and how much objectively real? Does the definition change so that the concern mounts and social interactions that were formerly perceived as benign are redefined as violent? Fighting, slapping, informal physical, and other such similar contacts in social interactions where there are no injuries or minimal ones, are found in most youth subcultures and in many families where "violence" and severe injury are certainly not intended. Of course the potential for injury is greater under those circumstances, but it still tends to be rare. Though aggressive, particularly tuned to the subculture and the situation, they are usually not the kinds of violence that threaten the fabric of society, nor ordinarily instill fear into the populace. Yet, when violence is a focus of concern, the interpretation is escalated to include these acts as serious, which in turn can be translated into popular fear. The fear then is greater than the threat. American violence is not morbid, it can be reduced, even without effort as it will ebb and flow with the historical tide, leveling off with the nature of the society as it evolves.

Homicide

Homicide is easily the most dramatic of the crimes of violence. American culture places a high value on life and sudden death is dramatic and shocking. With the exception of the more prominent victims and on occasion the law enforcement officer, the tendency is to quickly forget the victim and focus on the killer. The media of all types is replete with references to homicide plots: television drama, best selling books, classic literature (Hamlet and Oedipus), and it is even traditional to note the early references in the bible to the death of Abel at the hands of his brother Cain.

From all this coverage comes, for the most part, a good deal of misunderstanding about the crime of homicide. Contrary to the public presentation, homicides are not customarily perpetrated by clever schemers, or organized crime hit-men, random mass slayers, and gang and/or drug slayings, but by relatives, friends, or acquaintances caught-up in emotional situations that can arise from interactions among people who know each other – sometimes too well. Violence and homicide in the family can be related to its intimacy – the intensity of the social interactions. Adultery by a stranger may evince a smirk; by an acquaintance, interest; by a friend, concern; but by a spouse, passion. It is often said that locked doors keep out honest people, not burglars; it also can be noted that to avoid murder it might be more prudent to lock oneself out of the house, rather than in it. Nevertheless, though most cases of violence and homicide involve a prior relationship between the offender and the victim, violence and homicide between strangers may be more startling (Riedel 1993). Since this form involves strangers, there is an absence of strong feelings, perhaps suppressed for a long time, such as hate, jealousy, or resentment. In a robbery or a burglary, or an argument in a bar or in traffic, a confrontation can quickly erupt into violence or murder. Some writers argue that a fear of crime is a fear of strangers. The vision of an unknown marauder can inspire a greater fear than the specter of a confrontation with an acquaintance, friend or kin.

The Uniform Crime Report (UCR)

The FBI's UCR for 1993 (Department of Justice 1994) indicated some of the usual data but also some shifts away from the past. The UCR includes murder and nonnegligent manslaughter in the homicide category. In 1993 there were 24,526 homicides, a rate of 9.5 per 100,000. This was a 2.2 percent increase in the rate over 1992. Most homicides occurred in December, fewest, in February. The southern states had the highest rates (41%), the midwest the lowest (less than 1 percent). The rate for the metropolitan areas was 11 per 100,000 and only 5 per 100,000 for the rural areas and cities outside of the metropolitan areas. The majority of the homicide felons were Afro-American males; the majority of the victims were Afro-American males. Ninty-four percent of the Afro-Americans were slain by Afro-Americans; eighty-four percent of the Caucasians were slain by Caucasians; 88 percent of the males were slain by males; 90 percent of the females were slain by males. A plurality of the offenders were between 15 and 19 years of age. Seventy percent of the miscreants used firearms, 13 percent used cutting or stabbing weapons, 4 percent used blunt objects (clubs, hammers), 5 percent used personal weapons (hands, fists, feet), the rest used such objects as poison and explosives. The victim/offender relationship showed 47 percent either related or acquainted, 14 percent were strangers, and the unusual aspect was that 39 percent of the relationships were unknown. Twenty-nine percent of the female murder victims were killed by their husbands or boyfriends; only three percent of the male victims were killed by their wives or girl friends. There were 455 justifiable homicides by law enforcement in 1993, following a steady rise since the 363 in 1989. There were 356 justifiable homicides by private citizens in 1993, with a steady rise from 273 in 1989. The clearance rate, those offenders who were arrested, charged and turned over to the courts, was 66 percent. This is lower than previous years (91 percent in 1965), but still high compared to other crime categories.

Patterns Of Homicide

The homicide patterns between 1965 to 1992 showed both stability and some changes. The rates were 5.1 in 1965 rose to 9.4 in 1973, then stabilized ranging from 8.0 to 10.2. The most striking change was in the youth of the victims. Between 1975 and 1992, victims under the age of 1 year increased 46 percent and between 10-14 increased 64 percent. Although these changes are significant, the numbers are still relatively small overall. The most murder prone was the 15-24 age group, an increase of almost 50 percent. These three groups account for a 16 percent rise in total homicides between 1975 and 1992. The over 50 victims decreased 32 percent between 1975 and 1992. Homicide is the leading cause of death of young Afro-Americans, a circumstance confirmed in 1992. Afro-Americans have the most perpetrators and victims. Society's reaction to homicide is not uniform and depends on several factors such as the identities of the offender and victim. "Fashion often determines what is just," (Pascal). A number of studies indicate the unequal application of justice to Afro-Americans compared to its application to Caucasians (Garfinkle 1949; Johnson 1941; Wolfgang & Cohen 1970: 85-86). Between 1970 to 1992, the number of Caucasians arrested for homicide increased 67 percent; the juvenile Caucasian arrests rose 204 percent. The gender distribution for victims was virtually unchanged between 1975 and 1992. The weapons used in homicides shifted from the knife to the firearm. From 1965 to 1992, for firearms it went from 57 percent to 68 percent; the use of knives decreased during the same period from 23 percent to 15 percent. The change in circumstance/relationship is significant since the 1960s. In 1965, 5 percent of the circumstances were unknown; in 1992 this rose to 28 percent. In 1992, the victim/offender relationship was 53 percent in the combined categories of "by stranger" and "unknown". This was an historical high. In 1965, 31 percent of the victims were slain by persons in the family. In 1992, it was only 12 percent. Homicide seemed to become less family oriented than in the past. It is believed that the drug trade is a major contributor to the rise in murders whose circumstances are unknown. The fastest growing circumstance is juvenile gang killings, rising from 181 in 1980 to 852 in 1992. A study of job-related deaths from 1980 to 1994 by the Centers for Disease Control and Prevention showed that homicides rose to rank second to traffic accidents as the causes of workplace fatalities.

Homicide in the United States moved steadily upward from 1900 until the 1930s (Bloch & Geis 1970). Then the rate dropped from the mid-1930s to the end of World War II (Zahn 1980). This was followed by a brief upturn (3 years), then a drop to pre-World War II levels. Homicide was at its nadir during the 1950s (Farley 1980) then began to rise during the 1960s and 1970s. By 1980, the rate reached an historic high of 10.2 per 100,000 population, then declined again to 8.3 per 100,000 in 1984. From 1989 to 1993, the rates continued to vary. They were up sharply from 1989 to 1991, down in 1992 and up in 1993. From 1984 to 1993 the rates per 100,000 thousand were up 20 percent.

The varying trends in homicide rates are difficult to interpret. In more recent years activity associated with drugs contributed to increases. During World War II millions of citizens were in the military reducing the opportunity for lethal encounters outside of the battlefield. The trends can also be effected by the statistics and their interpretation. Rises and declines might be artifacts as better medical practices may produce fewer homicides and more aggravated assaults. Better police practices may identify more crimes as homicides.

In more recent times we may seem to be more violent, callused, and with less concern for human life. Some analysts suggest that the apparent shift to random victimization can be attributed to illicit drug traffic, disintegration of the family, and weapon proliferation. None of these suggestions, though candidates for cause, have been proven. For example, the murder rate among heroin users and traffickers is high. This does not mean that drug use or dealing causes homicide. It is more likely that the life style of those involved with drugs increases the opportunity and exposure to a lethal outcome of interpersonal relationships (Zahn & Bencivengo 1974). Zahn (1980) studied homicide in twentieth century United States. The significance of close relationships were obvious, principally domestic and love familiarity followed by friends and acquaintances.

Rates remained relatively low until 1965 when they began to increase sharply, peaking in 1974. Homicide has remained intramale and intraracial. Persistently the statistics show a male killing another male acquaintance. During times of increase, it is usually in the stranger and unknown relationship category with economic motivation. Finally, Zahn found that a relationship between homicide and firearm availability has not been established. But the tide of homicide will follow its history and have its minimal years to replace the elevated ones.

By 1997 the homicide rate dropped for the fifth time in a row (FBI 1998). All major categories of the reported crimes declined for the year. Violent crime was down 4 percent to the lowest rate since 1987. Since 1992 there was a steady decline in criminal activity. Murder declined nationally an impressive 8 percent between 1996 and 1997. Ironically, as the murder rates declined, the use of firearms increased to more than 2/3 of the 15,289 homicides. Although the perception remains that the streets and strangers continue to be dangerous, nearly ½ of all murder victims were known by their killers while only 14% were killed by strangers. It is difficult to identify the reasons for the decline. There are some who argue that the change in demographics – the aging of the population and decline of the crime-prone age groups – and good economic times are the causes of the decline. There is another cohort of people approaching the crime-prone ages that will test the above assertions.

Definition Of Homicide

California Penal Code 187 states, "Murder is the unlawful killing of a human being or a fetus, with malice aforethought." USC Title, Sec. 1111 states, "Homicide. Murder is defined as the unlawful killing of a human being with malice aforethought." Note the omission of the word fetus. Law schools often argue that after the words "human being" should come the words "by another human being." This makes it impossible for a machine, animal, or corporation to commit murder. Homicide is the killing of one person by another person. Usually homicide is divided into four categories: murder and manslaughter representing culpable homicide which can involve criminal prosecution, and justifiable and excusable homicide which ordinarily are not criminally prosecuted. Justifiable homicides are those which involve legal killings. The execution of a condemned prisoner, the policeman slaying someone in a shoot-out, and the guard killing an escaping prisoner, are all examples of justifiable homicide. Killing in self-defense could be justifiable or excusable homicide depending on the circumstances. In excusable homicide, the death is a result of an accident. The circumstances evolved out of lawful acts with adequate exercise of caution and restraint. For example, while disciplining a child or ministering to a sick person an unfortunate accident may occur.

Murder is commonly differentiated into first and second degrees, although in some jurisdictions there may be a third degree. The key consideration in determining the degree of homicide is whether there was premeditation and malice aforethought. Premeditation refers to the intent to kill prior to the act. For example an ambush, or one sets up elaborate plans to destroy another party. Malice aforethought refers to the desire to kill the individual while engaged in the act. For example, shooting someone a number of times is likely to indicate that the purpose was to kill and not just wound. First degree murder requires both premeditation and malice aforethought. Second degree murder includes malice aforethought but not premeditation. There is also a felony-murder doctrine. If a death occurs while committing a felony, the offender is chargeable with murder in the first degree. This may not be true of all felonies as the tendency is to precisely define those instances where it could apply. The most common ones are arson, rape, robbery, and burglary. An offender may be committing a robbery when he is confronted by the police. A shoot-out occurs and the person being robbed is accidentally shot by the police. The offender can be tried for a first degree homicide.

Manslaughter also is ordinarily divided into at least two parts. The first degree is often referred to as voluntary manslaughter while the second degree maybe referred to as involuntary manslaughter. In either case neither premeditation or malice aforethought need be present. It involves an unintended homicide. In the case of voluntary manslaughter, a death occurred under circumstances in which a lethal outcome might reasonably have been expected to occur. A sudden death in a knife fight or as a result of driving recklessly are examples of voluntary manslaughter. In the case of involuntary manslaughter, a fatal outcome in a particular situation is not usually expected. A death from negligent driving, or as a result of a fist fight, are examples of involuntary manslaughter.

Whatever the definition, historically it has varied. The variations occur in legal codes, interpretations, and the practices of those responsible for reporting deaths (Wolfgang and Zahn 1984). When cars were first introduced in the United States, deaths caused by them were classified by some coroners as homicides and others as accidental. Now they are defined as accidental unless negligence played a role. At different times abortions were considered a homicide or a women's right to choose. Devine (1978) suggested a moral definition of homicide. It is, he argued, a "presumption against killing." Thus he extended homicide to abortion and capital punishment.

Homicide And Suicide

Homicide has received considerable attention from a variety of disciplines. Several attempts at a typology have been tried. Durkheim's (1951: 338-359) famous study on suicide included references to the broad social context of homicide. He suggested that family life contains suicide but stimulates homicide. Homicides come from the opposite of the depression found in suicide. In general, societies with a high rate of homicide have a low rate of suicide. Durkheim examined types of suicide, social conditions, and homicide. Egoistic suicide is a result of social conditions emphasizing a low degree of social integration which is opposite to the condition necessary for homicide. Egoistic suicide is typified by feelings of depression and apathy. Egoism acts as a depressant on the homicide rate. Altruistic suicide is the result of conditions favoring a high degree of social integration. These conditions include strong family organization, strong religious and political faith, all generating the intense feelings necessary for homicides. Anomic suicide is related to conditions of normlessness, a breakdown in the regulatory functions, and is even more closely related to homicide than the other conditions. It leads to exaspiration and irritated weariness, states which may be turned against the person himself or others, depending on the circumstances.

The relationship between homicide and suicide, if any, has intrigued many researchers. The psychiatric approach views suicide and homicide as two sides of the same coin: in one instance the aggression is turned inwardly, the other, outwardly, (Menninger 1938: 71). The hypothesis of an inverse relationship between homicide and suicide rates (suggested by Durkheim under certain social conditions) was extensively tested by Henry and Short (1954). They concluded that suicide varied negatively while homicide varied positively with the strength of external restraints. Thus if external restraints are strong, suicides are lower and homicides higher. Richard Quinney (1965: 401-406) studied rates in 48 countries and found that suicide was high and homicide low in countries with a high degree of industrialization and urbanization. He concluded that suicide and homicide did not come from the same causes. Unnithan *et al*, (1994), formed an integrated model that makes a connection between homicide and suicide by depicting alternative presentations of the same motives and social forces. It is self and other-directed lethal violence – again, two sides of the same coin. Although not conclusive, it makes some linking suggestions in a worthwhile scholarly effort. Nevertheless it is still a moot and interesting question and further testing is warranted. Even more interesting would be the inclusion of all forms of deviance. Are rates of mental illness related to rates of homicide, suicide, and other deviant forms?

Johnson (1974: 152-154) used the Durkheimian typology of suicide and considered the relationship between homicide and the nature of sociocultural organization. Egoistic homicide involved those with a weak commitment to the social institutions. The society permits considerable variations in behavior and this enhances the possibility that homicide will be used to resolve conflicts. A similar notion was suggested by Bohannan (1960: 13) in analyzing suicide and homicide among Africans. He pointed out that egoistic homicide was closely associated with the less structured societies.

Altruistic homicide results from the demands of a well-integrated society for conformity to custom and expectations. This may lead to homicides in which there is a claim that the act served a higher purpose and was for the greater welfare of society. Anomic homicide is a result of a diminution of institutional controls. The social pressures and mechanisms of control no longer bind the individual to the rules. However, the distinctions between egoistic and anomic suicide are not clear. Both seem to arise from weak or diiminished social controls. Therefore, the same lack of clarity could be true of egoistic and anomic homicide.

Typologies

An early attempt to type murderers from a psychiatric perspective was offered by Manfred Guttmacher (1960). He studied 175 murder cases and classified them as follows

1. normal (no obvious pathology)
2. sociopath
3. alcoholic
4. avenging
5. schizophrenic
6. temporary psychotic
7. symbolic suicidal (in killing other, destroys part of self)
8. gynocidal (the murder of women by husbands or lovers)
9. homosexual
10. passive-aggressive
11. sadistic

This represents a mixed-bag of motives, situations, and mental states. Guttmacher (1967) edited a later book that went to the other extreme by suggesting very few possible types. It is asserted that most murders are committed by normal people, most do not have criminal backgrounds, and the crime occurs on impulse (like crimes of passion).

Another typology combining psychological and sociological considerations suggested seven types of murderers (Glaser, *et al* 1966: 23-32). The "ordinary" murderer usually reacts to affronts to his masculinity, reflects a tradition of violence, and has been drinking. The "professional" murderer is a killer by profession. The hit-man for organized crime is an example of this type. The "cultural" murderer is one who reacts to social pressures particularly from his subculture. The members of feuding groups or the Klu Klux Klan may murder to gain esteem within their own groups. The "inadequate" killer is driven by the need for self-esteem and cannot be satisfied by ordinary behavior. The “"brain-damaged" assailant with organic dysfunctions may react impulsively in an assaultive manner. The "psychopathic" murderer is one under continuous stress, with minimal conscience who readily erupts, occasionally in a lethal manner. Finally, the "psychotic" murderer is one who reacts to his distortion of reality.

One typology used motives as the criteria for classification (Tennyson 1952). Six types were delineated: murder for gain, murder for revenge, murder for elimination, murder for jealousy, murder for the lust of killing, and murder for conviction.

Gillin (1946: 56-60); (see also Banay 1952: 26) broadly classified the variety of murder situations:

1. Personal disputes of a prolonged nature such as feuds or family disputes.
2. A violent quarrel creating a crisis situation such as in marital discord, arguments while drinking or gambling, and in fights over girl friends.
3. In connection with the commission of another crime. (One might add the professional killer and cover almost all situations, broadly interpreted, connected with most murders. However, the bulk of the murders fell into the first two categories.)

Holmes & Holmes (1994), in an extensive analysis, proposed a general typology of killers.

1. Depressive. Depressed and often under the care of health practioners.
2. Child Killer. Sadism connected to sexual gratification.
3. Sexual. Often a serial killer and sexual sadist.
4. Psychotic. Mentally ill.
5. Organic Brain Disorder. Biologically prone to violence.
6. Psychopathic. Character disorder including a lack of conscience.
7. Mentally Retarded. Limited intelligence involves person in behavior leading to homicide.
8. Professional. The hit-man.

These types basically assume the psychological/psychiatric sick premise and thereby embrace their flaws.

Holmes and Holmes (1983; 1989) offer a typology of mass murderers. It is largely based upon victim characteristics, motivation, anticipated gain, and spatial mobility. It includes:

1. Disciple Killer. A follower of a charismatic leader.

2. Family Annihilator. A senior male in a family, often with an alcohol problem and periods of depression.
3. Pseudocommando. A stockpiler of exotic weapons, plans carefully and after a long period of deliberation, lashes out at society.
4. Disgruntled Employee. Fired from the job or on some kind of disability or medical leave, often under psychiatric care and with strong feelings of injustice, retaliates at the place of employment.
5. Set-and-Run-Killer. A person out for revenge or searching for anonymous infamy, or simply for profit. Though most mass killers commit suicide or are killed by the police, the Set-and-Run Killer attempts to escape, or is not at the scene as he may plant a bomb or poison a product.

Though types seem to offer mere descriptions, they are useful as indicators of heterogeneity. Sometimes each type will attract copy-cat offenders.

Studies Of Homicide

There have been several excellent studies of homicide. One early and very comprehensive one was conducted by Marvin Wolfgang (1958). His study provided a rich source of empirical evidence and prompted further inquiries by others. He analyzed the homicide records in Philadelphia for the five consecutive years 1948-1952. There were 588 victims. Wolfgang was able to present many of the patterns of homicide in considerable detail, coalescing what had previously been scattered through the literature, with original contributions. Of the 588 victims, 550 were slain by 621 known offenders (some cases involved more than one offender), and 38 cases remained unsolved. Some of the major findings are summarized as follows:

1. A disproportionate number of Afro-Americans were involved in the homicides. Seventy-three percent of the victims and 75 percent of the offenders were Afro-Americans, about four times their representation in the 1950 population of Philadelphia.
2. Homicides were concentrated among the males as women were infrequently involved. While males constituted 48 percent of the 1950 population of Philadelphia they accounted for 82 percent of the offenders and 76 percent of the victims. Women represented 18 percent of the offenders but 24 percent of the victims. The majority of the female offenders killed males.

3. Combining gender and race, the offender rates per 100,000 population were 41.7 for Afro-American males, 9.3 for Afro-American females, 3.4 for white males, and 0.4 for white females.
4. Only 6 percent of the homicides were interracial as Afro-Americans killed Afro-Americans and whites killed whites.
5. The methods employed were often brutal and the weapons easily attainable. Thirty-nine persent were stabbed, 33 percent were shot, 22 percent were beaten to death, and 6 percent were the victims of such diverse methods as poison, gas, and arson. The principle method of death for Afro-American victims was stabbing (47 percent), for whites, beatings (42 percent). Females tended to stab almost twice as often as males. These female stabbings were generally the outcome of domestic quarrels and included kitchen utensils. The methods used for homicides are probably a function of the particular subcultures and the availability of weapons.
6. There was a clear-cut temporal pattern. Saturday was the busiest day in the week for homicides (32 percent), and 8 A.M. to 2 P.M. the busiest time (50 percent). Sixty-five percent of the homicides were committed Friday night to Sunday midnight.
7. Alcohol was present in a significant number of homicides. In 44 percent of the cases, both victim and offender had been drinking, in 9 percent of the cases only the victim had been drinking, in 11 percent of the cases only the offender had been drinking, in 64 percent of the cases the offender or the victim had been drinking, and in 36 percent of the cases there was no evidence of any drinking on the part of either party. In spite of the apparent association between alcohol and homicide, caution is necessary before any significant connection is made. Alcohol may release inhibitions but as Wolfgang and Ferracuti (1967) have noted, there are more instances where alcohol interaction occur without violence.
8. Many of the participating parties involved in homicides had previous contacts with the police. Sixty-five percent of the offenders and 47 percent of the victims had a previous police record. Almost half of those offenders with a previous record had been arrested for aggravated assault.
9. As far as could be ascertained, the most frequent motives were: general altercations (35 percent), family and domestic quarrels (14 percent), jealousy (12 percent), money disputes (11 percent).

10. The majority of homicides involved people connected in some primary group fashion. Twenty-eight percent were close friends, 25 percent were family members, 14 percent were acquaintances, and only 12 percent were strangers. In 61 percent of the cases the victim was a close friend, family member, a lover, or a homosexual partner. Forty-one percent of the female victims were killed by their husbands. In homicide, one has more to fear from those who are known than from marauding strangers. This pattern has been repeated in several other studies, particularly in highly industrialized societies (Svalastoga 1956: 37-41; Morris & Blom-Cooper 1964; Driver 1961: 153-58). According to the President's Commission (1967: 18) about 70 percent of all willful killings, 65 percent of aggravated assaults, and a high percentage of forcible rape are committed by family members, friends and acquaintances. The risk of serious attack is only half as much from strangers on the street.

11. Twenty-eight percent of the homicides were victim precipitated. The suggestion here is that the victim was a major contributor to the act and triggered the event by initiating the physical force usually accompanied by verbal abuse. According to this study, also found elsewhere, extendable to other crimes, and theoretically implied by Von Hentig, criminal homicide often involves a personal interaction in which the victim's behavior significantly contributes to the outcome (Wolfgang 1957: 11; Von Hentig 1948: 383-385).

This excellent study suggests the various correlates and patterns in homicide. Most of these events are routine occurrences in the large metropolitan areas and considerably exceed the occasional turgid blow-by-blow journalistic accounts of the rare capricious case. Wolfgang and Ferracuti developed a theoretical framework for the "passionate" murders (Wolfgang and Ferracuti 1967). They propose that when certain psychological and social forms merge into a "subculture of violence" homicides become prevalent. The theory encompasses several major points.

1. Subcultures are never totally different from or in conflict with the larger society.
2. A subculture of violence does not require violence in all situations.

3. The pervasiveness of the theme of violence is attested to by the willingness to use violence in a variety of situations.
4. The ethos of violence in the subculture may be shared by all but is most prominent from late adolescence to middle age.
5. The adult male who does not defend his honor or female companion will be socially emasculated.
6. The incorporation of this ethos usually occurs through differential learning, association, or identification.
7. Violence is not perceived as illicit and thus precludes feelings of guilt.

Some studies support the idea of a "subculture of violence" while others do not. Schultz (1962) demonstrated the concern of Afro-American offenders about being attacked and the need to carry weapons for defense against others in the area who probably also carried weapons. Other studies proposed that the high homicide rates in the United States were related to the spread of southern cultural customs over much of the country from traditions developed before the Civil War (Gastil 1971; Hackney 1969; Doerner 1975; Hepburn 1971). In essence this constitutes the spread of a southern subculture of violence. Although this contention has been criticized because of methodological weaknesses in the studies, the general hypothesis of the importance of cultural variables in violence remains functional (Loftin & Hill 1974).

One study found no support for the subculture of violence (Ball-Rokeach 1973). There was very little relationship between the attitudes and violent behavior or values and violent behavior, neither distinguishing the violent from the nonviolent. Violence, it is argued, is primarily interpersonal, while attitudes and values are intrapersonal. Violent behavior comes out as an interaction and not out of one person or another person but a collaboration of both. The randomness of a lot of violence such as drive-by shootings and many manslaughter cases might belie the notion of a collaboration.

If there is a subculture of violence, contemporary experience would indicate that the ethos has reached downward from late adolescence to preadolescence. In addition, a national sample indicated that neither socio-economic status nor social class values were associated with violence. In short, it would seem that just about everyone has the capacity for violence and across-the-board many practice it, overtly or covertly. The concept of a culture of violence remains moot.

There have been other important studies on homicide, several corroborating Wolfgang's findings. Alex Pokorny (1965) replicated Wolfgang's study with an analysis of 438 criminal homicides in Houston between 1958 and 1961. Another replication was attempted with Chicago homicides in 1965 (Voss & Hepburn 1968). There were some differences, for example in Houston almost two-thirds of the deaths were by shootings compared to one-third in Philadelphia and one-half in Chicago. However, in general, the findings were remarkably similar. In each study criminal homicide occurred most often between members of the same race; those involved tended to be relatives or friends; males were most frequently involved; and the most likely hours were between 8 P.M. and 2 A.M. A U.S. Department of Justice (1991: 399) analysis found almost 78 percent of the homicides occurred between relatives or personal acquaintances.

Two other investigations involved 462 homicides in Greater Cuyahaga County (Cleveland, Ohio) between 1947 and 1953, and all homicides in Houston between 1945 and 1949 (Bensing & Schroeder 1960; Bullock 1955). The studies also found that most homicides occur on weekends. They also identified the ecological nature of homicides locating most of them in predominantly Afro-American areas, densly populated and manifesting slum conditions. The Cleveland study detected homicides linked to petty quarrels, marital discord, and sexual disputes, a familiar pattern in homicides. The Houston study recognized certain groups with lifestyles conducive to homicide, a contention similar to the notion of a "subculture of violence."

Gilliin (1946) assessed the background characteristics of imprisoned murderers. He found that they came from rural areas more often than sex or property offenders. More were from low income families, left school prematurely, had unstable employment records, and had fewer prior offenses than other prisoners. In general, they were relatively conventional persons, although they seemed to be detached and alienated. Palmer (1960) studied 51 New England prison inmates. He discovered a background of physical beatings by parents and an exceptional amount of frustrating experiences, particularly in the early years through adolescence. Waldo (1970) compared 621 murderers with nonmurderers in a prison population. His findings indicated that murderers had a lower "criminality level" than imprisoned non-murderers. Swigert and Farrell (1977) suggested that the popular conception of criminality in the adjudication of homicide defendents encompassed the stereotype of a "normal primitive." This refers to a person described as behaving normally in his own social setting. This social setting is then portrayed in a way similar to the notion of the "subculture of violence." The study concluded that this criminal conception along with social class has significant negative consequences for the defendant in the adjudication process.

Yarvis (1991) suggests that there are a number of factors relevant to the study of homicide – "proximate causal factors." They include such things as interpersonal relations, impulse control, reality testing, natural thinking, psychiatric disorders, stress, and intoxication. All of the factors are placed under the categories of baseline mental functions, interference from psychiatric disabilities, and effects of transient factors. This "explanatory model of murder" is obviously heavily influenced by the psychiatric model of personality. Added to the list are "long term causal factors." This contains negative family role models, childhood instability, disruptions of childhood environment. Each category is further elaborated. Other factors include demographic characteristics like sex, age, criminal history, and number of victims. Finally, there are childhood behavior patterns: psychiatric illness in childhood, behavioral difficulties in childhood, juvenile criminal behavior, school difficulties, interpersonal difficulties. Studies within this framework (prioritized) were 100 murderers in a *post hoc* methodolgical design. The results showed that the "proximate causal factors" accounted for the initiation of homicidal behavior. There also was considerable heterogeneity in the population of murderers. And lastly, there were seven distinct homicide clusters, but certain factors were universal.

As is true of most studies of this type, there are limitations. The author notes that a predictive model from these findings is unlikely. This would suggest the lack of a causal relationship. The psychiatric focus can be self-fulfilling. A search for difficulties in anybody's background is not difficult to find. Then, how does one account for those with similar characteristics who do not commit murder?

Holmes & Holmes (1994) elaborated the various facets of homicide. Race and gender were found to be important elements of the likelihood of becoming a victim. In 1988 the risk was 1 in 30 for the Afro-American male and 1 in 132 for the Afro-American female; for the white male it was 1 in 179 and 1 in 495 for the white female (Holmes & Holmes: 7). Most of the offenders were between 20 and 40, with the majority closer to 20. Most were males. While the female numbers were less (12 percent) they were increasing due to a more aggressive response to battering and adoption of similar motives for homicide as men (Holmes & Holmes: 9). There were geographical differences by city, county, and state and within each area as well. Rates fluctuated depending on the day of the week and month of the year with most occurring on the weekends. Afro-Americans were overrepresented in perpetrator and victim; most killers murdered within their race. Hand guns were most popular (43-59 percent), stabbing or cutting weapons were used 21 percent of the time, and the rest used blunt instruments, personal weapons (hands, feet), poison, fire, explosives.

All homicides are not alike. Neither the killers nor the crimes constitute a homogenious or unified concept. Some analysts believe that murder is fueled by drugs, dealers, and guns. Daly and Wilson (1988), from a psychological perspective, argue that killing is the ultimate conflict resolution technique. But the reasons, methods, and victims are varied. There are different motives and some times no motive at all, the backgrounds of the killers range from intelligent to dumb, educated to illiterate, thin to obese, all sexual orientations, both genders, and young through old to very old and very young; the settings vary from bedrooms to bars, and the methods from feet to bombs. Wolfgang (1958) showed this lack of uniformity as did the later studies by Falk (1990) and others.

Falk did an extensive study of murders in one specific area. He analyzed 912 cases of homicide in Erie County in New York between 1916 and 1983. The study was descriptive. That is, it involved an accumulation of facts that increase understanding of a phenomenon and set the stage for hypotheses. Different categories of murders were established. They included youth gangs, adult gangs (organized crime), rape-murder, parent-child, child-parent, jealousy, spouse, arson, self-defense, unknown killers, robbery, white collar, multicide (genocide, mass, serial) and many others. This is a mixed bag of motives, circumstances, methods, and participants. Nevertheless it is interesting to detail the different ways in which a lethal outcome can occur contributing to the difficulty in assigning causes to homicide.

The results showed few surprises. Saturday was the most lethal day and 2-3 A.M. the most lethal time. Wednesday was the least lethal with 6-7, 8-9, 11-noon, the safest times. In public places, they occurred most often in bars while in private places, most often in bedrooms. The higher the temperature, the higher the rate; it was highest for the Afro-American and lowest for

Asians. Most victims were 20-29, male, and laborers. Some of the demographics could be misleading because some of the categories were not patterned and probably spurious.

Falk also catalogued some of the conditions and dispositions of the cases:

1. Seventy percent knew their victims from casually to kinship.
2. Eighty-five percent of the cases involved alcohol, 12 percent some drugs, and three percent, both drugs and alcohol.
3. Forty-five percent were killed by some firearm, 30 percent by knives, 16 percent by hands, 9 percent by other means.
4. The motives were distributed among part of another crime (27.9 percent), sudden anger (23.9 percent), victim precipitation (11.2 percent), jealousy (10.8 percent), business dealings (7.2 percent); the rest included insanity, gang war, organized crime, drug deal, accident, divorce, racism, revenge.
5. Eighty-three percent were convicted, 4 percent pleaded guilty, 11 percent were not convicted.
6. Two percent were sentenced to death, 85 percent to prison, the rest were sent to a psychiatric hospital, given probation, or reversed on appeal.

These percentages are similar to other studies like Wolfgang (1958), Fisher (1976), and others in Chicago, Cleveland, and Houston.

Multicides

Assassinations, terrorism and multicides involve different patterns of action and reaction than the usual single homicide. These kinds of lethal acts are not new. But the contemporary scene with extensive media exposure makes it seem new, rampant, and spectacular, with everybody at risk. This reflects the consequence of embellishment and the old notion that we fear most those crimes that occur the least.

Assassination. – In the 11th century A.D., inspired by the conquests of a 9th century Iraqui peasant, the Ismaili Sect of Alamuit in Northern Persia, became a center for killings to further their religious cause (Durant 1950: 262; 310; Wilson 1972). They were called *hashshasheen* in Arabic from which the term assassin is derived. In general, an assassin can be described as one who murders because of disagreement with the victim's public position in politics or religion, or conflicting economic interests such as business rivals principally involving illegal enterprises (Falk 1990: 95).

Assassinations are murders, but different in a number of ways (Ellis and Gullo 1971). Assassination commonly involves a political figure, but could refer to any public figure. It is usually a politically motivated homicide, closely linked to internal political violence, external aggression, minority tensions, and high homicide rates (Kirkham, *et al*, 1969: 163-166). The United States ranks about fifth out of eighty-two countries in frequency of political assassinations. The assassin intensely disagrees with the view of the victim and feels that he is performing a valuable public service. On occasion, he is jealous, or he may hope to gain status, or the victim is a symbol of an intense hatred. The perpetrator rarely, if ever, has prior contact with the victim and only knows about him. The attack frequently takes place in front of an audience, perhaps dictated by opportunity or to gain instant recognition. Since there is an audience present, apprehension would seem to be desired by the assassin. They are often seriously distrubed and it has been suggested that with few exceptions, they tend to be psychotic (Kirkham, *et al*, 1969: 250). There are times when the political assassination involves a planned effort by some revolutionary group. This is more apt to occur in a country where the political system is unstable. As is the case in many types of homicide, little is known about assassins and even less about political ones.

Terrorism. – Terrorism has escalated since the 1970's. Forty percent of the victims are American or Canadian, but not necessarily as a result of an attack within either country. Acts of terrorism can include bombings, arson, and assassinations directed against specific targets. Unfortunately, the targeting spills over to innocent bystanders. Holmes and Holmes (1994) define it as "premeditated, politically motivated violence, perpetrated against noncombatant targets by subnational groups or clandestine state agents, usually to influence an audience." This is probably an adequate definition given how little is really known about terrorism and its practitioners. Some studies suggest elements of the unlawful use of force, such as assassination or kidnapping, with the intent to coerce or intimidate governments for ideological reasons. It is further suggested that the perpetrators are young, intelligent, industrious, committed, enduring feelings of persecution, and experiencing a sense of personal grandeur. Some may be psychotic. The recent bombings in Oklahoma City and the New York

World Trade Center have highlighted this form of terror. Although all bombings are not terrorist attacks, most of the devastating ones are. They go far beyond the adolescent prank of a bomb in a mail box. The Federal Bureau of Alcohol, Tobacco and Firearms reported a 76 percent increase in bombings from 1989 to 1993, a total of 6,574 cases and a jump to 2,400 incidents annually. Between 1989 and 1993 there have been 328 deaths, 3419 injuries, at a cost of over 641 million dollars. And all this before the disaster in Oklahoma City. The Bureau of Alcohol, Tobacco and Firearms suggested the following motives for bombings, from the most prevalent to the least: vandalism, revenge, protest, extortion, homicide/suicide, labore-related, insurance fraud. One could add that terrorism which may occur the least, can be the most destructive. It remains to be seen how the various government and policing agencies manage this growing threat.

Genocide. – There are different types of multicides with the common connection of more than one victim, ranging from two to millions. These include genocide, serial murders, and mass murders. Genocide can be illustrated with both historical and contemporary examples. In America there was the killings of the Native-Americans during the settlement of the West. Of those that occurred in Europe the holocaust is the most spectacular example of the deliberate killing of innocent people–over 6 million of them (Gilbert 1979).

Serial murders. – Serial homicides involve several victims over a span of time. For example, Ted Bundy, John Wayne Gacy, and Jack the Ripper, killed many people over time, either in one locale or scattered over many areas. Holmes & Holmes (1994: 73) differentiate the serial murderer from the spree murderer. Serial murder is the killing of three or more people with more than 30 days between the first and last kill. The spree murder is the killing of three or more people within a thirty day period. Where the mass murderer tends to die at the scene of the crime by his own hands or that of others, the serial murderer trys to avoid detection. In addition, the community response to a mass murder is usually immediate, fierce, and transient; while the community response to a serial murder can disrupt a community with fear for a sustained amount of time. The number of serial murderers in the United States is unknown but estimated at 35-200. The number of victims also varies with some estimates as high as 5000 (Holmes & Holmes 1994: 104). Spatially, some are mobile as they travel from one area to another while some are geographically stable. The serial murder starts with a fantasy, followed by the stalking of the victim, an abduction, the homicide, and ends with the disposal of the body (Holmes & Holmes 107). As is usually the case, a typology has been attempted by Holmes & DeBurger (1988). This one is based on the kinds of motives for the acts, The four types are:

1. Visionary. Voices told him to kill.
2. Mission. The goal in life is to eliminate certain people.
3. Hedonistic. This is the thrill killer.
4. Power/Control. There is gratification from the control over victims.

As seems to be true of so many typologys, the criteria are mixed and concepts barely defined. Still they have some descriptive and general value.

Mass murders. – Mass homicides involve many victims mostly in one place at one time. How many is many? Holmes & DeBurger (1985; 1988) suggest three as many. For example, in 1984 an unemployed security guard killed 24 people in a McDonald's Restaurant while in 1995 a bomb killed 168 people in the Federal Building in Oklahoma City. In recent years there were a number of these kinds of homicides – though still relatively rare. The explanations for such behavior remain debatable. They range from psychoses through poverty to brain damage. Some allege an unique combination of biological, sociological, and psychological factors; as root causes such explanations are useless as they can include everyone and no one.

Some Other Types Of Homicide

Spousal murder. – Partner or spousal homicide is a familiar form through its magnification by the mass media. This is where one spouse (or live-in partner) kills the other. Between 1976 and 1985, 8.8 percent of all homicides were partner commitments (Mercy & Saltzman 1989). The problem is international. In the United States, the female is more likely to be assaulted, injured, raped, or killed by a male partner than by a stranger (Browne & Williams 1987). It seems related to domestic violence and spousal abuse. Abusers and the abused have been studied, but it still is not well understood (Gelles 1974, 1979; Gelles & Straus 1989; Hansen & Harway 1993). There is general agreement that spouse abuse is under-reported to police, abuse centers, and other appropriate agencies. Many spouses may call the police, obtain court orders, and still become victims of homicide. Many times the perpetrator commits suicide. The causes are complex. Some writers believe it is a manifestation of a general devaluation of and violence against women (Stordeur & Stille 1989). However, this is too general a thesis to be valuable. Some of the reasons for the act include unfulfilled expectations, high stress due to poor health, loss of a job, or other kinds of trauma (Kratcoski 1987).

Parricide. – This refers to the killer of a close relative such as parents by their children. It could be the murderer of a person whose relationship resembles that of a father like the ruler of his country. It also has been applied to one that commits treason against his country. There is a small percentage of homicides where the children kill the members of the extended family. There is a new growing industry in middle America – the murder for hire. Husbands, wives, children, and other kin are hiring amateur hit-men, mostly from greed or anger. This represents a trend involving a radical response to a moral decay.

Infanticide. – The terms homicide and murder usually refer to the wrongful death of an adult at the hands of another adult. But it does not preclude the killing of an infant. Some parents murder their children, an act hard to fathom with no clear understanding of it in the literature. Some connect it to child abuse; some characteristics of the perpetrator are depression and alcoholism. The circumstances and motives for the act seem to be different for the father and the mother.

There is the case of the mother who kills her child, then commits suicide. This has been referred to as "altruistic filicide." It is believed that these women are usually mentally ill. There are those women who kill children under the age of one. Some experts believe this to be an abortion substitute. The mothers are often religious, naive, and feel the need to conceal their pregnancies from their families.

While most infanticides are committed by women, this is not exclusively so. Angry lovers and boy-friends kill the mother's baby on occasion whether he is or is not the father. And occasionally children kill children – playing with a parent's gun, beating another to death in a game gone awry, pushing or shoving in traffic or off a cliff or a bank into a stream or out of a window. But these are tragic misadventures, seldom true homicides.

Currently, one may catalog five kinds of situations leading to infanticide. A woman throws her baby into a sewer or a dumpster or leaves it in the rest room immediately after delivering it because she does not perceive it as a living creature. Another kills her baby out of an overwhelming sense of shame infinitely more powerful than any sense of guilt. The third has marked mood swings from loving and caring to a need to get rid of an irritant. A poor family has too many children, the last of whom is neglected and literally starved to death. Giving birth in a hospital, the mother sneaks away and abandons the infant. No one in the hospital is assigned to care for it, so it is not cared for and dies. (Piers 1978: 13-24). One dramatic and shocking example of hospital neglect was the case of a licensed vocational nurse who killed over thirty babies by lethal injection. Apparently this was because she hated some of the staff and had a compulsion to become a hero over all others in the hospital and in her community, (Moore and Reed 1988). She injected the babies and intended to succor them and bask in the accolades of the staff. Too often the plan went awry and a baby died.

Until about 1960, some doctors allowed hopelessly deformed and impaired infants to die at birth because they could not save them, given the state of medical science that prevailed up to that time. However, medicine made great strides in the next three decades to mitigate, if not to correct, birth defects. New discoveries and technologies made it possible for tiny premature infants to survive, as well as infants suffering from conditions long thought to be fatal. But the price has been high. Few if any ever lead normal lives. Many die early. Meanwhile, the financial and emotional strain on families for procedures to care for them is harrowing and sometimes stretches beyond the lives of parents and care givers. The consequence is an ethical, moral, and unrecognized social dilemma: what if support is withdrawn early – is this infanticide? What if it is not – does this promise a meaningful life? (Lyon 1985: 59-79). These issues are as ancient as mankind itself, now compounded by modern technologies that make their resolution as remote as ever.

Another contemporary anomaly is fetal homicide. This would be the result of a violent act that results in the death of an embryo or fetus. These acts are handled differently across the states. In some, killing an embryo from the moment of conception can be prosecuted as a homicide, (ie Ohio, the Dakotas and seven other states). In California it is a homicide if it occurs at 7 or 8 weeks. Eight states claim a homicide if the act occurs when the mother can feel its movement. Six states define it a homicide only after 24 weeks or the point when it could survive outside the womb. The rest cite the rule that the child must be born alive before death from fetal injuries can be prosecuted as a homicide. Fetal rights have drawn support from some and the chagrin of the abortion advocates. The attribution of these rules are by no means certain. The legal haggling over the issue should bring it before the public with increasingly shrill responses.

While not infanticide as strictly defined and understood, there have been current incidents where children were shot on school grounds by fellow students. Between October 1997 and May 1998 there were seven of these shootings. In all cases the assailants were boys. They killed one teacher and fourteen children. One shooter committed suicide. Forty-five pupils were wounded in these affrays. Some of the shooters bought or had been given the guns they used. Others took them from their homes where they were not secured or where there was a pervasive culture of guns and gun use.

Speculation and on-site statements give only meager clues to what motivate school children to shoot their class mates. One said it was evidence of power. One or two wanted revenge when a girl friend preferred some one else. One resented being expelled from school. He was also known to torture cats and said he wanted to kill people. While not a shooting but still in the scene where the young kill the young, eleven youths were involved in hanging a 15-year old companion for snitching. When she did not die, one of the group beat her to death with a rock. School yard deaths like these are unusual, but they should be noted in any summary of the history of homicide.

Female murderers. – Obviously, the female does not kill as often as the male and the reasons for the act also differ. In general, the typical female murderer kills in response to an abusive situation, the victim is someone she knows, and the event occurs inside her own home (Goetting 1989). Other reasons for the female's mortal acts include being spurned by a lover and involvement in cults (the Manson family). Some do become serial killers who tend to slay for money, insurance, or similar forms of profit.

Two recent books have chronicled the gruesome tales and details of female serial killers. From a feminist perspective, the writers hope for recognition that these kind of women can get away with murder because of the tendency to perceive and treat women differently in the criminological spectrum–another example of discrimination (Kelleher and Kelleher 1998). The authors consider different types of female killers such as the Black Widow and Angel of Death. The former includes those who marry and kill their spouses. They manage 10-15 murders before they are caught. The latter kill those in their care like children in hospitals and elderly patients in nursing homes. Pearson (1998) chronicles the female serial killer. The book is a polemic as it focuses on women's potential for violence and murder.

Lombroso & Ferrero (1915) described the born female criminals as more of a male than a normal female and that her crimes were caused by the masculine traits of the born criminal which are part of her physique. W. I. Thomas (1923) in *The Unadjusted Girl* alleged that offenders should not be punished but rehabilitated by careful treatment under indeterminate sentences. Women offenders are, said Thomas, less adjusted to the realities of their lives than male offenders are to theirs. Consequently they usually require longer periods of detention under indeterminance than do men for similar offenses. In *The Criminality of Women*, Pollak (1950) held that women's crime rates are masked by their social roles as wives, mothers, cooks, shoppers, home makers, church workers, their absence from commerce and industry, the secrecy of their menses, and other similar factors. Thus they are under detected, under reported, under arrested, under convicted, and under sentenced. Remove the mask and their crime rates would approximate those of men.

The social ecology movement held that crime was a product of ethnic and chiefly neighborhood cultures where crime was a norm that is learned in association with others. However, women if arrested are booked and incarcerated frequently for sex misconduct while men seldom are. Feminists ask why sex activity is an offense for females but not males. They object to all such themes in American crime studies. The rise in the feminist movement parallels the rise in female arrests but the former does not cause the latter. More women are arrested partly because of a widening fear of broad changes in society. Society reacts to this as it has to analogous changes by increasing law enforcement in its effort to slow down social change. More changes mean more arrests – in this case, of women. Some women murder with a feminist perspective as the motive (Jones 1980). Nevertheless, females are a very small percentage in the statistics of homicide.

Sex murders. – Sex related homicides are murders with a sexual component. It frequently involves fantasy, symbolism (a fetish or attachment to a certain body part like breasts or buttocks), ritualism (a particular pattern of behavior), and compulsion (a strong urge to repeat the crime and to kill). The act can include body mutilation. Some analysts distinguish lust murder as a type of sex homicide (Holmes & Holmes 1994: 161-162). The assaultive type of sex homicide is likely to involve a personality pathology often defined as a sex psychopath, a concept which has many critics.

Abortion. – Abortion is the deliberate termination of a pregnancy before the fetus is viable. There was a time in United States when this was illegal under most circumstances. It remains a contentious issue in United States with many opponents considering it a form of homicide. Legislative action in the 20th century has been aimed at permitting the termination of an unwanted pregnancy for medical, social, and personal reasons. The impetus for the change to legality was three-fold infanticide and the high maternal death rate associated with illegal abortions; a rapidly expanding world population; the growing feminist movement.

Hate killers. – One reason that some kill is simply hate. The potential is compounded by the formation of hate groups. There are as many as 71 such groups in the United States (Holmes & Holmes 1994: 53). The most widely known examples are the Klu Klux Klan (around the longest) and the Skinheads (Stohl 1988). Their doctrine encompasses "white supremacy," (White 1991). There are Identity Church organization espousing hate theology. They would include the Aryan nation and the *Posse Comitatus.* Their major targets are Afro-Americans and Jews which were expanded to include gays and lesbians. Violence is their theme; homicide an occasional consequence.

Conclusion

Homicide is a universal phenomenon with some similarities and many differences. The patterns change with time as well as place. The era of computers is upon us. Some people will kill to get one. Preoccupation with technology may make us focus on things and impersonalize relationships with a potential for deadly consequences. The opposite might occur where technology gives the opportunity for catharsis like nintendo games or channeling of hostility. As a crime of passion, homicide is found in many strata of society, yet may be concentrated in certain groups and areas. It occurs most often among persons with relationships and is best understood as social interactions within a cultural context.

The prohibition of homicide varies with the circumstances. In the past, heresy and treason were considered more detestable than homicide; in the modern era homicide became more abhorrent (Nettler 1982). The sacredness of life formulated in America places homicide at the apex of taboos. What is homicide and what is not derives from moral concerns.

The swarm of statistics describes the many aspects of homicide but does not explain why people kill. Attempts to explain it are legion, varied and at times contentious. Einstein once noted that when two people disagree, probably both are wrong. Daly & Wilson (1988) try to explain why people kill within a paradigm of evolutionary psychology. In brief, this refers to the expectation that two individuals will perceive themselves in conflict when the improvement of one's expected "fitness" contributes to the diminution of the other's "fitness." The adaptive characteristic of people is shaped by a "selection" process – the human psyche has been shaped by a history of selection (in the evolutionary sense).

If one accepts Durkheim's (1964) notion of the "normality of crime," without a perfect society there will always be crime. The less perfect the society, the more morbid the rate of crime. Homicide, as a crime, would fit into this notion. However, like most theories, this too is flawed, one reason being that societies do not kill, people do. There are many alternatives to action. Most often we tend to select a few of the vast array of alternatives available for each action. The array we select is significantly effected by our culture and subculture, our personality, and the structure of our society, all broadly defined and interactive as a system (Rudoff 1991).

Rudoff suggests a model of deviance that attempts to synthesize the various theories and with some modification and within a probability framework, one might be able to predict the kind of crime one is likely to commit as well as the chances of becoming deviant. Other theories suggest some internalize anger and develop psychosomatic illnesses. Others externalize it and assault the source of the anger or the symbolic representation of it, while still others neutralize it by redefining the situation in which the anger occurred. Nevertheless, the causes of violence in general and homicide in particular remain moot. Theorists search for explanations within a bio-anthropological, psychological/psychiatric, and socio-cultural framework.

The conceptual schemes may account for one aspect of deviance but not all. The searches for explanation continue.

Violence varies from society to society in its many aspects including the extent of its incidence and the forms it takes. In some cultures it is rare like the Arapesh of New Guinea and the Zuni Indians. The United States ranks high, uppermost among the highly industrialized societies. Most often, homicide is a crime of passion, seldom planned and carried out in cold blood. It tends to occur in conditions involving interpersonal tension and antagonism. These factors not only describe homicide in America, but in other countries as well.

CHAPTER FOUR

THE GENRE

Roots Of The Genre

The roots of the mystery detective (homicide) literature run deep. Some suggest Sophocles' *Oedipus Rex* as the prototype (Benevenuti & Rizzoni 1979: 1). There has been a brutal murder. Oedipus marries the victim's widow and becomes King. The victim implores the Gods for justice; they respond. The city must expiate the sin. Oedipus agrees to investigate the crime. He discovers the murderer – himself, with the additional crime of incest. Other sources include the bible, Herodotus, Arabian Nights, legends from China and Japan, and the real crimes occurring everywhere at all times. Other literary sources include Horace Walpole's *Castle of Otranto* 1764 and Mary Wollstonecraft Shelley's *Frankenstein* (1818). The ingredients were there, but did not come together until the 19th century with the advent of the professional investigator and police force.

However, mystery and detecting were scattered throughout literature before it blossomed into a genre. Writers such as Honoré de Balzac, Eugene Sue, Victor Hugo, Wilkie Collins, and Charles Dickens gave us a taste of what was to come. Dickens created Inspector Bucket in *Bleak House* and the *Mystery of Edwin Drood*. The Drood story was indeed a mystery with murder; unfortunately, it was never solved. Dickens died leaving the great mystery unfinished. Poe's *The Cask of Amontillado* focused on death for revenge. Of course, even the bible had its intrigue and murder. The story of the three Princes and the missing camel was told in the *Arabian Nights* (Ball 1976: 8). The term "detective police" was coined by Sir James Graham, the British Home Secretary in 1843/1844 (Ball 1976: 8). Dumas introduced the detective Monsieur Jackal who gave us the phrase *cherchez la femme*! Collins created Sergeant Cuff in *Moonstone*, drawn from an actual Inspector of Scotland Yard.

Lincoln read detective stories for "stimulation and solace;" President Wilson praised the *Middle Temple Murder* by J. S. Fletcher; Flemming's James Bond was read by President Kennedy with relish (Ball 1976: 17). President Roosevelt was another notable captivated by mysteries. The writers write within a cultural perspective. For example, if one writes during a period when torture is prevalent, it could be appropriately included in the story in different ways – in opposition to it, in acceptance of it, or objectively inserted. The definition of crime itself varies in time and place. The development of science produced contexts for hero or villain, new weapons and places, and other factors relevant to the story. Inductive logic became a tool of the detective. Even the heinousness of the crime desired by the author would be dictated by the cultural context.

The first professional detective to become famous was Eugene Francis Vidocq, the dashing founder of the Sûreté. He headed the French organization for twenty-eight years. This was quite an astonishing feat since he started as a galley slave. His renown served many detective mystery writers, especially Balzac. Hugo's *Les Miserables* fed the Gaelic distaste of the police with the character of Inspector Javert. Vidocq published his *Memoires* in 1829. Little did this famous detective realize that his autobiography would inspire Edgar Allen Poe and later Emile Gaboriau to write their trailblazing works in detective fiction. Poe is conceded the father of the detective genre with his *Murders in the Rue Morgue*. This was the first detective story while Gaboriau wrote the first detective novels. Poe noted that one could not combine a regular novel and a mystery story (Hillerman & Herbert 1996). The detective mystery introduced a puzzle and challenged the reader to solve it. The regular novel did not challenge the reader. *A Sudy in Scarlet*, with Sir Arthur Conan Doyle's Sherlock Holmes exploded on the scene, gilded Poe's lily and gave the mystery detective story respectability. Holmes was fiction's first consulting detective. The genre has attracted millions of readers since the beginning while the form has changed. Holmes is still a cult figure in Japan. In addition to the translations of Doyle's work, the Japanese have developed their own background books, adaptations, plays, films, children's versions, cartoons, parodies, and even an opera. Two of their most famous fictional detectives of the 1950s were inspired by Holmes – Kogoro Akechi, a dashing city sleuth, and Kosuke Kindaichi, a kimono-clad aristocrat rural detective.

In Poe's story the mutilated bodies of a mother and daughter were found in the area of an apartment in the Rue Morgue in Paris. One Auguste Dupin, a cavalier amateur detective, philosopher, and logical thinker, finally solves the mystery. He was aided by an unnamed friend who narrated the extraordinary exploits of Dupin. Dupin was the forerunner of a host of successful sleuths including Sir Conan Doyle's Sherlock Holmes, S. S. Van

Dine's Philo Vance, Agatha Christie's Hercule Poirot, and Rex Stout's Nero Wolfe (Benevenuti & Rizzoni 1979: 9). All of these famous detectives had their faithful companion and aid like Holmes's Dr. Watson and Wolfe's Archie Goodwin. Dupin reappeared in 1845 in Poe's *The Purloined Letter.* In some series, characters are developed and maintained. The character can achieve literary immortality if well-received by the public. Such successes are frequent, from Holmes to Poirot.

Poe's initial impact was most felt in Paris. The background for acceptance had been prepared by writers like Balzac, Victor Hugo, Vidocq and the success of novels of passion in the popular press. The chief adherent of Poe was Emile Gaboriau with *L' affaire Lerouge*. He closely followed Poe's *The Murders in the Rue Morgue*. The English version of the genre was heir to the Gothic novels and horror stories. Charles Dickens offered crime and detection in *Oliver Twist* (1837). *Barnaby Rudge* had similar elements (1841). A friend, a sergeant in Scotland Yard, became a model for several short stories and inspired Dickens to produce *Bleak House* (1853) and the Mystery of *Edwin Drood* (1870). Though one of his tales of terror (he called them crawlers), Stevenson's (1952) Jekyl and Hyde did contain some elements of the mystery. There was a homicide, an assault, a suicide, and indications of strange terrors that may have included acts of mayhem. The killer Hyde was pursued by police, there was suspense, signs of detecting and pre-Freudian psychological themes. It might be referred to as a psychological thriller with Gothic undertones allegedly borne out of nightmares.

Genre Writers

From the turn of the century up to World War I, detective fiction rose rapidly in popularity. Joining the early greats were an assortment of writers, not always as good as Doyle and Poe. Jacques Futrelle and R. Austin Freeman gave the genre an aura of intellectual and scientific credibility. Mary Roberts Rinehart shifted focus from the detective to the victim and the offender. The milieu was usually the wealthy and their entourages. Gilbert Keith Chesterton, a writer of note outside of the detective category created Father Brown, the sleuthing priest. He also dignified the genre and was largely responsible for the psychological detective novel as an independent type. A host of writers contributed contemporaneously with the leaders, and the category maintains its popularity today with many of the writers worthy successors to the pioneers.

French novels built around such characters as Arséne Lupin (early 20th century) elevated the style to literary distinction. They had elements of Greek tragedy and political and social themes (Benvenuti & Rizzoni 1979: 43). After World War I, the detective novels began to catch up with the technology developed during the war creating a new reality – cars, radios, airplanes, and movies. This period marked the golden age of the genre. Agatha Christie began to write and dominate the class for fifty years. In the 1920's, Christy and Dorothy Sayers brought finesse and cunning to the tech story. In America, similar developments appeared a bit later with Ellery Queen, Dashiell Hammet, Mignon Eberhart, and others. The contents widened to encompass the traditional methods but also adapted to the new times. Some writers introduced humor, turned to character description and psychological concerns. This period, lasting into the 1930's was dominated by the English writers. There was an interaction of influence between the English and the Americans.

The English. – The real architect of the English detective story was William Wilkie Collins (1824-1889). His novel *Moonstone* is thought to be the first real English detective story. The book is about a stolen sacred diamond, seized from an Indian sect and involving the murder of three Brahmins. The stone carries a curse and the culprit and his family become victims of this curse. The thief dies and a niece inherits the stone. The stone disappears and the police are notified. A Sergeant Cuff of Scotland Yard is assigned to the case and after several false starts, solves the mystery. Many critics (T. S. Eliot for one) lauded the novel, some as the greatest detective novel ever written.

For years the English dominated the genre, enriching it and spreading it around the world. Though the American's began to dominate, the English continued to contribute significantly. Ngaio Marsh, a New Zealander of English extraction produced many outstanding novels. She presented Inspector Roderick Alleyn in her first book, *A Man Lay Dead* (1934). He appeared in some thirty of her works. Ethel Lina White inspired two famous movies, *The Lady Vanishes*, a Hitchcock thriller from her book *The Wheel Spins* (1936) and the Spiral Staircase from *Some Must Watch* (1934). Edgar Wallace was very prolific with over 170 books, short stories, comedies, and scripts in his 27 year career. According to Barzun (Hillerman & Herbert

1996) the classic British tech stories are written by and for the educated upper middle classes. The setting usually is in an upper-crust milieu. The characters are types not persons; it is escape literature for the "intellectuals."

The French. – After World War I, detective fiction became fashionable in France. Numerous French writers followed the classic English style. But in the 1930s they turned away from the English rules and came closer to the pure novel. Care was taken with language and the character of the victim, criminal, and detective, both physically and psychologically. Most representative of this school is Pierre Véry. He published 28 mystery novels of people contending with reality. In 1932 a famous novelist, Claude Aveline (a pseudonym of Claude Avtzin) entered the field, the first time a French author of renown turned to detective tales.

There have been various partnerships in the writing of these type novels like Ellery Queen. One important example is that of the Frenchmen Thomas Narcejac and Pierre Boileau. They have produced extraordinary contemporary novels full of character studies and extreme tension. Their work has been filmed by Clouzot (*Les Diaboliques* 1954) and Hitchcock (*Vertigo* 1958).

The hard-boiled classics of Hammett and Chandler found their way to France in 1945. Stories of action, violence, and slang – the black novels – were soon adapted by many French authors. They included Le Breton, Sanantonio and Georges Simenon. A number of their stories found their way into French Cinema.

The Americans. – America produced the dime novel in 1860, precursor of the pocket editions and paperbacks. At the beginning the stories were about the expanding frontier with heroes like Buffalo Bill and Kit Carson. Later came other heroes, more successful than the previous ones. Most popular was Nick Carter, first as a detective, later as a James Bond type spy. They were created by a circle of writers who used aliases. The special American experience after World War I – the rise of organized crime, corruption in politics and law enforcement, the "Roaring Twenties" cultural phenomenon, prohibition, the Great Depression – structured a distinctive American version of the social scene. American stories can be in any local milieu – a rural farmhouse, streets of New York, a Montana trail. Dashiell Hammett, the former Pinkerton private detective, was not an effete product of upper or even solid middle class. He took us into the "mean streets." However,

America also had its snob in Van Dine's Philo Vance and perhaps a combination of upper and a less antiseptic class in the couple Nora and Nick Charles. The classic British form endured a myriad of modifications. In America it moved out of the privileged class into a focus on social purpose and realism. And at times, it linked the novel with the detective story.

The American detective fiction arrived on the scene and was highly successful and inventive. One of the most highly acclaimed mystery writers was Ellery Queen. Actually, the name is a pseudonym for two cousins, Manfred B. Lee and Frederic Dannay. The first novel (1929), *The Roman Hat Mystery*, featured an amateur detective named Ellery Queen. The novel was the beginning of the collaboration between Inspector Richard Queen of the New York Police Department and his son Ellery, a writer of detective novels. The cousins wrote 33 novels and many short stories. They received many awards for their crime fiction including five Edgars.

The Others. – In addition to the older pioneers and the new giants, there was a host of minor writers, many with fruitful contributions to the story type. The Englishman Eden Phillpotts was a master at composing tales of criminal intrigue. Philip Mac Donald wrote scripts for Charlie Chan and Mr. Moto (J. P. Marquand's creation) and took time out to write his own mysteries. Alan Alexander Milne introduced humor in his stories. Ronald Arbuthnot Knox was the first priest to produce this kind of literature.

Genre Styles

Benevenuti & Rizzoni (1979: 2-6) suggest 3 essential elements of the detective story. First there is the detective. The forerunner of the detective is found in Voltaire's *Zadig* who identifies a missing dog without seeing it, using the logic of deduction (shades of Sherlock Holmes). Then there is mystery. The most complex is the homicide perpetrated in a locked room. How did the killer do it? The puzzlement, riddle, enigma, connundrum, has always existed and always intrigued. The third element is the denouement – identifying the culprit. Hamlet used a play within the play where the murderer of Hamlet's father reveals himself. This ploy, though modified, has been repeated infinite times in the mystery genre. Christie's Poirot and Hammett's Nick Charles bring the suspects together and skillfully weed out the killer. Monsignor Ronald Knox in about 1928 introduced the "Ten Commandments of Detective Writing." The rules were technical and confirmed the role of detective stories as a genre. They included: introduce the criminal early; shun acts of God; avoid identical twins and doubles unless the reader is prepared for them; the detective can not commit the crime. Of course, the list reflects the prejudice of the time. The rules have since been bent if not broken.

Changes in style came in waves as one form was replaced by another. The variety of detectives and plots multiplied with ethnic detectives, blind ones and women; there arrived energetic detectives and couch potatoes, sophisticated ones and brutes, and many other kinds. Then the motives for the crimes ranged from killing for money to killing for fun. The mystery story has broadened considerably. It once meant detective story as a simple puzzle. It is now variously referred to as mystery fiction, crime fiction, detective fiction, suspense story, spy story, adventure story, and a gothic tale. Some writers make the distinction between a murder mystery and a crime story. In the former, we do not know who the murderer is until the end or close to it. In the latter, we know the murderer at or close to the beginning. The story concerns the search for the killer until apprehension. Not every mystery can be regarded as literary as not every painting is art; but, just as artists produce masterpieces, so mystery writers produce classics. Detective fiction ranges from the gross to the superlative. Many authors write these tales for what they consider "easy money." The public reads them because they challenge, they entertain, they relax, and like the movies, they offer escape.

The private eye is a type in itself, different from those working for some legitimate public authority. They often come close to knight-errantry, but unlike Quixote, they do strike a blow for justice. The 1940's and 1950's saw the advent of the private eye school. The earlier stories challenged belief and more realism crept into the narrative and began to dominate the genre. Sherlock Holmes was fascinating but his methods do not follow most, if not all, real-life crimes. The private eye school solves crime through action by hero types. The Saint, Mike Hammer, and even James Bond are extreme examples of this form. The classical type had "the puzzle" as the focus; the private eye type had the "action" as the focus. A typical puzzle type story included a locked room with a victim. How did the crime occur? Poe's *Murders in the Rue Morgue* was of that kind. A mutilated body of a young woman found in a locked and apparently inaccessible room. The crime was then solved with a rational and plausible explanation. A murder in a locked room and a master mind killer has received a modest amount of fictional attention. In fact, it is indeed a rare occurrence, if it happens at all.

The Gothic or romantic-suspense style started in the late 18th century, continued into the early 19th century and swept around the world in the second half of the 20th century (Whitney 1976). It emphasizes the grotesque and the mysterious. It was probably started by Horace Walpole with *The Castle of Otranto* in 1875. The tenor was initiated by such products as Mary Shelley's *Frankenstein* and Byron's *Vampyre*. The early ingredients of Gothic tales covered skeletons, mysterious beautiful women in trouble, creeking castles, and ghosts. The ambience was heightening terror. It was eventually brought down to earth with the works of the Brontës. It more or less disappeared until *Rebecca* (Daphne du Maurier). At first the field was dominated by the English writers. Later, more and more Americans began to write in the same mode. Gothic tales, especially when written by women, avoided the intrusion of the police. Detecting was done by an amateur, usually played by the heroine. This framework was subject to a great deal of deviation. The mystery detective genre can be combined with other genre like science-fiction or fantasy, the variations abound. The detective mystery occasionally includes the supernatural in the gothic style. Sax Rohmer, the British writer, incorporated the bizarre, exotic, and fantasy in the events and characters in his stories. He created Dr. Fu Manchu, out to dominate the orient and then destroy the occident. This type was, more or less, fashionable until the 1950's. Emphasis shifted to realism. Then psychological thrillers came to the fore. The new masters included such as Simenon and Highsmith.

A very important type of modern detective novel is the story with suspense. This variety is believed to have been invented by Cornell Woolrich. A fine writer, he started while a student at Columbia University. He became one of the most filmed authors with some twenty-five pictures including, *The Rear Window, Convicted*, and *Nightmare*.

The 1930's gave us Dashiell Hammet and the hard-boiled novel (*The Maltese Falcon, The Thin Man*). It was during this time that a distinctive American style emerged. It appeared first in magazines and then in books. Other portrayers of low-life were William R. Burnett (*Little Caesar, Asphalt Jungle*), Damon Runyan (*Guys and Dolls*), Raymond Chandler and Ross MacDonald. This was the realistic school of crime fiction. The stories were packed with violence and action. The language was abrasive and the moods and desires clearly stated.

After World War II, the new whodunit took off on another track referred to as the police procedure novel. This involved the hard working, humane detective plodding through his routine methods and solving crimes. This trend was probably started by Lawrence Treat's *V as in Victim* (1945). Treat started it with a series of alphabetized novels and short stories. (Sue Grafton started with A and continued through the alphabet with her titles.) The impetus for the popularity of this style came from the radio and television series of *Dragnet* with Jack Webb and the Broadway play *Detective Story* written by Sidney Kingsley. Others followed the course, including Ed McBain in the United States, and J. J. Marric in Britain. Marric was the pseudonym of John Creasey, the most prolific writer of all in crime fiction with 650 titles. He gave us Commander George Gideon of Scotland Yard who appeared in books, movies and television. McBain was the pseudonym of the well established author Evan Hunter (*The Blackboard Jungle*). Several of his 87th precinct novels were translated to cinema in United States, Japan, France, and Canada. Joseph Wambaugh, the former Los Angeles detective, is from this school of authenticity. His works also have been translated to the screen (The Blue Knight).

Both English and American writers have added to this category of literature with successful twists and turns, sometimes in pairs, sometimes alone, many times with pseudonyms, and usually for the money. Several of the detective fiction writers branched out into the spy variety with equal success. The writing, by the best, is often of a very high caliber, recognized as such by a considerable number of the traditional writers and critics as well.

Genre Protagonists

The greatest fictional detective, undoubtedly, is Sherlock Holmes. Perhaps debatable, equally famous is his sidekick John M. Watson. Created by Sir Arthur Conan Doyle, the initiation occurred in 1887 with *A Study in Scarlet*. Doyle, a medical doctor, received much of his training from the famous Professor John Bell who taught him deductive logic as a diagnostic tool. He was so impressed with the method that he applied it to other areas – eventually to the detective story. His spectacular success was due to the atmosphere of Victorian England, and the convincing characterization of a detective with his system of deduction and cleverness (Benvenuti & Rizzoni 1979: 17). Doyle established the genre of criminal fiction. The American Anna Katherine Green, the first woman to write detective stories (ten years before Doyle), coined the term "detective story" (Benvenuti & Rizzoni 1979: 30). Green and Doyle elevated the genre to literary status.

Christie's Poirot debuted while she worked as a nurse in World War I. Hercule appeared in thirty-three novels. Her other great character was Miss Marple. Modeled after the writer's grandmother, the first novel (after short stories) appeared in 1930 and the last in 1976 – twelve in all. Dame Christie gave us a total of 66 novels. Many believe her greatest work to be *Ten Little Indians*. The story involves ten people invited to an island and, one by one, are murdered by one of their number.

One of the first American detectives in crime fiction was Philo Vance. The author signed his products with S. S. Dine. It was quickly determined that this was not some promising newcomer but the distinguished journalist and art critic, Willard Huntington Wright. He used the pseudonym because he felt that the detective class of literature was inferior to his usual scholarly work. For this and various other reasons, many writers in this style used pseudonyms. Most of the writers did not feel that the genre was below them but were urged by publishers who feared the glutting of the market with the same author. The suave, invincible sleuth, Philo Vance, was created in 1926. Wright wrote twelve novels with Vance as the luminary. Vance has been described as the most aristocratic detective in American crime fiction. He was extremely intelligent, polished in theology, Greek and Persian classics, Sanskrit, Egyptology, and ethnology, and fluent in ancient and modern languages (Benvenuti & Rizzoni 1979: 85). These were just a few of his talents. Inheriting a fortune, he was able to live a leisurely life pursuing his many interests including detecting.

Perry Mason, perhaps the most famous of all fictional lawyers, was written by Erle Stanley Gardner, who also wrote under pseudonyms including A. A. Fair. Mason's first case was published in 1933. This was followed by many novels, television programs, and films. New and old adventures appear today and may embrace television forever.

About the same time as Mason, *Fer-de-Lance* appeared (1934), authored by Rex Stout. Thus was born Nero Wolfe, orchadist, misogynist, egotist, heavyweight, gourmand, and close to today's version of a couch potato. He lived in new York in a home four stories tall, with a greenhouse on the roof, right-hand man Archie Goodwin, butler and cook Fritz Brenner, and orchid tender Theodore Horstman. The public loved him.

In 1945 Mickey Spillane published his first Mike Hammer novel, *I, the Jury*. It sold over six million copies in America alone. The next five novels were close behind it in sales. Mike Hammer was the toughest of all the private detectives. The name itself evokes an image of force and power. The brutality of the stories, with the private eye dealing out hs own brand of justice, may have pleased the public but not the critics. Spillane wrote for the pulp magazines and continued the style of realism in his Mike Hammer novels.

One author, creative and prolific, who stands out as a master of his own style was Georges Simenon. Though Belgian born, he was French in culture. He produced over 400 novels, 200 under Simenon, the rest under 23 pseudonyms. To this flood he added over 1000 stories, about 15 volumes of autobiography and memoirs (Benvenuti & Rozzini 1979: 148). His most popular conception was Inspector Maigret, a protagonist in 102 adventures, novels, television, and screen. Simenon produced a Maigret novel a month.

In 1936 Peter Chegney published *This Man Is Dangerous* presenting Lemmy Caution, a very popular new type of character. A daring FBI agent, he was half hero and helf antihero. Another unconventional character was Simon Templar, known as the Saint. He was created by Leslie Charteris. The popularity of the personality was enhanced by the various television series chronicling the adventures of the Saint. Conceivably one of the best known contemporary private detectives is Philip Marlowe, created by Raymond Chandler with the popularity affirmed by stage and screen. The part was played by the best actors of screen and stage – Bogart, Montgomery, both Robert and George, James Garner, Elliot Gould, and Robert Mitchum. Marlowe was depicted as tired, cynical, disillusioned, but generous, moral, and sympathetic.

Some of the early writers in searching for the exotic mystery turned to the orient. Sax Rohmer created the evil Dr. Fu-Manchu. This turn was criticised and largely abandoned. Nevertheless, Earl Derr Biggers introduced the very popular Charlie Chan. Chan was a Chinese detective from Honolulu, very intelligent, well-mannered, and laden with Confucian quotes.

The ethnic detectives, Chan and Moto, were popular in the 20's and 30's. There are other more recent ones. Harry Kemelman created the detective Rabbi David Small. His first book was *Friday the Rabbi Slept Late* (1964). This was followed with six more for each day of the week. The novels contain much of Jewish customs and lore. The Native-American is represented by Lieutenant Joe Leaphorn of the Navaho police, produced by Tony Hillerman. His books have achieved a great deal of popular acceptance and have won two Edgars. H. R. F. Keating introduced Inspector Ghote of the Bombay C.I.D.; Arthur W. Upfield gave us Napolean Bonaparte from Australia: Max Freedom Long developed Kopmako Koa a Hawaiian cop; Joan Fleming created the Turkish detective Nuri Iskirlak; Robert L. Fish introduced José Maria Carvalho Santos da Silva of Brazil; Henry Klinger constructed Lt. Shomri Shomar of the Tel Aviv police. There are many others like Inspector Chafik of Baghdad, a gypsy in New York, detectives from the Caribbean Islands, Mexico, and Tibet. Many of these characters were created for their uniqueness and contribution to the search for money.

In the mid-sixty's the Afro-American detective came into prominence. Not the first, but most important, was John Ball's introduction of Virgil Tibbs in *In the Heat of the Night* (1965). The book won an Edgar and the movie an Oscar. Another successful Afro-American detective was John Shaft in Ernest Tidyman's 1970 book *Shaft*. As a private detective he was more like Mike Hammer than the plodding detective of Jack Webb. Tidyman also wrote the very popular *French Connection* (1971). Balll and Tidyman are white authors writing about black detectives. The outstanding black mystery writer is Chester Hines with his violent novels about Coffin Ed Johnson and Grave Digger Jones. His early fiction was first published in France.

From 1913 to the 1970's, many of the sleuths were auxiliaries helping some significant other – husband, lover, brother, father, employer. One of the earliest and most competent was the conception of G. H. Teed in 1913 (Craig & Cadogon 1981: 71). Most of these assistants were drawn into the trade by helping the professional investigator. Some became involved after changing from an adversary relationship to a confederate one. Nancy Drew, the American sleuth, started as an assistant to her father and then took off on her own. From Dashiell Hammet came Nora Charles, wife of Nick the retired private eye who continued to solve mysteries. Hammett's portrayal of the female operative abandoned stereotypes and was quite sophisticated.

Perry Mason and Della Street, the Erle Stanley Gardner creations were extremely popular in literature and television. Della's involvement was in terms of efficiency, concern for Mason's welfare, a companion in danger, and good thinking and good detective work. And of course, there was Dr. Watson who assisted Sherlock Holmes and Ellery Queen who assisted his father, a policeman.

Genre Women Writers and Protagonists

In 1861 a female sleuth was operating in Scotland Yard (Craig & Cadogan 1981). For over 100 years, the female detective has been a standard character in popular fiction. By 1900 young females were creating literary interest circling the globe solving mysteries. Later types included the spectacular detective, a philanthropist, a traveler, a comic, and a gifted one. Certain roles were symbols of feminine independence and daring – aviators, reporters, and detectives. The lady detective had its beginnings in the Victorian era. The choice of a lady as the detective was generated by its novelty, dramatic effect, potential for whimsy and humor and because intrusiveness is often considered a feminine trait (Craig & Codogan 1981: 13). The tradition of the woman operative started in 1861 in England with Mrs. Paschal in *The Revelations of a Lady Detective* by W. S. Hayward. This was soon followed by others. In the first two English novels, the lady detectives entered the profession to escape the alternative of genteel poverty. They also displayed eccentricity, a trait often attributed to detectives, both male and female.

The Victorian female tecs were romanticized as symbols of liberation (Craig & Cadogan 1981: 17). During the Golden Age of mysteries (1925-1940), certain rules for detective writing emerged. The standard was to eschew such plots as Divine Revelation, feminine intuition, and mumbo-jumbo. The writers focused on intellect, and interest in the intricacies of the plot, not the characters. Hugh C. Weir's *Miss Madelyn Mack, Dectective* (1914) introduced a female character modeled after Sherlock Holmes – with deductions and magnifying glass. The heroine in Arthur B. Reeve's *Constance Dunlap: Woman Detective* (1916), was an eaample of another popular type still available today in the male or female form – the ex-criminal in reformation. Some of the early novels focused on character, others on the investigation.

The first woman to write detective fiction was the American Anna Katherine Green. The book, *The Leavenworth Case*, was published in 1878 (Craig & Cadogan 1981: 38). Miss Butterworth was the first female detective to appear in America. Another woman detective to appear in American literature was in Harry Rockwood's *Clarice Dyke, The Female Detective.* The date of publication is unknown, but it appeared in print in 1883. The heroine was a detective's wife who helped him with his cases. Since then a number of husband and wife teams have decorated the genre. In 1896 Green created the forerunner of the most celebrated female detective – the elderly busybody. The legendary Miss Marple produced by Agatha Christie is the ideal example of this type. Green's successors included the likes of Agatha Christie, Dorothy Sayers, Mary Robert Rinehart, Carolyn Wells, Phoebe Atwood Taylor, Nagaio Marsh, Josephine Bell, Mignon G. Eberhart, and many others. After World War I, female detective fiction in the United States moved from the genteel to the gutsy crime-fighting stories with action and independence (and physical beauty) as the theme. The women were more professional and hard-boiled. They supplemented logic with hunches. A more contemporary era introduced Warshawsky, contrived by Sarah Paretsky. This investigator is a tough private eye different from the others only in gender.

Mignon G. Eberhart published her first detective novel in 1929. She soon became one of the best known American detective writers (Benvenuti & Rizzoni 1979: 115). Her first detective was a private one aided by a nurse. She created heroines like Susan Dare. Many of her over 50 books did not feature any of her fixed protagonists. The writers produced characters like the career girl (Susan Dare), the sweet young girl (Nancy Drew), the grandmotherly type (Miss Marple), the amateur (Harriet Vane). The more contemporary ones are more subtle, sophisticated, often with humor, at times dispair, occasionally the unusual (a nun) – all with the capacity for action and pragmatic intelligence.

Women mystery writers outnumber men mystery writers 3-1 (Benvenuto & Rizzoni 1979: 171). Many were not willing to disclose gender, until recently. Therefore, the ratio could be greater. Some hid the gender: Anthony Gilbert, M. V. Heberden, E. X. Ferrars. P. D. James never tried to hide gender, but used initials only. Her creations include the popular Commander Dagliesh of Scotland Yard. Some contemporary women mystery writers include Margaret Miller, Dorothy Salisbury Davis, Doris Miles Disney. Vera Caspary is primarily known for *Laura* (1943); Lucille

Fletcher is remembered for *Sorry, Wrong Number* (1948); Patricia Highsmith is identified with *Strangers on a Train*, Dorothy Uhnak with *Law and Order*, and Mary Higgins Clark with *The Cradle Will Fall.* Of course, there are the well-known ones like Agatha Christie and Dorothy Sayers. Like many others, The English woman Dorothy Sayers began writing detective stories for the money and was soon as popular as Christie. Her first novel, *Whose Body*? Appeared in 1923 and introduced Lord Peter Wimsey. This unusual character was a cultivated dilettante with a didactic presentation investigating crime. He was the son of a Duke, from a good background, with an Oxford education. After solving his first crime, he decided to spend his idle and useless life working as a detective. He soon gained the reputation as the Sherlock Holmes of the upper class crime scene.

Genre Contemporaries

Arguably, the most important contemporary writer is Ross MacDonald, pseudonym for Kenneth Millar. His wife's success with mystery novels encouraged him to pursue a similar career. He introduced private eye Lew Archer, perhaps a descendent of Hammet's Spade and Chandler's Marlowe. His products include *The Drowning Pool* and *The Chill.* Paul Newman has played Archer under the name of Lew Harper on the screen.

John D. MacDonald created Travis McGee for a seris of popular novels. Another American modern is Brian Garfield, author of such works as *Death Wish* and *Hopscotch.* Others include Robert B. Parker with his Boston private eye Spenser, Isaac Asimov noted author of science fiction and several volumes of detective stories.

A British mystery writer of recent vintage is Dick Francis. Once a jockey, he turned to writing and established a highly successful series of mystery-suspense novels within the horse racing milieu. Some other recent authors from Britain include Peter Lovesey (*Night of Wenceslas*), and Frederick Forsyth (*Day of the Jackal*).

CHAPTER FIVE

FICTION AND METHOD OF ANALYSIS

Introduction

André Gide coined the phrase "gratuitous act" in an 1912 novel *Les Caves du Vatican*. The protagonist in the story, on a sudden impulse, kills a total stranger on a train. Oscar Wilde wrote an essay about a forger who murdered his sister-in-law because she had thick ankles. There did not seem to be any motive. Such a system of behavior approaches Durkheim's notion of anomie – to the nth degree. Anomie refers to a normless society, one without rules. In a normal society, most murderers kill for a reason and thick ankles and impulses are not normative reasons. These kinds of homicides reported in fiction may have preceded the reality – or did they? Did fiction anticipate reality or adopt it to its own use? Some critics believe that fictional characters like Raffles, Arsene Lupin and Mike Hammer are romanticized and glamorized and eventually corrupt. Mike Hammer may be more destructive than the criminals he pursues. In many contemporary mysteries there is an increasing emphasis on the killings itself. Jones (1989) suggests that real murders are more extraordinary than fictional ones. It is often conjectured that fact is stranger than fiction. For the mystery genre it might be more appropriate to suppose that fiction is stranger than fact. There is a fascination with the grisly elements, wondered by the reader if he can do the same thing. The stories remind us of the dark side of life that exists though we may not be familiar with it. Detective fiction bears little relation to real crime. A dead body is smelly, messy, and indescribably banal. Crime fiction tends to skip over this. Yet, it is so popular. Sayers and Walsh (1998: 151) write that detective stories "...contain a **dream** of justice." They write further that these stories "...keep alive a view of the world which **ought** to be true. Of course people read them for fun, for diversion, as they do crossword puzzles. But underneath they feed a hunger for justice..."

Early American Fictional Violence

For almost 200 years America has shown much facination with homicidal violence. Our first serious novelist Charles Brockden Brown filled his book with comments on an irresistible urge to kill, killing of a wife and children, and a rape attempt beside the corpse of a victim. James Fenimore Cooper strew bodies within the virgin forests of America and Poe constructed grotesque homicidal incidents. All these authors were very popular, and to some extent, still are. They were the forerunners of writers such as James M. Cain and Mickey Spillane. In between there was murder by Nathaniel Hawthorne (The Marble Faun), murders witnessed by Huck Finn (Mark Twain), and violence in the works of Ambrose Bierce, Stephen Crane, and Jack London.

Davis (1970) suggests that a major reason for the American fictional violence is its sheer marketability. A mass market is less conducive to fine literature than violent sensationalism. For the harried citizen escapism is through a change of pace. De Tocqueville theorized that a democratic audience dotes on exaggeration and strong emotion which helps account for the violent sensationalism. Davis (1970) rejects the notion that the frequency of violence in American literature proves the violent nature of the society. However, it does reflect certain of American historical conditions and circumstances.

Writers refer to their time and place. They wrote through their history and experience. Pre-civil war, the American Revolution was popular for historical romances (Davis 1970: 56). It was hard to conceal the violence in which the nation was established. From the Age of Jackson to the Age of the Robber Baron the ideal encompassed self-sufficiency and individualism (Davis 1970: 58). The American hero was presented in the wide arena of the West. The heroic violence was reluctant but lethal. Cooper's Deerslayer (Hawkeye) and Owen Wister's Virginian are early examples of killers by code – survival of the fittest. The killings of Indians started early in American fiction and the incidents were bloody with the victims condemned as the cause and the perpetrators lauded as heroes. Davis (1970) proposes that the portrayal of violence in American literature reflects a shift in thought and values to what he calls "antirationalism," a celebration of "...mans passions, fears, and irrationality as an antidote to the classic virtues of prudence, decorum, and moderation." Spontaneous impulses become a driving force as Satan, Cain, and Faust became a fascination for the literati (Davis 1970: 63). Violence becomes a creative undertaking. American literature resonates the international disenchantment with the traditional view that life is rational and tranquil linked with the indigenous tradition of an individualistic hero proving himself through an act of violence.

Davis (1957) analyzed American beliefs, values and associations relative to homicide in fiction from late 1790-1860. The first serious fiction authors wrote under the influence of the European period of the Enlightenment. From the 18th to the mid 19th century the tendency was to perceive man as possessing the capacity for either good or evil. Some writers used allegories that turned to biblical drama with a conflict between good and evil like Nathaniel Hawthorne's *The Marble Faun*. Another biblical doctrine was that evil plants the seeds of its own destruction. Passions could drive violence outward or inward. After the middle of the 19th century, came the influence of psychiatric theory and the idea of mental and moral abnormalities. For example, irresistible impulse, moral insanity, psychopathy, and homicidal insanity became the driving force of evil. By the turn of the 19th century, there was the rejection of evil from Satan and the assumption that evil resulted from error – a violation of natural law or a breakdown of reason. Some of the traditional themes were largely embodied in religion and law; the biblical "blood for blood" was challenged. Man had the capacity to know the difference between good and evil. Therefore, the judgement was based on normal standards; the murderer willfully chose evil. What we have is the idea of rational man and free will.

Some of the early literature began to deal with urban villains from disintegrating slums socialized to brutality for economic survival. They were people who lacked moral sense. The characters of fictional villains were related to general social conditions. They were hardened criminals with an absence of remorse, a perverse criminal with no conscience and moral depravity. The fiction and fact did not necessarily relate to each other in copy-cat fashion. They just seemed alike because they arose out of a similar background of beliefs, values, and norms. The early motives for criminal activity were similar to those of today. They included individual notions like jealousy, insanity, the linking of sex and aggression, the immoral wife and the cuckolded husband or lover. Unlike the European literature, cuckolding was not funny. A common theme was the fallen women who is evil, seduces someone, and is slain. The moral code of the time justified murder for dishonor; extramarital adventures were a henious affair.

Much of fictional homicide involved revenge, implicit or explicit. An injury, real or imagined, is balanced with death. This exchange restores harmony. Some writers concluded that circumstances forged a criminal and if he revenged himself against society, he was no more responsible than a "wild beast." He was a victim of his own culture or subculture. Vengeance characterized men, but this was not extended to women. In the late 18th through the middle of the 19th century, two kinds of revenge were condoned – dueling and lynching. Dueling was likened to warring nations; the victims of lynchings were mostly traitors or criminals. The law did not apply. Similar to today's arguments, the death penalty was either retributive punishment essential to security for society, or a relic of barbarism. Literature followed the philosophical argument that criminals should be cured, not punished.

At any rate, this genre has been and continues to be very popular. Masters of the pure detective form like Christie, Sayers, and Queen have an army of fans. Why is this literary form so popular? Some would argue it is a relief from the Puritan morality. For Charles (1957) it is the modern man's Passion Play – the flaming sword of righteousness.

The Fictional Criminal And Protagonist

Do the criminals of fiction reflect those of fact? Some of the real early ones existed before detectives – Robin Hood, Dick Turpin. Since then we have had the likes of Fu Manchu, Count Dracula, Professor Moriarity, Arsene Lupin. These types evince a sense of grandeur, often an aberrant one. On occasion, the hero rather than the villain commits a crime to aid him in catching the bad guy. James Bond and the Saint practice this kind of ethics. Some, like Boston Blackie were dangerous criminals before reforming and becoming dangerous to criminals. In this last instance there is a parallel with fact. Eugene Francois Vidocq changed from criminal to founder of the Sûreté.

The fictional investigator pursues clues while the factual police bring in their informers. It is most likely that the facts of reality and the fiction of literature interact in a very complex way and not with equal impact or influence. Perhaps it is like the proverbial chicken and the egg, an unsolvable conundrum. Nevertheless, the reality seems more likely to invade the fiction than the fiction lead the way for the actuality. The crime may occur first in reality and then adopted and embellished in literature and then the embellishment (not the act itself) is adopted in the live act of homicide. For example, an author has a killer slay his wife by running over her with her car. Then he drags her body into their house and burns it to hide the crime. Another killer reads the story and adopts the method used in the kill, but also puts the wife in bed, beats the corpse with a blunt instrument, shoots her lover and puts the gun in his hand to look like a suicide-murder. Someone had, more or less, duplicated the crime with a few changes. But the story did not motivate the crime, but simply suggested a method. Instances of copying a crime occur occasionally as in the copy-cat murder. This occurs when one person duplicates, more or less, another persons crime or one from the mass media. However, the initial act, real or fictional, probably did not cause the copying. It simply suggested a method to someone who wanted to commit such an act. Mysteries, with their homicides, are extremely popular, and have been since their inception. Yet, killings by the readers have not become bounteous because of the stories. If they killed, it was very likely that they were already primed for such an act.

Real Homicide And The Media

Most homicides do not receive much media attention and hardly any literary response. They have become, more or less, routine events which are glossed over by media and consumers alike. At times a literary effort appears about a particularly notorious homicide like Truman Capote's *In Cold Blood*. On rare occasions there is a media frenzy matched by a rapt populace. The most recent such case was reflected in the O. J. Simpson murder trial. It was dubbed the trial of the century. There were other trials of the century. The first such event occurred in 1906 with the shooting of New York architect Stanford White. He was killed by the Pittsburgh railroad heir Harry K. Thaw during a musical performance at Madison Square Garden's rooftop theater. The motive was jealousy over White's attention to Thaw's wife showgirl Evelyn Nesbit known as the "girl on the red velvet swing." Another crime of the century occurred in 1932 with the reciprocal media frenzy and popular excitement. This crime involved the kidnapping and murder of the Lindberg baby by Bruno Hauptman. The furor reverberated worldwide. The 20th century is about over. However, there is still time for another "crime of the century."

Assessing The Problem

Trying to assess the interacting consequences of homicide in fact and in fiction is, at best, extremely difficult. However certain facts are available with which to make comparisons. Every literate society produces material for the population. Such material includes the mass media – newspapers, radio, magazines, television. These documents are available for research purposes. Such use of these media may require a technique of analysis called Content Analysis. Berelson (1952) defines Content Analysis as "a research technique for the objective, systematic, and quantitative description of the manifest content of communication." This technique is one form of unobtrusive research which involves the obvservation of social artifacts, especially any form of communication. It is not necessary to go about and initiate the information like that which is necessary in an interview because the data already exist. As a form of observation or interview, we can ask questions of a newspaper, or a book, or observe a movie or a television program. Then we can define categories so that the analysis can be systematic. One value of Content Analysis is the ability to translate verbal or written nonquantitative material into quantitative data. Another advantage is that the material examined is not produced for the benefit of the researcher and therefore, it is free from the influence of his biases. Furthermore, one can deal with the historical past as well as the present and it is economical.

Content Analysis was applied before it was systematized as a sociological technique. Historians examined documents to reconstruct the periods in which they were produced. Literary critics examined the works of Shakespeare to determine if he wrote them all. Some of the earlier uses of Content Analysis occurred in wartime with the monitoring and analysis of enemy newspapers and radio broadcasts. There is concern with violence on television, particularly with children's programs. One might compare violence in childrens's programs with that in adult programs. We can operationally define adult and children's programs, and define violence for each. Next we would develop a sample of those kinds of programs. Then we can formulate a plan to watch those programs and count the number of times violence occurs (and maybe severity as well). Lowenthal (1943) analyzed biographies in popular magazines from 1900 to 1941. His unit of analysis was the professions of the heroes of the stories. He searched for cultural changes over time. And change occurred from early heroes where 77 percent were engaged in the fine arts to the later periods where only 9 percent were so engaged. There was a decline in stories about politicians and an increase in entertainers. The heroes went from production to consumption. Thomas and Znaniecki (1918) used letters exchanged between Polish immigrants in America and their relatives in the old country. Seider (1974) studied speeches in order to assess the ideology of business elites. Berelson and Salter (1946) analyzed literature and classified characters in the stories they studied. They described them in terms of demographics and assessed how they were treated in the stories – for example, were they heroes, cynics, racketeers and such. They attempted to determine if minority Americans were treated differently in literature than majority Americans. Though a very useful technique, perhaps it is not used enough.

In order to compare homicide in fact and fiction, it was necessary to examine homicide in the pertinent literature and compare it with the data available on homicide in America. Content Analysis was the technique applied. Homicide was the unit of analysis, operationally defined to include such adjuncts as weapons used, background of victims and perpetrators, and other facets of the act. The study is essentially a descriptive one. As such, face validity should be sufficient. Reliability was assessed by two researchers agreeing upon manifest content pertinent to the study. The data for homicide in America came primarily from official documents such as the Federal Bureau of Investigation's Uniform Crime Reports. The data for homicide in literature came from a sample of a universe of literature in the detective/crime/mystery genre. The reason for this choice was the strong probability that this kind of literature would include an abundance of homicides. This type of story line is extremely popular and the number of books massive. Therefore, one can expect some well-done works and a host of mediocre to embarrassing ones. One way to compile a universe of books to choose from is to accumulate prize honored titles and/or authors plus the most popular writers, if not found in the prize list. Another category to consider is the classics from other literary genre that include a homicide like Theodore Dreiser's *An American Tragedy*. To make the list comparable to the collected facts of homicide, certain books had to be eliminated. First, the author had to be American and the book about an American homicide. This eliminated some prize authors like Agatha Christie. Some excellent books in this genre are biographical like Truman Capote's *In Cold Blood*. These were eliminated because they represented actual homicide cases and even though embellished, they could not be considered fictional. Some authors are listed in more than one category, or more than once in the same category. The rule that was followed was that each author was used only once, the selection by random – that is, whichever appropriate book was found first. The final universe of books totaled 588 sorted into categories A-L. The sorted categories are:

A. Classics of crime fiction from 1900-1975.
B. Best novel, Mystery Writers of America and Edgar Allan Poe awards.
C. Best first novel, Mystery Writers of America and Poe award.
D. Best paperback original novel, Mystery Writers of America.
E. Robert L. Fish award.
F. Ellery Queen award.
G. Edgar Allan Poe Grand Master award.
H. Best selling authors, 1990.
I. Best selling authors, 1975.
J. Authors with greatest appeal.
K. 1995 Pen/Faulkine award.
L. Classics.

A total of 115 crime novels written by American authors were chosen from the two periods 1912-1985 and 1986-1995. They were all prize winners or best sellers or both. The novels written in the 73 year span from 1912-1985 were examined against the data – fact in the 1981 Uniform Crime Report published for the year 1980. Similarly, those written in the nine years between 1986 and 1995 fiction were examined against the fact – 1995 Uniform Crime Report which covered 1994. The fiction dates encompassed the novels selected by the criteria. The division into the two groups was designed to be approximately equal in size. The Uniform Crime Report dates were selected randomly from the available reports to represent each of the two periods of the fictions. Each date was reasonably germane to these periods.

We see many interesting results when we look at the many ways crime novels compare with crime facts. Fiction and fact may be related in context, but fiction is more like a caricature of fact than a close image.

CHAPTER SIX

PALEOLITHIC HOMICIDE

Carl Sayers and George Vukinov, minor archeologists from the West Coast, struck Paleolithic gold some fifty years ago. They were deluged with honors. They found a small and ancient cave bountiful with bones and clues of life from the distant past. The cave was in the ancient and exotic land of Samarkand in mountainous Uzbekistan. The cave was called Teskik Tash, meaning "stone with an opening." The bones were the remains of a Cro-Magnon man. How did he live and how did he die?

The Evolution Of Man

The findings of paleoanthropologist Elwyn Simons support an adopid as the oldest anthropoid and common ancestor of apes, monkeys, and humans (Culotta 1995). Molecular biology enhanced theories of ancestry as DNA showed that it was likely that all humans had a common ancestor. Bones, some 3.5 million years old, were found in South Africa which indicated that the owners were adapted to bipedalism (Clark and Tobias 1995). The bones showed characteristics of both humans and apes. They probably belonged to an early member of Australopithecus africanus or some other primitive hominid species. The first upright, walking creatures lived some 2 million years ago in Africa. They are classified as genus Homo or Homo Habilis. They coexisted with the genus Australopithecus or Homo Hominidae. Their role in evolution is still debated. Homo Erectus emerged some 2 million years ago and eventually became the surviving Hominid species. Homo Sapiens came from Homo Erectus stock replacing all other populations of Hominids. They were stocky, with short but strong legs and carried blunt implements and/or long lance-like piercing ones. New dating of some old fossils in Java indicated that Homo Erectus was still alive as recently as 27,000 to 53,000 years ago (Gibbons 1996; Swisher, *et al* 1996). This is 250,000 years after they were thought to be extinct. The species first appeared in the fossil record about two million years ago. Now it seems they coexisted with modern humans and Neanderthals. Many of the different species of early humans were around at the same time like Homo Erectus, Homo habilis, Australopithecine.

The Neanderthals

Sayers and Vukinov had studied the Neanderthals and knew the little that was available about them. They studied the Teskik Tash cave carefully and began to unravel some of the mystery of their existence and demise. The Neanderthals appeared about 300,000 years ago and disappeared about 35,000 years ago (Johanson, *et al* 1994). They ranged from the sub-Saharan Africa to north of European Russia. Like those of today, those of the Stone Age lived in a variety of geographic regions and climates. Many lived in Europe in the shadow of glaciers. Their remains have also been found in North Africa and Asia. Environmentally, it was the ice and cold that effected their evolutionary development. This type human was first discovered in 1856 in the Neander River Valley of Germany (Stringer & Gamble 1993). The finds customarily included stone implements, especially scrapers to dress skins and triangular spearpoints. Though extinct, they had a long run and were not killed off nor did they succumb to some accident, mistake, or catastrophic event. They gradually disappeared. Anatomically they were similar to the great apes, chimpanzees, gorillas and orangutans. These species were less anatomically similar but reminiscent of humans, the lesser apes, gibbons, and siamangs, followed by monkeys and lower primates. They were not the only humans at that time, nor the earliest ones. The others were related but physically distinct from them. The long established Neanderthals encountered the newly arrived population (Cro-Magnon) which was just ahead technologically and anatomically more modern. They interacted, but lived in isolated groups with weeks spent seeing only kin or band members. Possibly, when they did meet, they competed for food, traded, and fought. The Neanderthals probably imitated some of the behavior of the Cro-Magnons without understanding. The two groups may have been closely related biologically and interbred but also fought. The Cro-Magnons were better able to cope with the environment and evidenced some language capability. The competition was disadvantageous to the Neanderthals, a major factor in their eventual extinction. It seems very likely that the Neanderthals were not part of our ancestory, but a parallel line. They belong somewhere in the human modern tree, but the exact place is uncertain. Some scholars believe that the Homo Sapiens developed in two directions, one leading to the Neanderthal and similar types, the other the modern races of man represented in Europe by Cro-Magnon of 30,000 years ago.

Archeologists established that the Neanderthals lived during the Ice Age or Pleistocene Epoch. They lasted through glacial and interglacial times and learned to cope with low temperatures and aridity. They rarely modified the environment, but took it as it was. Pleistocene is a geological term. European Paleolithic or old Stone Age is an archeological one for the same period. The Neanderthal evolved from European middle Pleistocene ancestors who were a late form of Homo Erectus or a descendant of that species. During the late glacial period their neighbors and successors were Cro-Magnon. The old Stone Age time had a variety of stone technology like pebble tools, flakes, scrapers, choppers and point forms for tools like a knife and a very versatile hand axe. The tools were made from igneous and metamorphic rocks and semi-precious stones. Stone points were attached to wooden poles and used as spears. The stone axe was blunt on one side and slightly sharpened on the other side. They probably possessed the skill and tools to creat leather clothing. The material culture was relatively complex and the tools made and possessed by the Neanderthals are referred to as Mousterian.

The Neanderthal anatomy was appropriate for the edge of the glacial environment. Anatomically adapted to a cold environment, they were able to conserve heat similar to the Eskimos. Physically they had a long skull flattened on top, eyebrow ridges in two arches, and large frontal sinuses. The most striking facial feature was a bulbous protruding nose well-suited for warming and humidifying cold air and radiating excess body heat. The mouth had large front teeth, and the cheeks were inflated. The hips were wide, the hands capable of a strong grip, fingertips broad, and toe bones strong and extensive. The tongue and larynx were inadequate; therefore, the speech was slow and limited. Though there was no language as we know it, there was rudimentary articulate speech compensated with gestures. Communication did occur within those limits. The anatomy was robust and potent. They were extremely active and the upper-body musculature was awesome. The arms and legs were thicker than modern humans; the knee and ankle joints were larger than modern humans; all was designed to sustain extreme stress. Squatting was the common resting position. They had large brains, bigger than modern humans, with some intelligence which they excerised very little. For example, their tool industry, known as Mousterian, remained the same throughout their existence – a technology that never changed. Some of their traits were endurance, stoicism, perseverance, and brute strength. Behaviorally they were stolid yet warm and family oriented, family as it was constituted at that time.

There was no nuclear family. The family groups occasionally split and thus the size of the family remained stable. Mating pairs spent little time together. The females were docile, subservient unpretentious, and humble. Men and women ate different foods, used different tools, and performed different tasks. They weaned their children at a later age thus limiting population growth. This too contributed to eventual extinction. They mastered fire for warmth and cooking and roasted and ate a lot of meat. Iron pyrites and flint or quartz were used to start fires and dried fungus was used for tinder. Studies described them in various ways from brutish and glowering fiends to gentle, religious, caring family members. In all probability they ran the gamut of behavioral characteristics very similar to modern humans and were not one large ethnic group.

The Neaderthal existed in small groups. The basic task was to establish group self-sufficiency. Social ties were of little interest to them. They lacked culture in the modern sense. There was little art and few symbols with the material culture dominated by stone tools. However, they did ornament themselves with paint. There was no need for art to help in ceremonies nor a social life to encourage language and enhance communication. Camp sights were varied. A base camp was used to prepare and consume food, make and repair tools. There were work camps to obtain food and new material. The overnight camp served as the place to sleep. There was much use of caves and rock shelters. The diversity of camps attested to their mobility. Over time and geography, there were differences in settlement, technology, and organization for survival and social life.

There was some symbolism and religion. They practiced ritual burial of their dead, indicating some feeling toward that person. Some of the bodies wore ornaments, evidence of some kind of status system. One person was found buried on a bed of brightly colored flowers woven into wreaths indicative of affection or status, or both (Shackley 1980). Some burial sights offered cooked bones for the dead. An occassional burial cave had bison horns at the entrance for protection. The rudiments of medicine were practiced with roots and leaves as they took care of the sick and injured. Some division of labor existed, particularly along gender lines, and they recognized and rewarded specific talents. There was the beginning of passing rites – naming a child, manhood, first kill. Some of the groups had an identification with an animal like a totem. The cave bear was important in this respect. They lived hard, physically active lives and died young.

Women died before 30, probably due to child birth; men died after 30, few passing 40 (Shackley 1980). They achieved a degree of "humanity." They involved spirituality in the burying of their dead; were the first to develop the use of clothing, fire, stratification, care for sick and wounded, proto-urbanis m, and the process of gathering – all in its simple form (Shackley 1980). Other species used similar elements of these attributes with increased sophistication. They remain a separate species from ours, "....an experiment in human evolution that ended in extinction," (Johanson, *et al* 1994: 285).

Hunting And Gathering

In addition to other humans, there was a variety of animals present. There were cave bears, lynx, hyena fox, bison, giant deer, fox, chamois, onager, hartebeast, mammoth, wooly rhino, hippopotamus, porcupine, rabbit, and beaver. Other animals included the aurock (huge reddish brown wild cattle), saiga (small sheep-like antelope), wild pigs, and red deer (later called elk), (Auel 1980). Essentially, food was obtained by hunting and scavenging. Salmon, silver trout, and sturgeon were fished from lakes and rivers using nets make from the hair of animals. There was some exploitation of plant food. The women gathered roots, stems, leaves, legumes, squash, yams, berries, fruits, nuts, some grains, and salt. Hunting involved such animals as deer and scavenging such as the mammoth. They often hunted with the spear and used the ambush technique. If lucky with stones, the hunter might hit a gannet or great auk (sea birds). Other hunting techniques included traps, pitfalls, snares for smaller animals, and bolas. Mollusk and crustacean shells were used as utensils and bowls. The hunting usually was done in bands of about 20-25. In severe winters they used the snow and ice to preserve food. Occasionally they combined with others to form large hunting groups cooperating on game drives. In general, they were proficient hunters killing the cave bear and wooly mammoth almost to extinction. They killed the cave bear for ritual, fur, and food. Widely hunted where it existed, the cave bear was embraced with totem-like symbolism. They relied heavily on ritual magic for success. Though proficient they were not always successful in the hunt. They did a lot of scavenging. The gathering was performed by women and they provided a good deal of the food. It was easier to be successful at gathering than at hunting. Therefore, women were in some demand. Hunters and gatherers still exist today but with a modern brain, different technology and life style.

Violence – From Animal To Man

In a recent five year study, Craig Stanford of the University of Southern California documented the behavior of chimpanzees. He gave compelling evidence that they are dedicated carnivores. The closest relatives to humans, the chimps use raw meat to procure sexual and political favors as a source of status and power. Their predatory behavior include hunting parties to catch smaller primates. Even defined within their own social system, it would seem plausible that they also practice, on occasion, homicide.

Applying game theory, a number of evolutionary biolgists assessed animal behavior. With a goal of reproductive prosperity, such behavior as fighting and killing was to some degree predictable. Many young birds, like the egrets, kill other young birds in the nest. It is triggered by sibling rivalry for food, especially when it is scarce. Komodo Dragons spend the first three years of their lives in trees. To keep from being eaten by adults including their own mothers. A Cro-Magnon could kill out of jealousy or over territory, Homo-Sapien because of arguments over cave pictographs. Homo Erectus could kill over competition for a food source, Homo Habilis over a woman. Any of them could have killed impulsively without motive or remorse. A Neanderthal too killed. Any homicide needs definition relative to the culture or group within which it occurs. To kill for a food source or woman could be approved by the group like justifiable homicide in our culture and time.

The archeologists Sayers and Vukinov were determined to discover the circumstances and cause of the death of the body they found. They turned paleocriminologists as they examined the scene and the dead body preserved in a cave effected by the Ice Age. It is likely that homicide is not a modern invention. As creatures moved from the trees to the ground and the knees to the upright stance they arrived with the capacity to kill. The investigators recognized that any account explaining the Stone Age homicide would be no more than a fictional core surrounded by a series of educated guesses.

The two archeologists went from the generalities of the Neanderthal existence to the specifics of a Stone Age killer. They had a number of clues, most from the Teskick Tash cave where the body was found. There was the partial skeleton, including the skull, of a Stone Age hominid. Carbon-14 dating established the time of death at approximately 38,000-40,000 years ago. The skull was explored and identified as that of a Cro-Magnon. The adult skeleton contained 96 identifiable bones, bone fragments, and 9 teeth. The cave was established as a Neanderthal one because of the several bodies of Neanderthals buried there and the large number of Mousterian tools. The age of the skeleton was calculated to be about 30. The Cro-Magnon skull had been battered by a blunt object. It was quickly established that the condition of the skull could only be accounted for by a crushing blow on the rear top and right side of the head, probably by the blunt end of a Mousterian axe. The Mousterian axe was known to be wielded by Neanderthals.

In searching the area around the partial skeleton, Sayers was able to detect a string-like artifact made from an animal skin. This type string was known to carry an amulet around the neck of the more experienced and successful Cro-Magnons. It served as a status symbol and as part of the magic rituals performed to ensure a successful hunt. It appeared that the amulet had been torn from the neck of the Cro-Magnon. A search for the amulet was futile. The ground was composed of light grey ashes from a hearth bed over dark brownish loam soil. The body held the remnants of an animal skin wrapped around the pelvic area. There was intermittent groove marks from the cave entrance to the site of the body suggesting that the body had been killed and then dragged into the cave. The remnants of the animal skin on the body showed a relatively heavy amount of dried soil and ashes similar to that in the cave. This seemed to verify the notion that the body had been dragged.

A recent finding in a small cave in Zawi Chemi Shanidar, a proto-neolithic village site in the Surdash area 22 miles north of Subaimaniya in Iraq revealed several pictographs. Cave painting was known to be practiced by the Cro-Magnon. This particular one portrayed two figures, each with weapons raised, one a Neanderthal with an axe, the other a Cro-Magnon with a spear. This would seem to confirm that the relationship between Cro-Magnon and Neanderthal was not always peaceful. In addition, Shanidar revealed a skeleton of a Neanderthal, apparently killed by a rockfall while recuperating from a knife wound probably inflicted in an unfriendly encounter. Another body showed signs of a spear wound, apparently a victim of a nasty conflict.

Shackley (1980) reported some evidence of ritual murder and cannibalism among the Neanderthals. Some charred bones were found with signs of being cut and some split lengthwise to extract the marrow. There was the suggestion of ritual murder followed by consumption of the brain (Shackley; 106). The victim is killed with a blunt instrument, decapitated and the brain removed and consumed.

Sayers and Vukinov held a meeting with several consultants pooling their knowledge of early hominids and applying it to the question of homicide. They developed a list of several scenarios for homicide during this primeval period.

1. In vying for top dog in such endeavors as hunting, an argument ensues over a kill leading to homicide.
2. Certain talents like hunting, manufacturing artifacts, confers high esteem and status and thus causes jealousy.
3. Woman kills mate to connect with more successful partner.
4. Unit moves to new territory, establishes camp, then finds competition from another unit, murder ensues.
5. Attempt to steal another persons technology thought to be superior (eg. Axe, spear, object for ritual magic), caught and killed, or perpetrator kills victim of theft.
6. Ritual murder of someone from other unit or other form of hominid to consume an organ associated with an admired trait – heart for courage, brain for skill. The correlation made between trait and organ would be culturally defined and does not need to be based on fact or knowledge.

The Mystery Solved

After much debate, the consultants concluded that homicide was a likely part of the Neanderthal culture. They also agreed that the motives and circumstances appeared very much like contemporary killings in an antediluvian setting. The clues gathered by Sayers and Vukinov – axe, skull fracture, amulet string, signs of dragging, pictograph of a fight, and other evidence of wounded or slain hominids of that period – were drawn together for a likely scenario of the events that led to the archaic homicide. The Neanderthal had observed the Cro-Magnon hunting with a high degree of success. He noticed further that each success was preceeded by a ritual grasping of an amulet tied around his neck, which was then used to strike his chest three times while kneeling on the ground. After the kill, the same amulet was placed against his lips and kissed three times. The Neanderthal had shown only sporadic success in his hunting quests. As a result his status in his group had declined and the women were less inclined to share their gatherings or their bed with him. He reasoned, as best he could, that success as a hunter would be possible if he had the thing around the neck of the Cro-Magnon and copied the ritual he had observed. His group had left the cave and were moving elsewhere because it was susceptible to falling rocks. He waited in ambush until the Cro-Magnon was returning to his group with a kill over his shoulder. The Neanderthal struck the Cro-Magnon on the head with the blunt end of his axe and dragged the body to his abandoned cave. He stripped the Cro-Magnon of his technology – amulet, spear, and flint, and hauled the body to the rear of the cave where some of his group were buried. After a good deal of discussion the paleoarcheologists conceded that this scenario for the death of a Stone Age hominid may have been the first case of an interracial homicide

CHAPTER SEVEN

THE LEGACY OF MYTH

The Meanings Of Myth

The Greeks enlightened mankind to civilization including their remarkable myths packaged in religion. As Tylor (1958: 274) noted, myth is an intellectual inheritance handed down from previous generations. Yet it effects feelings more than rationality. These inheritances were modified into new, arbitrary shapes effected by familiar processes and our own consciousness. It became our legacy; its influence still exists, subtly and in different forms; it is there in our culture like a social gene. It is our cultural and structural lineage. The past is in our present. Myths other than the Greek and Roman were also influential. The near-Eastern God-King Tammuz (Sumerian Dumuzi) established dates for the annual death-resurrection festival which are now assigned to Passover and Good Friday and Easter (Campbell 1972: 65). Western Asia had a god of vegetation named Attis who supposedly died and was resurrected annually and was mourned and rejoiced in a spring festival (Frazier 1970: 413). The worship of the Greek and Roman gods survived the establishment of Christianity through the many festivals, superstitions, and other manifestations, often in modified form with the original intent dissipated. Our calendar has months named after the gods in myth: January is named after Janus, one of the original Roman gods, "of good beginnings;" February is named after the Roman god Februus, in Roman mythology an Etruscan god for whom that month was sacred; March is named after Mars, the Roman god of war; June is named after Juno, the Roman Hera, wife of Zeus.

The word myth comes from the Greek *mythos*, meaning story, legend, word, or speech. It is a traditional story, fanciful, ostensibly of historical basis, usually to explain some phenomenon of nature like thunder and lightening created by Zeus hurling his thunderbolts, origin of man, custom, institution, religious rite, commonly involving the exploits of gods or heroes. Some are purely for entertainment like Pygmalion and Galatea perhaps as early examples of literature. As invented stories to tell a truth, they may take the form of a moral allegory, parable, or metaphor. As legends they may take

the form of monstrous fancies which could have a basis in fact. Mythology would be a collection of myths.
Tylor (1958: 278-285) questions how myths arise. Did they actually happen? Are they simply the misinterpretation of an event? Were they rationalizations of legends? The early stages of mythology were probably distorted by later ages and diminished into superstitious mysteries. Later stages retained some of the principles which formed a tradition and influenced the evolved culture. Foremost among myths is the animation of nature. This is the doctrine of Animism. Nature plays a significant role – an untamed nature requiring explanation and control. Even the stars, moon, sun, rainbow, waterfall have animate life – nature personified. In Central America some myths claim that monkeys were once human. In Africa it was the baboons who were humans. In the Mayan tradition, the first humans did not turn to well and the gods destroyed them and tried again. Whatever the myths, they are timeless, either in their original form or in their modified ones. Time is "the moving image of Eternity," (Plato).

Greek Mythology

As far back as the earliest of men life with nature was terror, magic, and sacrifice. To escape the terror, there was a magic rite or some offering to propitiate the gods. The Greeks, though descendants of these same primeval times, developed a different form of response to the terror with myths produced by the poets (Hamilton 1940). Their creations were fanciful and imaginative. Greek mythology presumably started with Homer's *Iliad*, written some thousand years before the birth of Christ. We are the intellectual descendants of the early Greeks. "In Greece man first realized what mankind was," (Hamilton 1940: 16).

There were no gods among the proto-Europeans five to six thousand years ago (Graves CF 1988). Common to all people of that time was the idea of an Earth Goddess. She took men as lovers, not as fathers of her children, since there was no concept of fatherhood. The Earth or Great or Mother Goddess went through three phases – maiden, nymph, and crone – which were then repeated endlessly and in a changeless cycle. These three phases were associated with the three phases of the year – spring, summer, and winter – all to be repeated forever. Like the cycles of the year, the Earth Goddess was seen as changeless, immortal, and omnipotent. She gave birth but was seen as impregnated not by male lovers but by the North Wind, by the sea, by coupling with a mystic serpent, or by eating certain plants. After taking pleasure with her male lovers, she tore them to pieces, devoured their parts, and sprinkled their blood across the land to fructify it. There were variations on this theme over time and space:

1. The male lover was allowed to perform limited offices in the name of the Mother Goddess, now personified as queen.
2. He was required to appear in her robes and to wear false breasts as signs of his office – a sacred and royal transvestite.
3. On completion of his duties, he was killed, to be followed by a selected successor in a later ceremony.
4. He was not killed, but his place was taken by an apparent twin, a look-alike.
5. Animal sacrifice replaced the queen's consort.

Strictly speaking, none of these consort sacrifices qualify as murder, as we see it. Homicide certainly; but not murder because the element of malice was missing. In its place was the faith that by these means the continuity of collective life was assured.

Either independently or by contact with other populations moving in from Asia, segments of Europe began to link the role of the goddess queen's lovers with procreation of her offspring. Gradually as this idea gained slow acceptance, the matriarchy receded and was replaced by the beginnings of a type of patriarchy. But with the exception of a few areas, the Earth or Mother or Great Goddess never wholly disappeared. She survived in most areas as a local figure and diety, enshrined in a sacred place and honored with calendric rituals. In time, the fear that her devoted worshippers might attempt to reenthrone her and reestablish the matriarchy led to the virtual imprisonment of all royal women as in the Roman Vestal college and the royal harem such as that established by King David in Jerusalem.

Before the Greeks, the gods did not resemble reality; the Greeks created them in their own image. Zeus committed adultry; Hera was the jealous wife. Greek mythology gave us a humanized world – rational, authentic regardless of the outlandish depictions, explanations and exploits. Hercules, constantly defeating monsters was said to live in Thebes; Pegasus, the winged steed would fly all day but rest comfortably in a stable in Corinth at night. A world of terror became one of grandeur. In some places, gods died. Greenland believed that a wind could kill a god and he could die if he touched a dog; Crete had a grave for Zeus, Dionysus was buried at Delphi, and some claimed that Apollo was buried there too (Frazier 1970: 314).

Most books on classical mythology depend on the work of the Roman Ovid (Hamilton 1940: 21). To him, they were silly tales; but to the early Greek poets like Hesiod and Pindar, they were truths of a religious nature. Virgil, the clever Roman who wrote the *Aeneid* to get on the good side of Augustus by tracing him to the gods, alluded to the myths. However, the chief contribution to the myths familiar to us came from the oldest Greek writings, Homer's *Iliad* and *Odyssey*. Another contributor is Hesiod's *Theogony*, an account of the creation of the universe and the gods. Pindar, who is known for his odes, made many references to the myths. Then there were the works of Sophocles, Euripedes, Aeschylus, Aristophanes, Herodotus, and Plato who often referred to the myths. Apollonius related at length the search for the Golden Fleece; Apuleius told the story of Cupid and Psyche.

The plays reflected the culture of that time and place which has effected the cultural pool of our time and place. They wrote tragedies involving passion, blunders, misery, and death – including homicide. It was dangerous to ignore the gods; prayers were not always answered. The various rites and ceremonies were devised to propitiate and please the gods and receive something in return – a birth, a crop, vengeance, whatever. Divine moral guidance was equivocal at best, man had only himself to rely on. They imaged the nature of the world and taught strength and truth. "Virtue gives no reward, but is still virtue; justice is uncertain in its pursuit of crime, but is still justice; ....that man's truest comfort comes from knowing he has only himself to rely on....," (Euripides 1953: X). For the ancient Greeks, this was life; this became part of our legacy. The time between the defeat of the Persians and the end of the Peloponnesian War, 480 BC to about 400 BC, saw democracy flourish with free thinking and the search for truth, but this turned to arrogance, her own tyranny and the sentencing of Socrates to death for teaching men to think independently on religion and morality. Greek gods did not embody an ideal like the Judaic-Christian god, but what existed in human nature. "Aphrodite, Artemis, Dionysus are primal instincts in man's blood,.... Gods are beautiful because they are eternal and unchangeable, ...morality ....is outside of the sphere of gods," (Euripides 1953: xii, xiii, xiv).

In Medea, the revenge extracted is brutal. Greek history is a series of revenges, often excessive. The desire for justice too often led to criminal excess. The biblical "eye for an eye" may have been an admonition for restraint. While the early Greeks interacted with their gods in myth and reality, they still looked after their own lives. Even though there was much treachery and injustice, the principle of reason and order dominated. They often asked the gods for forgiveness but it was rarely granted. *The Bacchae* (Euripides 1953) featured the arrival of the Dionysian cult to Greece. It represented the rebellion of a free spirit against civilization, a revolt against the beginning of urbanization. Dionysus became the god of license – the "beast in man," the id of Freud. Violence was featured even when suppressed by reason and sanity.

Mythology is full of horror, violence, blood, and homicide – an eager legacy for western civilization. Graves (1988: 9) was convinced that the gods used drugs – raw mushrooms – to induce hallucinations, rioting, prophecy, erotic energy, and remarkable strength. The intoxicant mushrooms were the ambrosia and nectar of the gods. The power of myth was substantial in ancient times. In its day it was as significantly influential as television is today. Some of the power still exists, mostly as a more subtle influence through metaphor and superstition. There are other myths besides Greek ones. But, the most pronounced influence on our culture came from Greek mythology. It is not the purpose of this book to deal with the legacy of mythology as a whole, but just the references and attitude toward violence and homicide for appropriate background.

Creation

In Greek mythology, the Universe created the gods (Cf. Hamilton 1940). Heaven and Earth were the first parents. The Titans were their children and the gods their grandchildren. Cronus, (Roman Saturn), was the ruler of the Titans. His son, Zeus (Roman Jupiter), seized power and took the throne. Other memorable Titans included Ocean, the river around the earth; Hyperion, father of the sun, moon, and dawn; Themis, justice; Iapetus, father of Atlas who carried the world on his shoulders; Prometheus, who gave earth fire. The Olympians, uppermost among the gods, succeeded the Titans. Olympus was their home. The heavenly family included Zeus the head, Hera his wife, two brothers Poseidon (Neptune) and Hades (Pluto), their sister Hestia (Vesta), Ares (Mars) son of Zeus and Hera, the children of Zeus, Athena (Minerva), Apollo, Aphrodite (Venus), Hermes (Mercury), and Artemis (Diana), finally, Hera's son Hephaestus (Vulcan). Greek gods were not the creators of humans. They came into being from the goddess Earth and "...were rather man's elder and stronger brothers than his makers," (Campbell 1972: 81).

Perhaps the most usual form of myth dealt with creation. In another version the world was created out of chaos (Hamilton 1940: 64). Love was born from darkness and death. Love generated light and day. Next came the earth and heaven. From Mother Earth and Father Heaven came children. They were monsters yet human. Some had many heads and more hands. Others were called Cyclops (wheel-eyed) with one large eye as big and round as a wheel in the middle of the forehead. Last came the Titans. These were large and as strong as the others, but not as destructive. After the struggle for dominance and the ascendance of Zeus, there was peace and the world was emptied of monsters and the earth ready for people.

Some suggested that the gods created men – the people then were men only. They experimented with five different races, all but the last disappeared. The last lived in evil times and were evil too, thus they were never free from work and sorrow. They too one day would become so bad that Zeus would destroy them. Others said that Prometheus and his brother Epimetheus (forethought and afterthought) brought forth the humans and animals. Prometheus stole fire from heaven and gave it to mankind. He also arranged it so that the men received the best parts of the sacrificed animal and the gods received the bones and fat. Zeus was angry and promised revenge on man and his friend. Zeus created Pandora, a sweet and lovely thing, but a great evil for men. She was the first woman with an evil nature.

In another version of Pandora, she was characterized as the source of misery, not wicked but curious. The gods gave her a box with something pernicious from each one and the admonition never to open it. She was given to Epimetheus, and her curiosity (said to be a womanly trait), lifted the lid and out came plagues, sorrow, misfortune, mischief, and other malevolence for mankind. One good thing that was released with the evil was Hope. In the Talmudic version of creation, Eve like Pandora, brings misfortune on mankind (Graves 1988: 35). Zeus had given men women as punishment. He punished Prometheus by binding him to a rock in the Caucasus. Eventually Prometheus and Zeus reconciled. Athenian society was generally misogynous. Women had no share in the democratic period of the Golden Age of Athens. They were dominated by men. Women, in myth and biblically as well, were identified as a source of evil, a legacy echoing down through the ages, growing fainter, but never disappearing.

There are many versions of creation. Most include very human-like deeds. One of the first murders occurred after Mother Earth emerged from Chaos (Graves 1988: 31-39). She bore a son Uranus who showered her with fertile rain. She produced grass, animals, rivers and then several semi-human children. Then she bore three one-eyed Cyclopes (whom Apollo later killed in revenge for the death of Zeus' son Asclepius by Zeus). Uranus fathered the Titans after throwing the Cyclopes into Tartarus, a region so distant that if you stood at the edge of the earth and dropped an anvil into space, it would take nine days for it to reach Tartarus. The angry Mother Earth persuaded the Titans to attack their father. Cronus, the youngest, led the pack. They attacked Uranus in his sleep and Cronus, with a flint sickle, castrated him. The Titans then released the Cyclopes from Tartarus and gave Cronus sovereignty over earth. Cronus married his sister, Rhea. He feared her children and killed and ate two of them. Her third son was Zeus. He was hidden and nursed by nymphs and goats. In gratitude, Zeus later gave one goat horn to the heavens where it became the constellation Cornucopia. Zeus poisoned Cronus who vomited up all of Rhea's children. Hades and Poseidon figure in this event as well. Together with Zeus, they overcame Cronus – Hades by stealing his weapons, Poseidon with his trident, Zeus with a thunderbolt which had been given to him by the Cyclopes in thanks for his having resorted them from Tartarus. Cronus and the Titans were banished to a British island, except Atlas. The Titan's leader was condemned to carry the sky on his shoulders forever. The Cyclopes were later known as the Cylops. Among other skills, they were the metal smiths whose guild mark was a series of concentric circles which they tatooed on their foreheads. They also wore a patch over one eye when working with hot metals. Both practices gave rise to the perception of them as one-eyed.

Finally, creation almost had an early end. Apollo was the charioteer of the Sun. His son, Phaëthon, seized the chariot and tried to drive it across the heavens. He lost control. The horses dragged the Sun off its course. This threatened Heaven and Earth. Zeus struck Phaëthon with a thunderbolt and killed him. Creation was saved. The mad and fatal journey left a scar on the sky in the form of the Milky Way.

God-like Traits

Though immortal and powerful, the gods often misbehaved in a fashion unacceptable to mortals just as misbehavior of mortals were unacceptable to mortals. The gods could act cruelly and perfidiously, and did. But they still maintained a powerful influence. Zeus was amorous, promiscuous, vengeful, cowardly, and ridiculous. Sisyphus betrayed a Zeus secret and was sent to Hades where he was doomed to roll a stone up a hill forever. However, Zeus did change to a guardian of mankind – it seems as if he grew up. Hera was full of anger and revenge punishing Zeus' liasons. Poseidon controlled the storm, wind, and surging of the sea and used them as a weapon. Hades was King of the Dead, brutal and terrible, but not evil. In the image of men, the gods too possessed a mixture of good and evil. Athena sprang from the head of Zeus. This birth unfolded when Zeus lusted for Metis the Titaness but learned that she might give birth to a boy-child who would kill him. When Zeus got Metis to bed, he swallowed her. He immediately developed a raging headache. Hermes or Prometheus split Zeus's head open and out sprang Athena fully armed and with a mighty shout. She was fierce and ruthless.

Apollo, beautiful, master musician, archer, healer, god of Truth and a link between gods and men, was also pitiless and cruel. Apollo earned the anger of Zeus whose son Asclepius, a physician, had the temerity to resurrect a dead man. This robbed Hades of a subject and he lodged a complaint on Olympus. Zeus killed Asclepius with a thunderbolt. Apollo, in revenge, killed the Cyclopes. Zeus was enraged at the loss of his armourers. He would have banished Apollo to Tartarus for ever if Leto had not pleaded for him and undertook to mend his ways. The sentence was reduced to one year's hard labor to be served in the sheepfolds of King Admetus of Therae. Taking the advice of Leto, Apollo carried out the sentence humbly and conferred great benefits on Admetus. He preached moderation in all things and such phrases as "Know thyself!" and "Nothing in excess!" were always on his lips. He brought the Muses down from their home on Mount Helicon to Delphi, tamed their wildness, and led them in seemly dances. It seems the gods broke rules, were judged, appropriately punished, and some even, rehabilitated.

Artemis, fierce and vengeful, was a slayer of women. Aphrodite was treacherous and malicious with deadly power over men. Hermes was shrewd and cunning and a master thief; Ares, god of War, was detested by Zeus and Hera and according to Homer, a murderous, ruthless, bloodstained coward. He loved battle for its own sake. He had great contempt for litigation. He was charged with the willful murder of Poseidon's son Halirrhothius. Ares claimed he saved his daughter from being violated by Halirrhothius. There were no witnesses except Ares and his daughter. Naturally, his daughter confirmed his claim. He was acquitted. This was said to be the first judgement pronounced in a murder trial, (Graves 1988: 73-74). Hephaestus, god of Fire was ugly, lame, kindly and peaceful. There were many lesser gods: Eros, Ocean, Naiads, Furies, Pan, Satyrs, Centaurs, and Gorgons. The gods were usually not beneficial to humans and often were burdensome. Two of man's best friends were Demeter (Ceres), goddess of the Corn (agriculture) and Dionysus (Baccus), god of Wine (pleasures). The behavior and misbehavior of the immortals was in the image of the mortals.

Divine Misdeeds

Persephone (Proserpine), daughter of Demeter, was kidnapped and raped by Hades (Pluto), the brother of Zeus, lord of the underworld. Demeter was terribly angry and grief stricken. She wasted away in mourning and longing for her daughter. Because of the neglect of her domain, nothing grew and man was fated to die from hunger. Zeus had to intervene and instructed Hades to free Persephone, which he did. Though returned to her mother, Persephone was required to spend four months a year in the Kingdom of Darkness. Elated, Demeter filled the earth with food.

Dionysus (Bacchus) was born in Thebes. His mother was mortal, his father, Zeus. Zeus killed the mother because she saw him, which no mortal could do. Dionysus could be very kind, but also very cruel. The Maenads (Bacchantes) were women driven mad by Dionysus with his wine and engaged in frenzied dancing. They rushed around the woods tearing the wild animals to shreds and devouring them. This was the way to worship Dionysus, ecstatic joy and brutality. In Euripides' (1953) play *The Bacchae*, Dionysus arrives in Thebes, home of his mother, now dead. He recruits the women for the wild worshipping with wine, dancing, and other pernicious behavior. Pentheus, grandson of Cadmus, King of Thebes, is outraged at the foolishness – Bacchus emulating a god and the cavorting of the frenzied women. He locks up many of the women. His grandfather, founder of Thebes, and the father-in-law of Bacchus, are about to join the revelers to propitiate the god. They are joined by a seer when spotted by Pentheus.

Again he is irate. The seer argues that Bacchus gave us wine and wine is the cure for the weariness of life. Bacchus, like other gods, was happy when men celebrated his rites and honor him as a god. Pentheus, not at all placated, orders his men to find Bacchus and bring him back in chains.

Dionysus is brought forth and derided by Penthius. Dionysus slowly takes over the mind of Penthius convincing him to watch the women cavorting in the mountains and to dress like one. The god plans on shaming him in the woman's dress and having him killed by his mother who was one of the Bacchae. Dionysus makes the Bacchae think that Penthius is a lion cub and, led by his mother, he is torn to pieces. Pentheus' mother recovers her senses and sees what she has done. Cadmus, the founder of Thebes and his wife are turned into beasts. The entire house of Cadmus is destroyed because Dionysus was not acknowledged as a god and his revenge was terrible.

Dionysus killed many enemies in battles which he fought across Greece, Egypt, the Tigris and Euphrates rivers, and India (Graves 1988). When he returned to Europe, Rhea, his grandmother, "purified him of the many murders he had committed during his madness, and initiated him into her Mysteries." On a later occasion, he killed Hippasus, the son of one of the three sisters who declined to join him in ritual revels. This murder was annualy atoned in a feast called Agrionia (provocation to savagery). Women devotees pretended to look for Dyonisus, decided he was away with the Muses and sat in a circle asking riddles. Then the priest of Kyonysus rushed from the temple with a sword and killed the one he caught first.

So many of the myths involve the interaction of man and gods with the heroism and baseness of both. The tale of the golden Fleece is well-known. The story of kings and gods and ambition, jealousy, and death has been told by the ancient poets like the third century B.C. Apollonius and Pindar the odist. The return of Jason with Medea is one of Euripides' (1953) most powerful and famous poems. The hunt for the Golden Fleece started with the Greek King Pelias who was tired of his wife, shunted her aside, and married Princess Ino. The first wife was afraid the second wife would kill her son Phrixus so that Ino's son would inherit the kingdom. This happened in typical sinister fashion. Ino managed to manipulate the sacrifice of Phrixus. At the altar Hermes sent a remarkable ram with a fleece of gold to snatch Phrixus and his sister and fly them to Colchis. During the journey, the girl Helle, slipped and fell into the water and drowned. The strait was named after her – Hellespont. The boy arrived safely. Phrixus sacrificed the ram to Zeus in gratitude for his escape and gave the fleece to the King of Colchis.

When a child, Jason's right to his father's throne was usurped by Pelias. When adult, he returned to claim it. Pelius agreed if Jason would first recover the Golden Fleece, thinking it impossible. Jason agreed to what he considered a great adventure. Aboard the ship Argo with a crew of heroes (including Hercules) and a series of bizarre adventures, Jason with the help of Medea, including the murder of her brother, recovers the fleece. Returning home, Jason found that Pelias had forced Jason's father to kill himself and his mother died of anguish. Medea, with her usual cunning, caused the death of Pelias in revenge. They then left for Corinth. It was there that the story concludes as Medea slaughters her two sons and Jason's new wife. "Hell hath no fury like a woman scorned." All the evil and good by Medea was for the love of Jason. He was a traitor as he tossed her aside to marry another to fulfill his ambitions. This launched a flood of hate and the appalling revenge. It is rather amazing that 1000 years before Christ, the troubles and arguments between hsuband and wife rings so familiarly. Aside from the royal nature of Medea's situation, the consequences may be rare in our time, but it has occurred with abandonment, jealousy, hate, and revenge with murder.

An example of the interrelations of the gods which hardly qualified as role models occurred when Zeus fell in love with Io. He feared Hera's reaction. He wrapped the earth with a thick dark cloud to hide Io and himself. Hera knew something was afoot. She found him down on earth beside a lovely white heifer. Zeus had been quick enough to transpose Io into the animal. Zeus lied to Hera but she did not believe him. Cleverly, she asked him for the heifer as a gift. Zeus gave it to her because to refuse would expose his lie. Io was turned over to Argus who had a hundred eyes to watch over her. Zeus sent Hermes, the messenger, to kill Argus. He found Argus, played his shepherd's pipe and told him stories in a monotonous fashion. This caused the eyes of Argus to close, a few at a time, until all were shut. Hermes then slew Argus. Hera, not to be daunted, took the eyes and placed them in the peacock's tail. Then she sent a gad-fly to plague Io who was stung to madness. She wandered endlessly. One sea was named after her – the Ionian sea. At last, she reached the Nile where Zeus returned her to human form. She gave birth to Zeus' son Epaphus. Hercules was one of her descendants. One Zeus escapade in which the woman was more fortunate than Io was the indiscretion with Europa. Hera apparently was not aware of this adventure. The encounter was as usual with Zeus, trickery, divine promises, and a celestial form of rape.

Poseidon too practiced seduction. He did so with Arne who produced two sons, Aeolus and Boetus. They were exposed on a mountain to die but a herdsman rescued them. The King Metapontus was married to Theano who was barren, for which reason Metapontus threatened to divorce her. He went to consult an oracle when the herdsman gave the two foundlings to Theano. When Metapontus returned, Theano passed the foundlings off as her own. Later she became pregnant by Metapontus and bore him two sons. As all four children grew up, Metapontus favored Aeolus and Boetus who, being of divine origin, were more handsome than their foster brothers. This enraged Theano. She instructed her sons to murder Aeolus and Boetus. This misfired as Aeolus and Boetus killed their foster brothers. Theano stabbed herself to death with a hunting knife. The mischievous deeds of the gods often led to terrestrial disasters.

Myths covered the beauty of flowers and even there embraced tragedy. Persephone, daughter of Demeter, was drawn to the Narcissus by the work of Zeus to help his brother the Lord of the Underworld who had fallen in love with the girl. She wandered over to pick the beautiful flower and was snatched by Hades. Also, there was the beautiful lad Narcissus who fell in love with his own image (arranged by the Goddess Nemesis) and gazing at it in a pool pined away to his death. On the spot where he pined, a flower bloomed and it was named after him.

The gods also created birds, but tragedy struck first. Tereus, a powerful king of Phocia and Thrace, married Procne. She bore him a son, Itys. He later fell in love with Philomela, Procne's sister. Tereus locked Procne away, cut out her tongue so she could not talk, said she was dead, and married Philomela. Tereus then murdered his brother to keep his throne. Meanwhile the sisters, Procne and Philomela, discovered each other. Procne killed her son, Itys, boiled him, and fed him to her husband. When Tereus realized what he had eaten, he tried to kill Procne and Philomela but the gods intervened. They changed all three into birds – Procne into a swallow, Philomela into a nightingale, and Tereus into a hoopoe.

Some of the myths became a part of the heavenly landscape. Orion, a mighty hunter, was eventually killed by the goddess Artemis. After his death he was placed in heaven as a constellation. The Pleiades were the seven daughters of Atlas. They were pursued by Orion but he could never catch them. Nevertheless he kept pursuing them. Finally, Zeus pitied them and placed them in the heaven as stars.

The Iliad told the tale of that most famous of cities – Troy. The legend started with the dispute of three jealous goddesses. Eris, the evil Goddess of Discord was not popular in Olympus. Resentful, she was determined to cause trouble at an important wedding (to which she was not invited). She threw a golden apple into the banquet hall marked for the fairest. All the goddesses wanted it, but the choice was narrowed down to three: Aphrodite, Hera, and Pallas Athena. Zeus wisely refused to judge them and recommended Paris for the job. Rather than look at them and choose, he was asked to consider the bribes offered and then to choose. He chose Aphrodite's offer of the fairest woman in the world. Thus, the snatching of Helen, the "face that launched a thousand ships," the siege of Troy, and a ruthless war with godly interference.

The sack of Troy was followed by two other legends – the Odyssey and Aeneid. Odysseus put out to sea and faced tribulations as arduous as those brought upon the Trojans. The gods Athena and Poseidon who helped them conquer Troy, became their bitterest enemies on the trek home. Aeneid was Virgil's account of the defeated Aeneas and the remnants of Troy and their struggle and complications leading to the founding of Rome. Virgil contrived this legend for Augustus to show a relationship between the Caesar and the gods.

Famous Greek Families In Mythology

Conceivably, the most famous family in mythology is the House of Atreus. Some of the members were Agamenmon, head of the Greek expedition to Troy, Clytemnestra his wife, and Iphigenia, Orestes, and Electra his children. Menelaus, husband of Helen, was his brother. All their misfortunes started with Tantalus, a King of Lydia. His baneful deed placed a curse on the family that continued beyond his death. It made men sin against their will and brought suffering and death upon the innocent as well as the guilty. Tantalus was a son of Zeus, honored by all the gods and given privileges usually not available to mortals. He was atrocious; he had his only son boiled and served to the gods. He did it to scorn the gods as cannibals as he hated them intensely. They were not fooled and decided to punish him. They put him in a pool of water in Hades. Whenever he was thirsty and stooped to drink, the water disappeared. He stood up and it reappeared. Hanging over the pool were fruit trees laden with pears, apples, figs, and pomegranates. Whenever he reached for one the wind blew it out of his grasp. Thus, with eternal thirst and hunger in the midst of plenty, he was never sated. The gods restored his son to life, but had to fashion an ivory shoulder for him as one of the gods inadvertently ate it. He became the only descendant of Tantalus who was not marked by misfortune. In contrast, his sister Niobe met with disaster. At first, highly successful, she ruled Thebes with her husband. Then she took after her father by arrogantly and openly defying the gods. Apollo and Artemis killed all fourteen of her children. She turned into stone which was eternally with tears. And so it went with the family.

> "Woe springs from wrong, the plant is like the seed –
> While right, in honour's house, doth its own likeness breed."
> (Aeschylus 1961: 34).

Zeus sent the Greeks to Troy to avenge the rape of Helen. To speed the ships on their way to Troy and to appease the gods, Agamenmon sacrificed his daughter. The gods were divided, some for the Greeks, some for Troy. After Troy fell, there was sacking and violence. Those gods sympathetic toward Troy now sought revenge for the brutality while other gods sought justice for the crime against the Greeks. The returning Greek fleet was battered by a storm induced by heaven, sinking and scattering many of the returning ships. Menelaus got Helen back, returned home and lived happily ever after. For Agamemnon, the story was quite different. He finally arrived home. He received a great welcome from the townspeople. His wife maintained a grudge ever since he sacrificed their daughter Iphigenia. She had taken a lover, Aegisthus. Agamemnon had brought with him from Troy, Cassandra, daughter of Priam, a gift from the army of the comeliest of the women captives. Apollo was enamored of Cassandra. He gifted her with visions of the future – an ability for prophesying. However, she rejected him. Therefore, he allowed her to keep the gift, but no one would believe her oracles. She envisioned her death and that of Agamemnon. Nobody payed attention to her prophesy. Clytemnestra fulfilled the oracle and assassinated both.

"He who lives by the sword, dies by the sword," (Aeschylus 1961). The children of Agememnon and Clytemnestra, Orestes and Electra, plot revenge against their mother. Orestes slays Aegisthus and Clytemnestra, then seeming to go mad, flees to the Temple of Apollo at Delphi. Apollo assigns Hermes to guard Orestes and guide him to Pallas where he can find atonement for his deed. Apollo protects him because it was he who urged Orestes to his action. The Furies come from Hell to demand revenge for the matricide. Athena is called to judge between the Furies and Orestes. A jury is set-up of 12 Athenians. Apollo is a witness for Orestes. Apollo and the Furies argue their causes. The panel votes and splits 50-50. Athena casts the final vote and frees Orestes. Athena placates the Furies and the curse on the house of Atreus is lifted.

In the old account Iphigenia was sacrificed by Agamemnon. The later Greeks did not like stories of human sacrifices to appease the gods. They felt it slandered the gods to practice such events. Therefore, they concocted another story in which Iphigenia simply vanished when she was about to be sacrificed. She was taken by Artemis to the land of the Taurians where she was made priestess of Artemis's temple. Years later, Orestes and his friend Pylades landed in that country. This was after Orestes was absolved of guilt for the assassination of his mother. He still felt dispair, went to Delphi where he was told to go to Taurian country and bring the sacred image of Artemis to Athens. This would heal him and he would be at peace. Orestes and his friend were captured and were to be killed as the Tauric people hated the Greeks. Iphigenia and Orestes eventually recognized each other. Using a clever ruse, and with the help of the gods, the three escaped. A furious Thoas pursued them to the Island of Sminthos where Thoas was killed by Orestes and Chryses, (Graves 1988: 74-76).

The Royal House of Thebes rivaled the House of Atreus in fame and tragedy. Again, with the help of the gods – in both directions. The house was founded by Cadmus with the help of Apollo. Cadmus married Harmonia, daughter of Ares and Aphrodite. They had four daughters and one son. All the daughters met with some misfortune. One of them was Semele, the mother of Dionysus, who was killed for catching sight of Zeus, the father of Dionysus. Another was Agave, driven mad by Dionysus and killing her own son. Ino's husband went out of his mind and killed their son. She jumped into the sea with her son's dead body. The gods saved them both. Autonoe endured the terrible and undeserved death of her son. The one son Polydorus was the great grandfather of the great tragic figure Oedipus. His daughter Antigone guided the blind Oedipus when he was exiled. His two sons later vied for the throne of Thebes.

Perhaps one of the more positive figures in myth was Theseus. Although the gods intervened with his adventures, it was a tenuous and more subtle influence. He sailed on the Argo with Hercules and Jason in the search for the Golden Fleece. He brought democracy to Athens and spent much of his life as the protector of those who were helpless. He received the aged Oedipus and sustained and comforted him until he died. When his cousin Hercules lost his mind and killed his wife and children, Theseus comforted him and persuaded him from suicide when he returned to his senses. It was as penance that Hercules took on the Twelve Labors of legendary fame. This included the freeing of Theseus from the Chair of Forgetfullness in the lower world. It was in the later years of his life that he married Phaedra and tragedy (abetted by Aphrodite) fell upon his son Hippolytus by the Amazon Hippolyta (also called Antiope).

The calamity unfolded when Phaedra was smitten by Aphrodite to fall in love with Theseus' son Hippolytus. Aphrodite resented Hippolytus' neglect and hated his purity. At first hesitant, she soon became more aggressive under the spell of the goddess. She was rebuffed. To avoid dishonor, she hung herself. Tied to her arm was a note accusing Hippolytus of ravaging her. She turned the suicide into revenge. Theseus banished his son as punishment. On his way to exile Poseidon, father of Theseus, carried out the curse on Theseus to kill his son. Along the seashore in his chariot, the horses were frightened by Poseiden and panicked. The chariot was upset and Hippolytus was tangled in the reins and dragged to his death. Artemis appeared to notify Theseus of the tragedy. He was passionately contrite. Aphrodite destroyed three lives: Theseus the King, Phaedra his wife, and Hippolytus his son. Artemis promised revenge on Aphrodite. She struck down the man that Aphrodite held dearest in the whole world. "To find pleasure in power is to be corrupted by it....," (Euripides).

Mortal-Immortal Affiliation

The affiliation between the mortals and immortals must have given a sense of power to the mortal outcomes. One such example of corruption was in the legend of Bellerophon and Pegasus. Bellerophon was rumored to be the son of Poseidon. His mother was Eurynome, a mortal taught by Athena until she was said to be the equal of the gods. The extraordinary horse Pegasus, a winged steed tireless in flight, sprang from the Gorgon's blood after being slain by Perseus, the son of Zeus and a mortal mother. With the help of

Athena, Bellerophon was able to saddle and mount Pegasus and fly wherever he wished. There followed a series of adventures involving the accidental killing of his brother and attempts on his life for spurning a queen. His success went to his head as he thought himself equal to the gods and tried to ride Pegasus to Olympus to join them. The steed knew better and threw Bellerophon. Thereafter he wandered alone, hating the gods, until his death.

"A thing of beauty is a joy forever," (Keats). There was a great deal of promiscuity in the mortal-immortal interaction. But, there also was love. Endymion was immortalized by Selene, the Moon, and Keats, the poet. Endymion was a shepherd (or King, or hunter) of transcendent beauty. He was seen by Selene and loved. She came down from heaven and kissed him. To keep him forever for herself she cast a spell and he never awoke again. Though immortal, he sleeps forever, never conscious and she visits him nightly and covers him with kisses. For the gods, the affairs of the heart could be heartless.

Cupid, son of Venus, and Psyche, daughter of a mortal king, is a story of love, wealth, sibling jealousy, terror, and tragedy. But in the end, love and soul (Cupid and Psyche) found their happiness and Psyche was given the ambrosia of immortality.

Orpheus was the son of one of the Muses and a Thracian king his mortal father. The gods were the earliest musicians. He inherited the gift from his mother. He sailed with Jason on the Argo. He saved the crews from the Sirens by drowning out their seductive and fatal voices with his lyre. He fell in love with Eurydice, they married, and as she walked with her bridesmaids she was bitten by a viper and died. Orpheus, grief stricken, was determined to go down to the underworld and bring her back. He so shamed the Lord of the Dead and all others, they agreed to free her. There was one stipulation. He was not to look back at her as she followed him until they reached the upperworld. As soon as he left the underworld he turned around, but it was too soon for her. She disappeared back to the underworld. He was not permitted to return. Devastated, he wandered in solitude through Thrace playing his lyre to the rivers, and trees. Eventually, a band of Maenads (women put into a frenzy by Bacchus) slew him and dismembered his body. The Muses buried his head in Lesbos and his limbs were gathered and buried at the foot of Mount Olympus where the nightingales continue to sing more sweetly than anywhere else.

Other Myths

Though the Golden Bough (Frazier 1970) was written as a "Study in Magic and Religion," it included a great deal of mythology. It is a book full of extraordinary ceremonies. They capture a "tragedy of human folly," and many of the picturesque ceremonies are still in abated force today, usually hidden sources of continued tragedy. The ceremonies are gathered from around the world. For example, the Aztec use of sacrifice was the product of the mistaken notion that the sun was fueled by human blood, not nuclear fission.

In the legend of Diana and Virbius there is a sacred grove and sanctuary of Diana of the Wood. Here we see an ancient event, passed down in myth and legend, still influential, even through modification and metaphor. Virbius was formally known as Hippolytus who was the son of Theseus so unjustly slain. He was raised from the dead by Aesculapius, son of Apollo and a mortal woman. He was said to have visited the grove. In this grove was a certain tree which always has a prowling figure carrying a drawn sword. He was a priest (also a King) and a murderer. He achieved his status by killing his predecessor. Sooner or later, his successor would kill him. That was the system of succession. Frazier attempted to explain this phenomenon. One such explanation states that the Tauric (Crimea) Diana (Greek Artemis) was worshipped at this grove (Nemi) after being instituted by Orestes who fled with his sister to Italy after slaying King Thoas. He brought with him the image of Diana hidden in a bundle of sticks. It was said that every stranger who landed on the shore of her Tauric temple was sacrificed on her altar. When translated in Italy it was modified. Within the sanctuary at Nemi there was a tree from which no branch was allowed to be broken, except by a runaway slave. If successful, the slave was entitled to battle the priest. If he won he became the King of the Wood. The fateful branch was the Golden Bough. The flight of the slave represented the escape of Orestes; the combat represented the human sacrifices once offered to Diana. This rule of succession endured into the times of Imperial Rome.

The combination of king and high priest was not unusual in ancient times and survived into more modern ones. Thus we have the combination of royal authority and religious functions. In earlier times the combined functions included magic. This early society of kings and priests was thought to be endowed with supernatural powers – the incarnation of a deity (Frazier 1970: 199). Thus the acts attributed to gods could be duplicated by mortals allegedly endowed with the attributes of gods, ironically imputed to the gods by men.

While the Greek gods were immortal and invincible, how could they be heroic? The Norse gods were constantly in danger and fated to be doomed. Their choice was to go down fighting – heroically. The day would come when they would be destroyed; the fate of the gods would be the fate of the mortals. The gods were called Aesir; their enemies were the Giants – good against evil. Their home was in Asgard. The mortals knew that they could not save themselves, but they would never quit, but die resisting. A brave death entitled them to entrance into Valhalla, one of the halls of Asgard. Even there they must look forward to final defeat. In the last battle between good and evil they will fight with the gods and die with them.

The writings of Norse mythology were destroyed by the christian missionaries combating paganism. A few survived like Beowulf in England and the Nibelungenlied in Germany (Hamilton 1940: 301). Like the Greek and Roman myths, the Norse ones reached America through the early settlers and later immigrants. Odin, like Zeus, was the chief god. He is an aloof and solemn figure. Two ravens perch on his shoulder. Each day they fly around the world and bring him the news of all that men do. One is called Hugin (thought), the other Munin (memory). Odin's main concern is the postponment of the day of doom – destruction of heaven and earth. His attendants are the Valkyries. Their chief task is to decide who wins and who loses, who lives and who dies on the battlefield. They then carry the brave dead to Odin.

Balder was the most beloved of the gods, on earth as well as heaven. His death was the first of the disasters. He dreamt of danger. His mother, the wife of Odin, determined to protect him. She exacted an oath from everything, dead or alive, not to harm him. The other gods, thinking him safe, played a game where they tried to hit him with a stone, dart, arrow, or sword. All fell away harmlessly. This was fine with all but Loki. He was not a god but the son of a giant. Trouble followed him everywhere. He was allowed to visit Asgard in spite of his tendency to be vexatious. He was jealous of Balder. He discovered that everything had sworn not to harm him except one little shrub – the mistletoe. He took the shrub to where the gods were amusing themselves. He went to Balder's blind brother and asked him to join in the fun. Loki told Hoder he would guide him and give him something to throw. He gave Hoder a mistletoe branch, helped him aim, and Hoder hurled the branch as hard as he could. It pierced Balder's heart and killed him. Loki was punished. He was bound and placed in a cavern with a serpent above him dropping venom on his face causing great pain.

Some of the other gods were Thor the Thunder-god, Freyr the caretaker of the fruits on earth, Heimdall the guardian of the rainbow bridge to Asgard, and Tyr the God of War. Goddesses were not as important as in Greek and Roman myths. One place where a goddess ruled was in the Kingdom of Death. This belonged to Hela. "The fierceness of men rules the fate of women," (Elder Edda c 1300). Sigurd is the most famous of the Norse heroes. He plays the Norse version of the German Nibelungenlied hero Siegfried in the story of Siegfried and Brunhild.

The tale of Isis and Osiris in Egyptian mythology (parts related to Greek and Roman mythology), is an example of more benign deities. They were brother and sister. They married and had a son Horus. Isis was worshiped as the protector of children. Osiris was murdered by his brother Set. Isis searched for and retrieved his dismembered parts and revived him. She was the epitome of faithfulness and maternal devotion. Horus avenged his father's death. Osiris was the god of the dead, son of Geb the earth and Nut the sky. He was worshiped as the corn-god, buried and coming to life with the new crops, and the sun-god as well (Frazier 1970: 449; 458).

The Legacy

There were many other myths told by the Greeks, Romans, and others. Some told the same story differently. But the intrusion of the gods was constant and tragedy dominated. These myths became part of the Western culture inherited by America. Their effect on character is not known, but they do make suffering and illicit death, as well as heroics, part of normal life for both mortals and immortals. Many of the stories from the first five books of the Old Testament are from various dates and authors and are likely mythical and similar mythical tales are found everywhere. Biblical accounts are still taken literally in the face of their impossibilities as demonstrated by science. They come from imagination. Cultures interpret their own symbols literally and they support their, "Moral order, cohesion, vitality, and creative powers," (Campbell 1973: 9). Their myths are their symbols. Science demolishes or modifies myths logically and this, Campbell argues, unsettles the society which can lead to an increase in vice and disease. This happened to the primitive communities when they were beset by "civilized" intruders.

Campbell avers that the moral order is founded on myths. When myths are questioned, especially by science, the moral order is also questioned. From this comes social disorganization. In the earliest emergence of Homo Sapiens, there was already evidence of myth shaping the world of those people. Apparently myth is traceable to Neanderthal caves with ceremonially disposed bear skulls and burials suggestive of some kind of life to come (Campbell 1973: 31). Fire goes back to the Neanderthals and even further to the Pithecanthropus. Probably it was not used for cooking but for heat and also as an altar. Ritual has a significant role in society. It brings people together. As it fades, disorganization may ensue. Myths and rites unite us. The fundamental themes of mythology are constant and universal – "mortality and the requirement to transcend it," and the perseverance of the social order. In short, man will die, he must adapt to the culture in which he is born, and there will be others after him just as there were others before him. Another factor shaping mythology is how one relates to the natural world in which one finds oneself.

The legacy of myth is a legacy of violence and death. In primeval East Africa there were two kinds of hominid – a vegetarian and a meat-eater. The former is extinct. It is the latter, a killer maker of tools and weapons from whom present humans descended. "Man is a beast of prey," (Spengler). It is a dominant mythological theme of many peoples from tropical zones that one increases life through killing, (Campbell 1972: 177). Greek mythology involved a polytheistic pantheon where, in war, some favored one side, some the other. In the Old Testament, we have a single minded single deity who chooses one side and is merciless, (Deuteronomy 7: 1-6). As Campbell (1972: 181) puts it "...we have been bred to one of the most brutal war mythologies of all times." War and its atrocities have been practiced since ancient times. Even in recent times, Hitler practiced genocide, religious wars wrecked havoc, the Inquisition slew many, and today we hear "Praise Allah' before gunning down of civilians. In most recent times, peace was sought with armed might – be strong and peace will prevail.

Some of the myths, in modified form, have come to us from ancient times and have become mechanisms of social control. This is particularly true of rites and ceremonies. In many instances they bring harmony, control, and cohesiveness to groups of different structures. Rudoff (1971) devised a functional model of deviance which described mechanisms of control present in the personality, culture, and structure of a social system. The personality may use fatalism to escape from trouble – a trait that may very well come down to us from mythology. Freud has implied that we are born animals and learn not to be one. Culture may include the legacy of myths in the way it faces challenges of social provocation. Spencer (1897: vols. 1, 2) suggested a theory of ceremonials that generate from dominant-subordinate relationships. These relationships can allay fears and preserve inequality through symbolic control. Van Genep (1908) outlined the rites of passage, usually along the life cycle, that integrate one into the group at a certain age, or integrate the group at the death of a member. Structurally we still have mechanisms like sanctuary, legal fictions, and legitimate non-normative roles that can relieve stress and preserve harmony.

Thus we have the difference between a normal amount of deviance and a morbid amount. We possess a repertoire of mechanisms across the social spectrum for the control of misbehavior. The goal beyond a low normal rate of crime, like zero, can not be achieved. It would be an Eden before the fall – again.

CHAPTER EIGHT

THE BIBLICAL LEGACY

It is often noted that the bible is the best seller of all time. It is old and has been pored over for over two millennia. Its influence is monumental. It is the soul of the Judeo-Christian influence. It is easy to concede its moralizing influence. Yet its content is teeming with violence. "The murderer rises before daylight to kill some miserable wretch," (Job 24: 10). Does it constitute a legacy of encouragement of heinous behavior when it is interpreted by some as a divine instruction?

Cain And Abel

Most suggest that the first case of murder involved Cain and Abel. Cain was a farmer and Abel a herdsman (Cf. Kugel 1997). Both made offerings or sacrifices to God. Abel's was a prized animal. Cain offered some of what he grew. God accepted Abel's offering but rejected Cain's. Cain became angry and from here on the story is hazy. These are four accounts from Genesis 4:8 –

> King James: Cain rose up against Abel his brother, and slew him.
> New Jerusalem: Cain set upon his brother Abel and killed him.
> New English: Cain attacked his brother Abel and murdered him.
> Revised English: Cain attacked and murdered his brother.

Was it a slaying, a killing, or a murder? There is a difference between killing and murder, and slaying is ambiguous. Note too that in tradition, all versions of the bible, and God Himself say that Cain brought about the death of Abel. But, no where does Cain admit it. He is accused and condemned by circumstance, not evidence. Of course, being omniscient, God does not need evidence. And of course too, all generations need to have Cain guilty.

Why did Cain kill Abel? The general answer is that Cain felt a jealous rage toward Abel over God's favor. If so, why did he get mad at Abel? Why not at God? Did Cain and Abel have a fight? The bible does not say; we do not know. How did Cain kill Abel? Did he stone him, cut him with a sickle or a knife, or beat him to death? Again, we do not know.

Whatever happened, was it somehow due to Adam and Eve? Edwin Friedman, a present-day rabbi and family counselor, blends both professions in describing the first family as dysfunctional (Public Affairs Television 1996: 54-55). Adam forever complained that he had to work too hard. Eve complained that Adam never knew what it was like to bear children. Abel, the younger, was more successful than Cain, the elder. Cain resented this and saw Abel as the cause of his failures. Both parents were discontented with each other and neither could handle the friction between the two boys. It was inevitable that some day Cain would kill Abel over any incident, large or small.

It was quite clearly a killing, but was it murder? If it was a killing in self-defense, it was not murder. If it was a murder, what was the intent and where was the malice? If it was there, God ignored it. He made Cain leave the area – to be "a vagrant and a wanderer on earth," (New English 4: 13). This was a severe and dangerous punishment and might have been a death sentence. But when Cain pleaded for leniency, God listened:

> "So the Lord put a mark on Cain in order that anyone meeting him should not kill him. Then Cain went out from the Lord's presence and settled in the land of Nod to the east of Eden."

In essence, the Lord withheld his wrath from Cain just as He did when He banished Adam and Eve instead of destroying them. What was the mark that He put on Cain? No one knows. No version of the Bible describes it. We do not know where it was nor what it looked like. As one conjecture, God's mark on Cain might have been a personality trait – perhaps a pugnacious posture or a bearing so humble that all would ignore him.

There are other views. Christopher M. Leighton, (Public Affairs Television 1996: 50-53) writes that the mark of Cain was originally a sign of God's mercy but over the centuries, it was reinterpreted. Augustine taught that Cain and Abel were allegories – Cain for the Jews and Abel for the Christians. The mark of Cain, said Augustine, signified the people who killed Christ. It could be removed only when the Jews became Christians. In the Middle Ages Pope Innocent III ordered the Jews to wear a special badge so that Christians could avoid them as pariahs. This was reinstated by the Nazis in World War II and smoulders as one of the secret prejudices many people retain today. Thus, the mark of Cain is a grim reversal which man has worked with God's original protective symbol.

In general, we are left with questions like these –

1. Did Cain kill Abel or murder him?
2. How did he do it?
3. Why did he do it?
4. Did he admit it?
5. Why was the Lord lenient with him?
6. What mark did the Lord put upon him?
7. How did the mark work?
8. Apart from Abel's animal sacrifice, this was the first death. What did Cain know about dying or death? (For an entirely different interpretation of the Cain and Abel encounter, based on ancient sources, see Kugel 1997.)

Violence And Death In The Bible

The story of Cain and Abel reflects a God who tempers justice with mercy. This contrasts with later accounts where killing and murder thread their way thorughout biblical history. The Revised Standard Concordance Version shows 597 entries for the words kill to killing and 81 for murder to murders. A few have to do with the killing of animals but most concern the murder and killing of people. Fact, myth, and legend are woven together either to instruct or frighten the faithful or to report to them what happened in their common past and by inference what might happen again. A random sample of the references to violent death in the New English Bible may be divided into at least nine rough groups although with overlap. These suggest some of the reasons for killiing and murder beyond what might be learned from the story of Cain and Abel.

Revenge. – Revenge is certainly a contemporary motive for murder. But it has its many moments in Biblical lore. Joab quarreled with David at Hebron for releasing Abner, an accused spy (II Samuel 3: 26-30). "On Abner's return to Hebron, Joab drew him aside in the gateway as though to speak privately with him, and there, in revenge for his brother Asahel, he stabbed him in the belly and he died." Gideon (Judges 8:13-21) killed two men who killed his brother.

In II Kings 14: 3-7, Amaziah "...did what was right in the eyes of the Lord, yet not as his forefather David had done; he followed his father Joash in everything. The hill-shrines were allowed to remain; the people continued to slaughter and burn sacrifices there. When the royal power was firmly in his grasp, he put to death those of his servants who had murdered the king, his father; but he spared the murderers' children in obedience to the Lord's command written in the law of Moses: 'Fathers shall not be put to death for their children, nor children for their fathers. A man shall be put to death only for his own sake.'" Summarizing Jeremiah 41: 1-8, Ishmael, son of Nathaniah, and ten men assasinated Gedaliah, governor of Judah, while at dinner. They also murdered the Judeans who were with them and the Chaldeans who happened to be there. He and his men then murdered eighty visitors and threw their bodies into a pit.

The New Testament portrays similar pernicious events. Mathew 22: 7, (Jesus: the parable of the king and his son's wedding feast.) "...But they took no notice; one went off to his farm, another to his business, and the others seized the servants, attacked them brutally and killed them. The King was furious; he sent troops to kill those murderers and set their town on fire." Then in Revalation 21: 8, (God speaking to those about his throne,) "But as for the cowardly, the faithless, and the vile, their lots will be second death, in the lake that burns with sulphurous flames."

Breach of mores. – Another corollary of homicide extant today is a breach of mores. Abridging Judges 16: 2-3, the people of Gaza plotted to kill Samson for spending the night with a prostitute. He escaped by pushing the house down and carrying it to a hill near Hebron. In Samuel 3: 26-30, David heard the news that Joab killed Abner and said, "I and my realm are forever innocent in the sight of the Lord of the blood of Abner son of Ner. May it recoil on the head of Joab and upon all his family. May the house of Joab never be free from running sores or foul disease, nor lack of a son fit only to ply the distaff or doomed to die by the sword or beg his bread!" In Psalms 10: 7-8, "His mouth is full of lies and violence; mischief and trouble lurk under his tongue. He lies in ambush in the villages and murders innocent men by stealth." (He refers to any wicked man.) Again in Psalms 94: 6-7, "They (i.e., the arrogant and wicked whom the Lord must punish) beat down thy people, O Lord, and oppress thy chosen nation; they murder the widow and do the fatherless to death..."

Jeremiah 7: 8-9 notes that God commands Jeremiah to warn the people of Judah: "You gain nothing by putting your trust in this lie. You steal, you murder, you commit adultery and perjury, you burn sacrifices to Baal, you run after gods whom you have not known..." Hosea 6: 7-9 conveys the Lord's displeasure with certain cities of Israel. "O Admah, they have broken my covenant. They have played me false. Gilead is the haunt of evil doers, marked by a trail of blood; like robbers lying in wait for a man, priests are banded together to do murder on the road to Shechem..."

"But what comes out of the mouth has its origin in the heart; and that is what defiles a man. Wicked thoughts, murder, adultery, fornication, theft, perjury, slander – these all proceed from the heart; and these are the things that defile man; but to eat without first washing his hands, that cannot defile him," (Mathew 15: 18-20). In Romans 1: 28, Paul contrasts the faithful with the godless "...who break all rules of conduct. They are filled with every kind of injustice, mischief, rapacity, and malice; and they are one mass of envy, murder, rivalry, treachery, and malevolence..."

Deterrence. – The Bible proposes deterrence – punish deviance, insure conformity. From Exodus 20: 13 we have "You shall commit no murder." (King James-"Thou shalt not kill."). Further commandments (Exodus 22: 24) include: "You shall not ill-treat any widow or fatherless child. If you do, be sure that I will listen if they appeal to me; my anger will be roused and I will kill you with the sword; your own wives shall become widows and your children fatherless." Again in Exodus, 32: 19-29 – Moses on seeing the golden calf: "He took his place at the gate of the camp and said 'Who is on the Lord's side? Come here to me;' and the Levites all rallied to him. He said to them, 'These are the words of the Lord God of Israel: Arm yourselves, each of you, with his sword. Go through the camp from gate to gate and back again. Each of you kill his brother, his friend, his neighbor.' The Levites obeyed and about three thousand people died that day."

Summarizing Leviticus 18: 6-20 – The following were to be put to death: a man who reviles his father and mother; those who commit adultery; a man who has intercourse with his mother or daughter-in-law; or with another man; or with both a woman and her mother; or with an animal, or a woman who does so; or incest with his sister, or a menstruating woman; or with his uncle's wife, or his sister-in-law.

In II Kings 9: 30-37 – After killing the King of Israel and the King of Judah, "...Jehu came to Jezreel. Now Jezebel heard what had happened; she painted her eyes and dressed her hair, and she stood looking down from a window. As Jehu entered the gate, she said, 'Is it peace, you Zimri, you murderer of your master?' He looked up at the window and said, 'Who is on my side, who?' Two or three eunuchs looked down, and he said, 'Throw her down.' They threw her down, and some of the blood splattered on the wall and the horses, which trampled her under foot. Then he went in and ate and drank. 'See to this accursed woman,' he said, and bury her; for she is a king's daughter.' But when they went to bury her they found nothing of her but the skull, the feet and the palms of her hands; and they went back and told him. Jehu said, 'It is the word of the Lord which his servant Elijah the Tishbite spoke, when he said, 'In the plot of ground at Jezreel the dogs shall devour the flesh of Jezebel, and Jezebel's corpse shall lie like dung upon the ground in the plot at Jezreel so that no one shall be able to say: This is Jezebel.'"

In Numbers 35: 16-21 – "If a man strikes his victim with anything made of iron and he dies, then he is a murderer; the murderer must be put to death. (Similarly with anything made of stone or wood.) The dead man's next-of-kin shall put the murderer to death; he shall put him to death because he attacked his victim. If the homicide sets upon a man openly or malice aforethought or aims a missile at him of set purpose and he dies, or if in enmity he falls upon him with his bare hands and he dies, then his assailant must be put to death; he is a murderer. His next-of-kin shall put the murderer to death because he attacked the victim." Also in Numbers, 25-5 Moses ordered the judges of Israel to kill everyone who worshipped Baal at Peor. Moses also ordered his commanders to kill every woman who had intercourse with any man who worshipped Baal at Peor (Numbers 31: 16-19). Jehu killed all in Ahab's house who had worshipped Baal. Then, all ministers and priests of Baal were crowded into a temple and killed. They then made a privy out of the temple.

Jealousy. – Jealousy is an universal and ancient passion and motive for homicide. So it was in biblical times. In Genesis 20: 11, Abraham said to Abimelech, "I said to myself there is no fear of God in this place and they will kill me for the sake of my wife." He then pretended that Sarah was his sister to foil the Grears from killing him. Again in Genesis 26: 7, "When the men of the place asked him (Isaac) about his wife, he told them she was his sister; he was afraid to say that Rebecca was his wife, in case they killed him because of her; for she was very beautiful."

In Genesis 27: 41 "Esau bore a grudge against Jacob because of the blessing which his father had given him, and he said to himself, 'The time of mourning for my father will soon be here; then I will kill my brother Jacob'." Rebecca warned Jacob and urged him to flee from the area. In Genesis 37: 17-24, Joseph is saved by Reuben from being killed by his brothers and is instead thrown into a pit from which he is soon sold to a traveling caravan of Midianites. Joseph was his father's favorite. His brother had long hated him for this. Finally, in 1 John 3: 11-12, "For the message we have heard from the beginning is this: that we should love one another; unlike Cain, who was a child of the evil one and murdered his brother."

Mercy Killings, Superior Orders, And War

There were other fatal outcomes reported in the Bible which were not murders but for some, the interpretation was moot. This could be labeled mercy killings, death decreed by superior orders, and wars. The Bible also describes limitations on the explication of murder.

Mercy killings. – An Amalekite youth reported to David that he killed Saul who was mortally wounded in combat but still alive. He was suffering and asked to be put out of his misery. The youth brought Saul's crown to David (II Samuel 1: 1-11). David later killed him.

Superior orders. – Genesis 22: 1-14 reports killings based upon orders by a superior – God. Similar alleged orders occasionally lead to slayings in contemporary times, usually carried out by mentally ill persons. Abraham obeys the Lord and prepares to sacrifice his son Isaac. The Lord relents, stays his hand, and substitutes a ram. Some scholars have interpreted this story as indicating the end of sacrificing the first-born to Moloch. Exodus 1: 15-16 "...the King of Egypt spoke to the Hebrew midwives, whose names were Shiphrah and Pah, 'When you are attending Hebrew women in childbrith,' he told them, 'watch as the child is delivered and if it is a boy, kill him; if it is a girl, let her live.'" The midwives disobeyed and let the boys live. They told Pharaoh that Hebrew and Egyptian women differed in that Hebrew women gave birth before the midwives could get to them. Thus the Jews increased in numbers in Egypt. In Exodus 4: 19-23, The Lord ordered Moses to return to Egypt and plead with Pharaoh to let the Jews go out into the wilderness to worship him. Pharaoh would refuse. Moses is to say that the Lord would kill Pharaoh's first-born son.

War. – Wars are reported with a horde of contestants and a multitude of casualties. Judges 19 through 21 reports on such a battle. A Levite left Bethlehem with his party of a young man, a concubine, several asses, and houseware. They headed for his home in Ephraim. On the way, they spent the night in Gilbeah, peopled by the tribe of Benjamin. An old man let them stay in his house for the night, but during the evening some rowdies from Gilbeah pounded on the front door. They demanded the host to release the Levite so they could sodomize him. The host refused but offered them his own virgin daughter. The mob rejected her, so the Levite sent his concubine to them. They raped and abused her all night. In the morning she crept back to the house and died on the doorstep. The Levite loaded her on one of the asses and took her to his home in Ephraim. There he dissected her body and sent the parts to all areas of Israel as evidence of what happened at Gilbeah. Thousands of Israelites gathered from most of the tribes and swore vengeance against the tribe of Benjamin. There were many battles. The Benjamites won all of them until the Israelites developed a strategy in which they ambushed the Benjamites, defeated them decisively, and won the war. The Benjamites lost 50,030 men. The Israelites lost 40,030 men. The Israelites then swore they would never intermarry with the Benjamin tribe survivors.

However, the Israelites realized that their oath would mean that the defeated Benjamites would soon disappear as one of the nation's tribes. To prevent this, they searched for an out. The Israelites found that the residents of Jabesh-Gilead had not participated in the recent war. They killed all the men and women there as punishment but spared four hundred virgins whom they brought to a vineyard near Shiloh. They encouraged these women to stage a festive dance in the vineyard and secretly urged the surviving Benjamites to capture them while the dance was in progress. This was done. The Benjamites intermarried with their captives and eventually their tribe was restored. Thus, the Israelites preserved the integrity of their vow that none who had participated in the war would marry a Benjamite.

The battles between the Israelites and the Philistines provided horrific casualties except in the confrontation of David and Goliath (I and II Samuel and I Kings). Samuel was sent to be raised by Eli, priest of Shiloh. Eli had two sons killed in a battle with the Philistines where Israel lost 4,000 men. The Israelites brought the Ark of the Covenant from Shiloh to the battle site but were again defeated losing 30,000 men. After suffering a devastating plague, the Philistines mobilized to attack the Israelites, who fled. Saul attacked and defeated the Philistines several times. Samuel, speaking for the Lord, directed Saul to exterminate all Amalekites since they attacked the Israelites during the Exodus. Saul did so, and eventually killed their king.

Saul permitted David to fight Goliath a nine foot Philistine giant. David killed the giant and the Philistines departed. Saul became jealous of David's continued success and David fled to the wilderness. The battles between the Israelites and the Philisitines continued. In one of them, Saul was killed. Wars continued between David and the forces of the deceased Saul. David was eventually annointed king of Israel. David continued the battles against the Philistines. After returning the Ark to Jerusalem David and his forces defeated the Philistines, the Moabites, and the Rhobites, from whom he captured 1,700 horses and 20,000 foot soldiers. The Arameans tried to relieve the Rhobites but David killed 22,000 of them. He slaughtered 18,000 Edomites and was victorious everywhere. In a later battle with the Arameans and Amonites his troops slew 700 of their charioteers and 40,000 horsemen.

David had a son Absalom who undermined the people's allegience to David, so he fled. Absalom allowed a force of Israelites to attack David in the wilderness. David knew they were coming and defeated them with his loyal forces. They killed 20,000 of Absalom's army. Other wars with the Philistines were fought. There is no way to judge the accuracy of these reports. However, they do depict David as mighty in battle, as champion of the Lord, and a fit subject for myths and legends.

Limitations

Even in Biblical times context helped define an act. An unnatural death was not always a homicide. The verdict was shaped by limitations. Numbers 35: 22-29 established that in an accidental death the man could seek sanctuary in a city of refuge and remain there until its high priest dies. After that, he was free. Again in Numbers 35: 30, "The homicide shall be put to death as a murderer only on testimony of witnesses; the testimony of a single witness shall not be enough to bring him to his death." Then, in Deuteronomy 22: 25-27, "If a man comes upon such a girl in the country and rapes her, then the man alone shall die because he lay with her. You shall do nothing to the girl for she has done nothing worthy of death; this deed is like that of a man who attacks another and murders him, for the man came upon her in the country and, though the girl cried for help, there was no one to rescue her." (The rape is equated with murder).

Conclusion

The passages identified above lend credence to the view that violent death was a prominent concern to the authors of the Bible. The motives for homicide in fact or in imagery in those ancient days ring a contemporary note and fall into several groups such as:

Revenge – A man kills those who killed his brother, his father, his servants; pariahs; hated foreigners.

Breach of Mores – Sexual misconduct; misdirected hostilities; heretics; foul talk; blasphemies; groundless animosities.

Deterrence – Punishment for mistreating the helpless; idolatry; forbidden matings; unfair fights; worshiping false gods; sorcery; law breaking.

Mercy killing – Helping a man to die who was mortally wounded and in great pain.

Superior orders – Obedience to God; evasion; threat of death.

War – War of revenge by tribes of Israel against Judah for rape; thousands killed on both sides; many wars with high casualties.

Jealousy – Lust for another's wife; sibling rivalry.

Limitations – Sanctuary following an accidental death; required witnesses; innocence of a rape victim.

> Still others – A more complete analysis of the many references would add still other motives for killing and murder. For example there was theft, possession of too many mates and slaves, gambling debts, escape, trade deals gone awry, and others. The result of any review of the Bible makes one pause to wonder why so many people killed each other in those ancient days and did so frequently for so long after Cain and Abel.

Homicide was both approved and disapproved as in the Present Era. It is difficult to fudge whether the statements about violent death in the bible are to be taken literally, or whether they are embellished reports of past events designed either to illumine legendary heroes, or to warn those who might stray from prevailing conventions. In all events, they serve as devices for social control.

Killings and murder actually did occur on occasion. But how often and how massive were they? Were three thousand men, women, and children really killed for beholding, let alone worshipping, the golden calf? Were over 90,000 men killed in the war between the tribes of Israel and the Benjamites? Are these and many other battle counts plausible? Only three weapons were employed in the days before David – swords, stones, and clubs. Any conflict like that at the foot of Sinai or any war like the one reported in Judges could hardly have caused so great a slaughter. The figures were compiled after the fact and were probably inflated to reinforce the impact of myth and to insure the stability of later societies.

Doubts persist about what happened between Cain and Abel. Doubts persist about the frequency and massiveness of violent death among those who came after them. The gospels of the New Testament focus on the death of Jesus, while the Epistles and the Act emphasize His resurrection. But even here, while condemning violence, accounts of killing and murder show that all later writers used these as lessons and themes as did their ancestors centuries before. The sixth commandent says, "Thou shalt not kill." Later versions change this to, "Thou shalt do no murder," perhaps because in Leviticus the Lord prescribed death – i.e. killing – to the children of Israel for many transgressions far less serious than Cain's. Whatever the reasons for the semantic shift, it is quite clear that killing and murder preoccupied the contributors to the Holy Writ of Judeo-Christianity.

In general, homicide as a practice, however condemned and discouraged, is prominent throughout the bible. Certainly it happened on occasion, but hardly as much as stated or there would have been no Palestine, no Israel, no Judah. These reports of what may have happened and these threats of what could happen to the disobedient seem most likely to have been the stuff of legend on the one hand, and of measures to insure conformity on the other. If they occurred as many times as written, there probably would have been no culture and no one to write about it. Yet many readers take it at its word. Even if meant to deter and control, it must have offered encouragement for motive and deed. Does the bible, in its interpretation offer to some the various aspects of homicide? What effect has it had on cults? Does homicide find its source in the bible and religion; is that one of its legacies?

CHAPTER NINE

THE LEGACY OF IMMIGRATION

Introduction

Every society has a category of people whose culture is dominant. For some societies, like Scandinavia and Japan, the populations are quite homogenious. Other societies foster minorities, so labelled for one or various reasons – cultural differences, racial differences, religious differences, and perhaps things like life style or gender. The United States is quite heterogenious. How does a society develop a minority? There are a number of ways such as conquest, annexation, and immigration. One country's conquest of another caused upheavals in ancient times and is repeated in contemporary ones. Examples include the Romans ravaging other nations and Hitler providing similar upheavals. Annexation achieves the same thing through war and other means like the Poles in Russia, Greeks in Turkey, and Mexicans in America. Migration, a typical source of minorities, has come about voluntarily and involuntarily. Slavery, ethnic cleansing, innocents in war, famines and a search for a better life feed migration.

When people move from one place to another they bring with them their life patterns including how they love and cherish and how they hate and kill. All these patterns present a legacy to the host country – exemplar handed down from those who came before to those who are there now. The legacy requires a digging into the past like a cultural archeologist searching for the contributions – the good and the bad – of the forebearers. Former Prime Minister Thatcher noted that British culture might be swamped by an alien one (Ferrell and Sanders 1995: 198). This may be jingoistic but the argument assumes culture can be at least effected if not overwhelmed. If so, would this include crime including homicide? The consequences of cultural diffusion could include all facets of homicide, its extensiveness, and perhaps such factors as weaponry and motive. Gertain graffiti has spread from America to Europe (Ferrell and Sanders 1995: 279). These may be minor crimes, but serious ones also might scatter. Napoleon's army in Egypt left graffiti on some classical structures. What else did they leave? Immigrant styles, in some instances, are diffused to the host country, and again it could include homicide (Ferrell and Sanders 1995: 181). Of course, most if not all nations have homicides; it is not the crime that is diffused but certain parts of it – the weapon, motive, target, vileness, and others. Ferrell and Sanders (1995: 199) strongly suggest that in Britain the punk movement with its legacy of hate, rage, and Nazi fetishism, among working class youth, and the rhetoric of nationalism and subsequent racism, and self interest, created a "new authoritarianism." Some of these factors were indigenous, some either directly or indirectly a reaction to immigration. Many people looked on with dismay attributing the killings and other crimes to the nature of the immigrant culture in spite of the parallel behavior of the host country – "Why can't they be like us?" – which they may become with acculturation.

Each geographic region and historical period has its own criminality (Rousseaux 1996). Eighteenth century criminality is not the same as 13th century criminality. British crime is different from Italian crime. The idiosyncratic criminality enters with the immigrant. It will change with the impact with the new culture. But until it does, it could lend its influence and effect on the existing criminality – for a moment or an era. What influence has brigandage in Italy and Spain had on America? Did the Robin Hood tradition in England and the bandits in Mexico and South America effect America? What has the American gunslinger wrought for other countries?

Mass Population Movements

Hardly anyone can trace his deep roots to where he is now. The history of the world is one of migrations. In preliterate times when the geography was different, movement occurred for survival – away from the threats of others, the weather (Ice Age), a search for food, to alleviate crowding. With larger communities came conquests. The ancient Greeks would conquer an area and then set up colonies and much later they became a minority, or the people conquered did. The Romans did the same on a larger scale. Chaka, the Zulu Chief, conquered other tribes, expanded his empire and caused a ripple effect as those ousted, ousted others, stirring a great deal of movement and mixing. Some searched for a better place to live and found it at the expense of others. Some failed in their search like the Helvetii who came down from the Alps to find a more palatable home, were met by Julius Caesar and his legions and were driven back to the Alps where they still remain. The land they were driven from was part of the Roman conquests. Attempts at "world" domination by such conquerers as the Romans,

Genghis Khan, Napoleon, Hitler and others dislodged many populations. Some of the conquests succeeded and decayed, others were temporary successes, and time seems to belie most such thrusts.

The extensive slave trade uprooted millions, the diaspora still causes occasional changes in residence. Nebuchadnezzar conquered Jerusalem in 586 BC and transported the Jews to Babylon. There were times when whole cities were destroyed and the population that was left was placed elsewhere – perhaps Troy suffered that fate. Some groups developed basic skills and were hired or captured by others where they made their homes. Some of the examples are the Turks as ironmongers, the Mamelukes first as slaves then warriors, and different tribes as mercenaries in the Roman Empire and other places and times as well. More modern wars, particularly World War I and World War II, evidenced significant boundary changes and forced migrations. In Africa today similar changes still occur.

There were several great mass population movements: slaves from Africa estimated at 10-20 million, Europeans in the 19th & 20th centuries when probably the largest migration in history occurred when 70 million people were involved. In America in 1910 one quarter of the country was racial and ethnic minorities: there were 9.5 million foreign born whites in 1850 and peaked to 14.5 million in 1910. Reconstruction of territory caused the upheavel of millions in places like Pakistan and India with the movement of Hindus and Moslems; the breakup of Yugoslavia and "ethnic cleansing" continues to cause changes in population construction.

Native-Americans. – The Paleoindian was the first to enter the New World. The occupation of North America by man occurred during the latter part of the Pleistocene ice age. The introduction of the land bridge permitted movement from Asia through what is now Alaska 30,000 to 1500 BC. The Native-Americans were essentially hunters and familiar with killing both animals and each other. Before the contact with the Europeans, the various people interacted, had bursts of creativity and moments of stagnation leading to the cultural diversity met head on by the earliest immigrants. This intrusion found a people with a long history in this hemisphere.

The contacts were, at first, fairly peaceful but soon the encroachment on territory and way of life was met with resistance. From Columbus' landing on San Salvador through his four voyages to the New World, antagonism, fear, and exploitation became the essence of the Indian-Explorer relationships. Within the context of the place and time it was palpable as the Indians were threatened and defending their land and the Europeans defined them as at best primitive and so fair game to conquer. In the earliest contacts Columbus and his cohorts met with a number of Casiques (Chiefs). These contacts ranged through peace, fear, and violence. This set the tone for subsequent confrontations that eventually decimated the American-Indian. When Columbus arrived in Hispaniola there was a population of over 100,000. By 1520 only about 1000 survived. This was a tragedy caused by violence and disease – measles, influenza, and smallpox. The Indians learned a great deal from the early immigrants – diplomacy and intimidation, coalitions among the tribes, and strength to remain faithful to their culture.

In the early 1600's the French made contacts with the Algonquin and Huron tribes. The tribes furiously fought each other at times supported by the Europeans. As early as 1622 the Natives killed 347 Englishmen. This was interpreted as inferiors refusing the offer to "civilize" them. In the 18th century, French and English fisherman commonly landed in Newfoundland and killed the natives there. Contact with the Europeans was oftern lethal and occurred throughout most of the Western Hemisphere. There were many bloody collisions from which the American attitudes toward the "Indians" coalesced. In the Journals of Lewis and Clark, the Indians were said to have a "merciless system of warfare." Tribal warfare was not unusual and more than just ceremonial. Every stranger was regarded as a potential enemy. Spousal abuse was not a remarkable exception among the Plains Indians. But many of the early immigrants were familiar with violence too, many times as victims. There was violence here before they came and was quickly extended between the two groups.

From Columbus to the present the Native-American has been exploited, ill-treated, deprived of his cultural heritage. The Native-American legacy is extensive. It includes tobacco, cotton, turkey, pharmaceuticals, moccasins, rubber, trails *cum* roads, water transport, canoes, guerrilla warfare, and perhaps a more tolerant attitude toward violence.

Immigration to America. – The earliest pioneers to America were chiefly from the British Isles. The earliest mass influx was from Africa when slaves were transported mostly to the south to work the plantations. In the late 19th century up to the 1960s saw a tide of immigrants involving some 40 million people – Germans, Irish, Italians, and Russians predominated. But every

European country was represented. Their contributions invigorated the country's life and accelerated its economic growth. Their presence and intermarriages produced a diverse ethnicity. Before 1890 they came primarily from the British Isles, Germany, and Scandinavia – of Anglo-Saxon Protestant stock. After 1890 they came primarily from eastern and southern Europe – Roman Catholic and Jews forced to leave due to famine, lack of opportunity, political instability, or religious persecution. The degree of influx varied depending on the economic cycle – high with prosperity, low with depression. The Chinese were restricted by the Exclusion Act of 1882 and the Japanese in 1908 by the so called Gentleman's Agreement later replaced with the Immigration bill of 1924. A quota system was established in 1924 (Johnson Act) favoring northwestern Europeans. The system was reaffirmed in 1952 in the Immigration and Nationality Act then abolished in 1965.

Immigrants are not always welcomed with open arms. In many of the countries that permit immigration the usual accusation is that they carry diseases, are corrupt, cause crime and all other forms of deviance. But studies do not substantiate such accusations (Harris 1995). In the 1840s nativism, an anti-Roman Catholic political movement occurred in America. With the influx of German and Irish immigrants, the so called Native-Americans feared that the immigrant growing influence might effect the American culture. Several organizations rose like the Native American Party, Order of Star Spangled Banner, Know Nothing Party, and American Protective Association. Immigration offered the mainstream a variety of life styles and values and encouraged cultural borrowing. Each group was exposed to their own brand of crime including homicide. Some participated; most observed. The effect was latent or manifest. By now, we are the legacy they left. And what legacy did they leave for homicide?

Accommodation

In the interaction of the indigenous people and the immigrants an accommodation process occurred. It took different forms. In acculturation, the two cultures fused. The immigrant group adopted the new ways with its language and values, and other symbols. However, this process is not a one way street. There is some exchange. Most of the change occurs in the immigrant, but some of their culture is passed on to the indigenous group. They pick up some words, foods, certain behaviors, and other aspects of their culture. This could include some of the criminal behavior and various aspects of homicide. The host might adopt a motive like honor, a weapon like a machete, or a situation like a vendetta. These could represent a legacy from the immigrants.

Integration is another form of accommodation. The fusion is social as well as cultural. Assimilation is the process of fusion into a social unity and common culture. By and large, acculturation is necessary for integration to occur; but there can be acculturation without integration. Ironically, if the immigrant group accommodates, they may introduce some addition to homicide, then subsequent generations assume the Americanized version of it. Amalgamation is a biological fusion through intermarriages. Although the aim is uniformity, the outcome is usually unity in national interest, but the maintenance of identity in special areas – food, language, holidays, religion, certain values, and other cultural demeanors. This is often referred to as cultural pluralism, a concept popular since World War II.

Ruth Benedict has noted that assimilation is a three generation phenomenon. The immigrants start the process, their children embrace the new culture with tension, and the grandchildren take their culture for granted. Acculturation is not a simple happy affair. The immigrant who comes as an adult finds it painful, his children are pulled by two cultures which means rejection of family with shame and guilt and anxiety. The third generation feels belongingness, is secure in identity, and may reidentify with the old. The Chinese return to the Chinatown with a camera around the neck. The Russian searches for a samovar, the Afro-American travels to Africa, and genealogy becomes a craze.

Immigration And Cultural Transfers

Montell (1986) suggests that there is a sub regional culture that tolerated violence including homicide. He did a historical ethnographic study of homicide from 1850-1979 in a specific region of the Kentucky-Tennessee state line. The study was influenced by the Wolfgang and Ferracuti (1967) notion of a subculture of violence. The ancestors of this region migrated largely from the British Isles during colonial times. The economy was mostly marginal or single family farms. There is a history of extensive moonshining. It was hypothesized that lethal violence was an acceptable way to handle disputes. The violence began after the Civil War. The author describes the events as murder connoting viciousness, but perhaps is better described as killings for integrity. Homicide followed a pattern formed and bolstered by such factors as motive, relationship, weapons, alcohol, attitude toward law enforcement and courts. The men dominated the community and homicide involved male on male. They raised hell but were not physically abusive and violent. There was no child abuse and very little spousal abuse. But they used killing to settle disputes with other males. This was code-like behavior and was transmitted to generations. Was this a legacy from British colonists modified by the American experience?

Cultures or subcultures tend to have idiosyncratic situational or other factors related to homicide. Montell (1986) suggests four types of situations in his study: confrontation, ambush, brawl, unknown. These types are known to occur elsewhere but the way it is distributed can identify a culture or subculture. In this case, confrontation accounted for ½ of the deaths where each knew the other with malice. The subculture did not distinguish situations but accepted all types given the proper circumstances. The motives included to protect property (1/3), domestic quarrel (almost 1/4, revenge (1/5). The rest were unspecified, drunken altercations, avoidance of arrest, and paid manslaughter. The two factors most important in perpetuating violence was the high value on gun ownership and the widespread use of alcohol. Also crucial was the relationship with law enforcement. Many killings were unreported at the time. Attending doctors tried to avoid involvement in court hearings. There was ineffective law enforcement involving some corruption, geographical isolation, and political fragmentation. Montell describes it as "Folk Justice." The heritage in this example could involve structural and subcultural effects on social control with consequences for homicide.

There are other examples of cultural transfers that could effect violence and homicide. Phillips (1996) details the French transplantation of their system to Quebec while the British transplanted theirs everywhere else in Canada. An interesting phenomenon is the ubiquitous presence of bandit heroes. They come to us through ballads, folklore, fantasys, imagination often perverted, and in more contemporary times through literature, comic books, radio, cinema, and television. From fact or fiction they are reconstructed into heroes or villains and used for personal or political purposes. In any case, they may effect part of the attitudes towards violence. Perhaps at the top of the list would be Robin Hood while the American West had its James boys among others. At the core of the chimera is a belief that sometimes it is necessary to break the law to achieve justice. Academically it is sometimes referred to as social banditry. In some instances they establish a symbiotic relationship with the society in which they operate and even exploit. Some of this kind of banditry is transported through immigration and may lose something in the translation. The Asians in America have a rich history of contributing to the well-being of the country. The deteriorating social, economic, and political conditions during the latter part of the Manchu dynasty coupled with tales of the "Gold Mountain" gave impetus to the early Chinese immigration to the United States. The old Chinese Triad societies found there way through Hong Kong to America. Quite different from the original organization, it has since been warped from the political force that drifted into banditry and emerged in Hong Kong as delinquent and criminal gangs. It lost the original purpose and Taoist influence but kept the secretiveness and ritual. Some of their crimes have taken on an overlay of the American criminal subculture – extortion, drug trafficking, loan sharking, and occasional violence. What did it give in return?

Australian colonization by British convicts is a notable example of the legacy of criminality for a society (CF Garton 1996). They were the ones who populated a land of aborigines. European colonization began when the American colonies declared their independence and the overcrowding of the hulks (ships used as prisons). The first transports arrived in 1788 and the last in 1868. Some 160,000 convicts were transported and their descendents formed a significant part of the population. Keeping them in check powerfully effected the structure that emerged. They were largely from an urban criminal culture. Part of that culture could have intruded into that of the host country influencing the formation of the nature of their underworld. The idea being presented is that a class of people historically immigrate with their culture, national character, and structural experience and interact with the host country. There is bound to be an exchange, a cultural diffusion, even if the host attempts to destroy or integrate the newcomer. In Australia, the convict influence must have been vital in that their mere presence and numbers required a structure dominated by that presence and focusing on protection and control. Their skills were needed as they were used as a labor force and this too helped mold the nation. They contributed a great deal to the success of the nation; they also must have contributed to a criminal subculture defining the various aspects of violence including homicide.

Like Australia, America too received its share of debtors from the English gaols. It became a repository for the dispossessed. It was the policy of King Charles II in 1733. By 1770 20,000 British prisoners went to Maryland and artistocratic Virginia got its share of indentured servants. They became part of the achieve and possess syndrome of the American character and both traits required aggression.

Crime Among Immigrants

It is highly unlikely that a causal relationship can be made between the contribution to homicide from the country of origin to the host country. But some associations might be possible. The relationship between immigration and crime is of some theoretical interest. In America criminality among immigrants received considerable attention in the first half of the twentieth century. During the height of immigration it was thought to be the chief cause of crime. Several reasons were suggested (without evidence) that immigrants came largely from inferior racial stock; they were unaware of American norms; their crimes were committed out of ignorance; they often were poor and frustrated; they were highly mobile and lacked control from primary groups (Sutherland & Cressey 1978: 148). The rise in urban crime and xenophobia led popular opinion to believe immigrant groups responsible. This relationship was diffused by careful studies, especially by Thorsten Sellin, that belied those claims (Ferracuti 1968). Other explanations replaced those assertions such as mobility as a source of normative conflict leading to violation of laws (Cressey 1968).

Crime rates of foreign born compared to native whites varied from one immigrant group to another. For example, at the peak of immigration persons of Irish heritage had rates 3-5 times higher than German immigrants. Adult Puerto Ricans and Japanese immigrant rates were exceptionally low (Sutherland & Cressey 1978: 150). Native white sons of immigrants tended to have higher crime rates than their fathers, but lower than other native whites. A comparison of first and second generations of Italian immigrants for personal violence including homicide in Massachusetts in the early 1900s indicated a drop in rates for the second generation. Conviction rates for the Irish showed that the types of crime committed by the sons were different than those committed by their fathers. The homicide rates were lower for the sons but higher than the native whites. Certain crimes of the immigrants are traditional in their original country but is not passed on to their children in the host country. The children take on the traditional crimes of the host country. Italian and Turkish immigrants living in Germany in 1965 had higher rates of conviction for murder and assault. This was similar to their home countries (Shannon 1969). The criminal traditions of the home country are carried to the new country and are replaced by succeeding generations. Do some of these traditions become part of the traditions of the host country?

There may be some associations possible, but the process is extremely complex, difficult to establish, and the data too convoluted to trust. Homicide is an act almost if not universal. Different cultures may perform the act differently and for different reasons. One culture may do it most often out of jealousy and use a knife, another for greed and use a gun. However, it is reasonable to assume that a style and reason captures a host country and becomes a part of its culture. Assimilation is not a one way street where the immigrant takes on the new themes while the host rejects everything foreign. The immigrant learns the lost language, adapts to the food, clothes, and values. But the host culture picks words out of the other's language, some of its food and clothes, and perhaps adopts a value or two – maybe just a shift in value hierarchy or value variation, all to a much lesser degree. One example of crime imported with immigration is the professional one.

Professional Crime

Professional crime is not a modern phenomena. With the disintegration of the feudal system in Europe in the fifteenth and sixteenth centuries, a class of rogues and vagabonds emerged (Inciardi 1975: chapter 1). Many of these bandits were attracted to the new urban centers. They eventually produced the professional criminal. These early professionals practiced such criminal activity as highway robbery, swindling with dice, cards, or false gold, horse stealing, shoplifting, and cutpurse (pocket picking). England transported many of these criminals to the colonies and France to New Orleans. Their influence was noticed as early as 1672. Their trades blossomed into an American version. There must have been an occasional homicide with a foreign twist which took on an American inclination. Inciardi (1975: chapter 1) analyzed professional criminality within a contemporary setting and including a comprehensive historical assessment. He found many similarities with Sutherland's (1937) classic study of the professional thief.

Inciardi distinguished three categories of such criminals: the professional; the professional heavy (armed robbery and hijacking); and organized criminal or racketeer. It is within organized crime that one can trace some importation of the homicide process.

Organized crime. – The Black Hand, L'Unione Siciliana, Mafia, Camorra, Cosa Nostra, Syndicate, are all terms used to describe some secret, conspiratorial group of gangsters preying on the American public. Although much is myth and there is disagreement among the experts, one thing is certain and consensual; there exist in America groups of people, highly organized and exclusive, who deal in illicit goods and services involving large sums of money, kill when deemed necessary, and who act with a great deal of impunity. What is organized crime? The answer comes largely from occasional interviews with informers on the fringe of the organization, intelligence reports from various enforcement agencies, rare desertions of "made" members, and highly publicized legislative hearings. The President's Commission on Law Enforcement and Administration of Justice states: (1967: 187)

> "Organized crime is a society that seeks to operate outside the control of the American people and their governments. It involves thousands of criminals, working within structures as complex as those of any large corporation, subject to laws more rigidly enforced than those of legitimate governments. Its actions are not impulsive but rather the result of intricate conspiracies, carried on over many years and aimed at gaining control over whole fields of activity in order to amass profits."

The Commission avers that the basic criminal activity involves the supplying of such illegal goods and services as gambling, loan sharking, narcotics, and other vices. It also embraces illegitimate methods in legitimate business and labor unions such as monopolization, terrorism, extortion, and tax evasion. To protect their designs, they minimize governmental interference by corrupting officials. Many, not all of the groups, were started and are or were dominated by a very small number of those who were immigrants.

The expression "organized crime" is an ambiguous one. Sometimes it is used to identify groups of criminals who happen to be working together over a long period of time in criminal ventures. Extortion rings and car theft rings are examples of these types of organized crime. An Attorney General of California had, for administrative purposes, dubbed organized crime as any criminal activity involving two or more people. Thus, motorcycle gangs, drug rings, and prison gangs are included. Some experts have carefully examined the conception of a criminal organization (Cressey 1969, 1972; President's Commission 1967: 25-60). It was noted that a broad range of informal and formal organizations exist among criminals. In some groups there may be understandings, agreements, common standards and attitudes, and communication. But the affiliation is very loose. They may be organized, like a street corner society, but they are not an organization. An extortion ring is not organized crime; the brigands of southeastern Europe and smugglers in America are early examples of organized crime. The smugglers might have learned their trade from the British. The contemporary associations referred to as Cosa Nostra families qualify as organized crime.

The Mafia. – The Mafia is said to have developed in Sicily and is referred to locally as *Onorata Societa* (Ianni 1973: 59-60; Ianni & Ianni 1972: 31). Emerging as a political power after aiding Garibaldi in the unification of Italy, a symbiotic relationship grew between the Mafia bands and the central government – a delivery of votes for a relatively free hand. At the turn-of-the-century the Mafia families formed a loose alliance and pursued their illegal activities – mostly extortion. These groups performed various community functions and the members were viewed with respect as men of honor. The concept of Mafia refers to a sense of pride, a person of respect and dignity, one who gets things done, and one who can be counted on when in need (Ianni & Ianni 1972: 26). The structure of the Mafia as it was in Sicily in the early twentieth century is similar to the way it is today. However, the illegal activities, social functions, and attitudes of the people and government toward the Mafia has changed becoming less accepting and more hostile.

A second bandit society developed in Naples, Italy at about the same time as the Mafia and was known as the *Camorra* (Ianni & Ianni 1972: 30-40). It started as a prisoner's union in the dungeons of Naples and their activites were largely strong-arm crimes. They too developed political clout and some trappings of organization. But they were unable to survive because of their inability to adapt to changing times and a lack of respect or support from the people (Smith 1975: 55-61). The *Camorra* never caught on in America but the Mafia did.

The Cosa Nostra (Mafia) governs its members, or more appropriately, controls its members and maintains the power of the bosses through a code of conduct similar to that of the Sicilian Mafia and at least parts of it infiltrated with Sicilian immigrants (President's Commission 1967A: 195-196; Cressey 1969: 175-178; Ianni 1972: 135-139; Presidents Commission 1967B: 40-50). In summary, the code consists of several rules:

1. Be loyal to other organization members do not interfere with each members interests.
2. Be rational; keep your cool. Be a member of the team and conduct business and settle disputes quietly and calmly.
3. Be a man of honor; respect womanhood and elders.
4. Be a stand-up guy; your mouth shut (omerta-silence) show courage, don't whine or complain, "if you can't pay, don't play."
5. Have class, be independent; don't be a sucker.

Such admonishments might be fairly universal among young male groups. The code is similar to "ethical systems" attributed to prisoners and thieves as well as the Mafia. The code, of course, is not a written formalized document but a reflection of the values that these groups pursue. The organization's code sustains the power of the leaders: loyalty, honor, respect, absolute obedience. The members are socialized with these values through various mechanisms such as initiation rites and sanctioned through material rewards and violence. When loyalty, or honor, or respect, or obedience is breached, the violence could be homicidal. All of these things might not have been introduced to America, but they could have been aped and adopted by others including idiosyncratic themes.

Daniel Bell (1962) insists that organized crime is an "American way of life" for certain groups whose members are poor but ambitious, especially immigrant groups in urban slums. Organized crime is functional since it provides an opportunity for upward mobility. Organized crime has given members of various ethnic groups an opportunity to achieve the American Dream, albeit a somewhat perverted version of it. From an historical perspective, there has been the succession of one ethnic group by another in organized crime (Ianni 1973; 1978: 673-689; Tyler 1962: 10-15, 343-344). In the nineteenth century organized crime was dominated by the Irish, followed by the Jews, and then the Italians. Today, Afro-Americans, Puerto Ricans, Cubans, Russians and some Latino groups appear to be developing their own versions of the Mafia and any or all might succeed the Italians.

The American experience with crime including homicide is as old as America itself. But the roots of organized crime as we know it today probably started with Prohibition. Prior to this period the public demand for illicit goods and services was provided by a variety of immigrant groups. These nineteenth century racketeers were the prototypes of syndicate crime (Inciardi 1975: 105). They largely emerged from the street gangs of Chicago, New York, and New Orleans. They struggled for territory and the lucrative trade in saloons, gambling, prostitution, and extortion probably with occasional unanticipated needs for homicide.

Between 1820 and 1930, about 4.7 million Italians immigrated to the United States. Almost one-half came between 1900 and 1910, mostly from southern Italy and Sicily (Ianni & Ianni 1972: 48-49). Mostly poor and illiterate, the southern Italians quickly segregated in the eastern urban ghettos forming the little Italys of the early twentieth century. One avenue of upward mobility was crime; like other immigrant groups a few took that route; most of them distinguished themselves as constructive contributors to America. The crimes – extortion, vendettas and the kidnapping of brides – mimicked the culture of the old country. Their victims were other Italian immigrants. This was the onset of the Italian involvement in organized crime. As these early criminals became wealthy and powerful, they expanded their activities and recruited others. Extortion was a major activity and a loose association of small independent gangs referred to as the Black Hand was formed. They terrorized the vulnerable immigrants. By no means a true organization, this American invention with an Italian twist sent a threatening letter demanding money that was signed with a drawing of a black hand. These crimes declined from 1915 to 1920 as the target population diminished, and more importantly, the Volstead Act established the Prohibition Era.

The beginning of modern organized crime probably started with Johnny Torrio shortly after prohibition. He had an extensive criminal background. After assasinating his boss Colosimo he organized the Chicago territory vice industry and developed an alcohol syndicate with investments in numerous illegal breweries. He had a good reputation with and knew many of the important gangsters around the country. One of Torrio's employees was Al Capone, first hired as a bouncer in one of his whorehouses. Torrio was arrested in 1924 and convicted of bootlegging. He eventually abdicated his empire to Capone, an empire with a gross value estimated in 1927 at about $100 million. The Torrio-Capone gang was just one of several powerful criminal groups. Capone did not have the stature of Torrio nor the ability to minimize the internecine warfare. Such characters as Frank Costello, Dutch Schultz, and Lucky Luciano were also providing alcohol for a thirsty nation. Capone's ascendency was punctured by considerable rivalry, especially with the Moran-Aiello gang, culminating in the 1929 St. Valentine's Day Massacre in which seven members of the Bugs Moran gang were lined-up in a garage and raked with machine-guns. The futility of such measures forced a compromise with a meeting producing an agreement in the form of the organization that exists, more or less, to this day.

The violence soon turned inward as conflict erupted between the old-country Mafia types, the "Greasers" or "Mustache Petes," and the second generation Italians. The latter, the "Young Turks", Americanized Italians, used the Jewish entrepeneur gang leader as their model rather than the old timers' feudal parochialism. The conflict between the generations exploded into a 14 month struggle, 1930-1931, known as the Masseria-Maranzano or Castellammarse War. Originating in New York between Salvatore Maranzano and his "Greasers" and Guiseppe Masseria and his new generation allies, the fighting soon spread to Chicago and other cities. Maranzano's faction was the winner, but the victory was a Pyrrhic one. Many of the old timers were killed and irreplaceable. The Americanized mobsters emerged as the powerful leaders in the Italian syndicates. Many of the old ways were altered, but some remained and became part of the Mafia legacy as well as spilling over into the American stream. Central to explaining the Mafia is the violent honor code and instrumental friendships transferred to America and used more or less successfully by the crime families (Hughes 1996). Parts of this seeped into the general criminal culture.

The FBI identifies four main groups in organized crime. At the apex is the Mafia, still dominant and with some control from lesser groups. Next is an assortment of local criminal elements in different parts of the country. Boston boasts the "Irish Mob" in control of gambling. Others include the "Greek Mob" in Philadelphia, a "Syrian" Mob in St. Louis, Cuban refugee groups, Russian groups, Canadian groups, certain elements within the Chinese community in San Francisco, the "Mexican Mafia" in Los Angeles, and various Afro-American and Puerta Rican groups in New York City. The third division includes the outlaw motorcycle gangs such as the Hells Angeles of Oakland, the Outlaws from Chicago, Bandits in Corpus Christi, and the Pagans based in Long Island. Their focus is illegal drugs. The final division involves huge narcotic cartels that peddle billions of dollars worth of such drugs as heroin, cocaine, and marijuana. The homicides perpetrated by these groups as part of their criminal culture must owe something to the criminal culture transported by some members of the immigrant groups.

American history is replete with references to immigrant groups and their contributions to the greatness of the country and its pluralistic nature. Their special position in society and their cultural and subcultural characteristics contribute to the amount and pattern of their crimes. Deviance in America is multicultural. The cultural legacy could be indigenous or alien. The native culture develops and emerges; the alien culture diffuses part or whole aspects which can be modified and become part of the native culture.

The Afro-American Immigrant

Afro-Americans were among the first immigrants coming to America in large numbers. They first appeared in numbers as slaves. The majority came from the West Coast of Africa. Many had an admixture of Mediterranean people. Added to this was an American and Indian combination. With the advent of the plantation system a stable slave culture emerged organized around unstable families and arranged "marriages." They were concentrated in the rural south where they settled into a caste status. After Emancipation there were four places to go. They could leave America and some did. Most emigrated to Liberia and Haiti. They could go west and a few did but there was strong opposition. They could go to the urban south and many did. Finally they could go north and a large number went to the big cities. The great migrations started in 1915 and continued in waves. First the movement was to the urban south and then to the big cities in the north. In World War II the movement turned westward. The impulse to move was jobs – economics was a driving force. In more recent times, there has been some minor movement back to rural areas and to the south.

There are instances where the mere presence of immigrants serve as a perverse invitation to homicide usually incited by the prejudice of the majority group. The legacy is arguably universal – a distorted notion that one's group superiority is threatened. In this case the victim is Afro-American and the felon is white. The crime is homicide; the method is lynching. Between 1900 and 1960 there were 1992 lynchings. In the 1890's they averaged 154 lynchings a year. In 1913 it dropped to 13 a year, in the

1940's to 4 a year. Many attempts failed. Between 1937 and 1946, 200 attempts were prevented. The events usually occurred in rural areas and were perpetrated by young, unemployed whites, many with police records. It rarely occurs now; however, perhaps the traditional use of lynching has been replaced with more subtle forms of violence.

Race riots involving the Afro-American (and other groups as well) occassionally serve as the condition for a homicide. It can involve the death of either the Afro-American or the white majority. This is not a new phenomenon, it has occurred in the past, the present, and will be repeated in the future. Just one example is the Detroit riots of 1943 where 34 people died and 433 required treatment. The Watts riot is a more contemporary example.

The Mexican-American Immigrant

One group that became part of this country through the process of annexation was the American of Mexican descent. This was followed by immigration both legal and illegal. The circumstances that might permit a cultural contribution to crime is the gang. Though their gang life is not dedicated to homicide, violence and occasional lethal outcomes occur. Gangs are part of the American scene, still concentrated in the urban areas but showing signs of entering the suburbs and rural areas as well. Gangs were not introduced into America by the Mexican culture. But the significance of certain cultural traits like *machismo* did infiltrate the American cultural scene and interacted with the existing characteristic of masculinity. Some of these factors may have affected deviance in general and homicide in particular. Culture as well as personality and structure can determine a relationship to deviance – involving either the predator or the prey. This would include the nature of the act and its various aspects.

In Mexican culture the first break with the family is to the gang (CF Rudoff 1971). The focus is gang-mindedness rather than group mindedness. There is little experience in the give and take of group life as every man is a world in himself. Life is better with the lead and follow of the gang. It offers a *confidante* one with an uncritical attitude and a defender and protector. Otherwise the gang is impersonal. One can achieve status and gather experience. At the same time one can abrogate decision and judgement making responsibilities – a group life with minimum obligations and a sanctuary for avoidance and withdrawal. It begins at adolescence and one is socialized as a *macho*. Machismo is measured by sexual prowess then by physical strength and courage. Status with peers involves being as *macho* as possible. These cultural themes are showing signs of change as the group is more and more entering the cultural mainstream.

The Chinese-American Immigrant

Due to restrictions, the Asian population increased slowly until more contemporary times and the liberalization of the immigration policies. The 1990 census showed 1,645,472 Chinese, 1,406,770 Filipinos, 845,562 Japanese, 815,447 Asian Indian, and 614,547 Vietnamese. This last group is the most recent large immigration. They got in trouble here by using gill nets in fishing and eating squirrels in Golden Gate Park. Gangs and gangsters came here on the later waves of refuges. They feared the local police at home and maintained the same fear here. They also came with a mistrust of banks and hoard their money. What might be transferred is too early to tell but the new generation brought up in the American culture has followed the usual route of acculturation. The Chinese have been here for a long time and contributed considerably to the development of America. The early Chinese society that was established in the United States mirrored that of China in many ways – food, dress, queue, bound feet, Confucianism, ancestor worship, revered past, respect for elders, filial piety, male domination. Along with the similarities, there were differences. The population in United States contained mostly sojourners, overwhelmingly males, few families, and the development of institutions and practices around the needs of a bachelor society. Organizations were established around village or district. The "Company" flourished offering social and charitable services, protection, and mediation in disputes. There were rivals to the "Company" – clans and tongs. Clans were family associations based on lineage. Tongs were secret societies translated as "meeting hall." They were formed for mutual aid and protection disregarding social status, clan ties, or locality of origin. The early ones derived from the Triad – Heaven, Earth, Society. They were widespread in southwest China and were an anti-dynasty group instigating rebellions. Many were established in California. Several were involved in gambling, prostitution, and opium trafficking. All these activities prospered in the bachelor society. Some of these rival groups occasionally clashed. There was competition, private quarrels, fights and assassinations carried out by Hatchetmen or highbinders. There were also guilds patterned after those in China and organized around craftsmen and merchants.

Their collective experience was different from the European immigrants. They were singled out for discrimination through laws and in 1882 the first immigrant group targeted for exclusion and denial of citizenship (Vecoli 1995). They were recruited to extract metals and minerals, construct the railroad, reclaim swamplands, build irrigation systems, as migrant agricultural workers, for the fishing industry, and labor-intensive manufacturing. After World War II their plight eased and acceptance grew. The 1960s saw changes as Civil Rights restored many rights and opened up opportunities. The 1970s experienced new Chinese immigrants, well-educated, and those escaping political instability in East and Southeast Asia. They prevailed in the up-hill struggle. They started as sojourners, moved to Chinese in America, to Chinese-Americans, to Americans of Chinese descent. The contemporary crime history is different than the early one of opium and gambling. Today the crime rate is very low paralleling that of other middle class Americans. The advent of tongs and hatchetmen was distinct to that period. The method for homicide was idiosyncratic but the motive (economic rivalry) ubiquitous. The motive exists in all cultures today, the method never caught on. What they contributed to homicide is more likely to be latent than manifest.

Conclusion

America became multicultural as it was nourished with immigrants from most places on the planet. Each brought with them their distinctive way of life. These characteristics covered the gamut of social traits including nefarious behavior. Violence and its occasional lethal outcome was part of their baggage. How much of it coalesced with the American scene shaping the criminological spectrum? What was the legacy? So much of their contributions were good and this is quite transparent; but the bad remains cryptic. Our early pioneers brought the conservative branch of Protestantism with a fundamental religious focus. Virtue was emphasized; morality and control was dominant. Yet, we produced the Salem witch trials, supported by belief in demoniac possession, with hangings that can be described as homicides. Those that followed made their contributions dominated by rectitude with a modicum of baseness. There are several significant immigrant groups that have interchanged culture with America.

Those mentioned above are some examples of those likely to have left a legacy including violence and homicide. The legacy could include all or parts of the process of homicide but also could include all or some aspects of amity and forbearance. The Chinese example might be closer to forbearance than violent death.

CHAPTER TEN

FACT AND FICTION COMPARISONS

Summary Of Results

A series of analyses was completed, examining the data from the UCR 1980 and UCR 1994 and the mystery genre of fiction divided into the 1912-1985 and 1986-1995 periods. Each category of fact and fiction was assayed and then fact and fiction were compared where similar data were available. The following summarizes the results.

A. Fiction

1. There were 115 books in the fiction sample; the male authors comprised 62 percent and the female authors the rest.
2. The 1912-1985 period comprised 46 percent of the books and 1986-1995 contained the rest.
3. There were 529 victims, 4.6 per volume.
4. Male authors depicted 69 percent of the victims while the female authors portrayed 31 percent.
5. Sixty-five percent of the victims were males, 35 percent females.
6. Male authors killed 54 percent of the male victims and 16 percent of the female victims; female authors killed 11 percent of the male victims and 19 percent of the female victims.
7. The early period killed 36 percent of the victims; the later period did away with 54 percent.
8. The victims' gender for each of the two periods showed no significant differences.
9. Female authors had a significantly higher percent of female victims and a lower percent of male victims than the male authors.
10. The distribution of the class of the victims was 16 percent upper, 37 percent middle, 18 percent working, 29 percent lower; the middle and upper class victims significantly dominated the stories.
11. Female authors chose upper and middle class victims significantly more often than the male authors; the male authors chose lower and working class victims significantly more often than the female authors.

12. The two periods also showed significant differences with the later period focusing more on the lower and working class victims then the earlier period.

13. The victims were exposed to sordid experiences by the offenders two-thirds of the time.

14. The female authors inflicted somewhat less nastiness on the victims than the male authors.

15. The later period displayed harsher treatment of the victims than the earlier period.

16. Firearms were the most frequently used weapons.

17. The choice of weapons was similar for gender and period.

18. There was an overwhelming presence of some kind of relationship between the offender and the target.

19. The female authors were less likely to use a stranger as a killer than the male authors.

20. There was a high percentage of culpability on the part of the victims for their own demise.

21. A plurality of the homicides occurred in the residences of the victims.

22. A similar amount of homicide occurred on the job and in the street.

23. The female authors created significantly more homicides in the home and less on the job and in the street than the male authors.

24. Homicide in the older novels was centered in the home and the later ones branched out to job and street.

25. Almost half of the offenders came from a culture of violence, almost as many came from a culture of manners, and the least from a culture of madness.

26. The male authors pictured the offenders from a violent culture significantly more often than did the female authors.

27. The periods showed no significant differences in cultural backgrounds.

28. The distribution of motives, in descending order was; profit, "other," passion, cover-up, and revenge.

29. There was no differences in the distribution of motives for gender or period.

30. A bare majority of the offenders were in the lower classes, but almost half of them were in the upper and middle classes.

31. The female authors selected significantly more middle and upper class killers and less lower and working class ones than the male authors.

32. The class distributions were insignificant for the two periods.

33. About two-thirds of the fictional offenders had no criminal background.

34. The female authors had significantly fewer offenders with criminal backgrounds than the male authors.

35. The periods indicated a significant increase in offenders with a criminal background for the later period.

36. For the final resolution of the homicide, most of the offenders were killed, about one-third were arrested, and the rest either committed suicide or escaped.

37. The above distribution of outcomes had no significant distinctions for gender or period.

38. Seventy-seven percent of the offenders were males, 23 percent females.

39. There was a significant increase in male killers in the later period and a decline in female killers.

40. Only 34 percent of the homicides were solved by the police, 5 percent by a private investigator, and 61 percent by everyone else.

41. The apportionment of the crime solvers was similar for gender and period.

B. Fact

1. In 1980 there were 23,044 homicides, 10.2 per 100,000; in 1994 there were 23,305 homicides, 9.0 per 100,000.

2. In 1980, 77 percent of victims were males, 53 percent white, 42 percent black, 4 percent "others;" in 1994, 79 percent of victims were males, 47 percent white, 51 percent black, 2 percent "others."

3. In 1980, 77.3 percent of the offenders were male, 51 percent white, 48 percent black, 1 percent "others;" in 1994, 78.4 percent were male, 46.2 percent white, 50.8 percent black, 2.3 percent "others."

4. In 1980, firearms were used 62 percent of the time, 19 percent were cutting instruments, 13 percent other dangerous weapons (poison, blunt object, explosives), 6 percent personal weapons (hands, fists, feet).

5. The 1994 distribution of weapons was 70 percent firearms, 13 percent cutting, 12 percent other dangerous or unknown weapons, 5 percent personal.

6. The 1980 victim-offender relationships were, 51 percent relatives, friends, acquaintances, 13.3 percent strangers, the rest unknown.

7. The 1994 relationships were 45.7 percent relatives, friends, acquaiuntances, 13 percent strangers, the rest unknown.

8. The victim is likely to know his/her killer.

9. In 1980, arguments accounted for 45 percent of all homicides, 25 percent were the result of a felony or suspected felony, the rest were unknown or "others."

10. In 1994, arguments accounted for 28 percent of homicides, 19 percent were the result of a felony or suspected felony, 5 percent were gang killings, the rest were unknown or "others."

11. In 1980, 72 percent of homicides were cleared by arrest; in 1994, 64 percent were cleared by arrest.

C. Fact vs Fiction

12. In all comparisons, fiction slew more females than occurred in real homicides.

13. Although firearms were the dominant weapons in both fiction and fact, fiction was significantly more diverse in choice of weapons.

14. Fiction used significantly more strangers as killers than occurred in fact.

15. Though more males were offenders than females, and this difference increased over the periods studied, fiction still used more female offenders than fact.

16. In fact, the usual motives for homicide were arguments and during the commission of a felony; while in fiction, the usual motives were profit, passion, cover-up and revenge.

17. In fact, the homicides were usually solved by the police; while in fiction, the protagonist not the police resolved the case.

18. In fact, a large majority of the cases were cleared by arrest; while in fiction, only one-third were cleared by arrest and the others by killing the offender, suicide, or escape.

The Process

The comparisons involved several variables. In the category of fact, two periods were selected purposely to share periods from which the fiction was selected. The fiction was divided into two periods and the genders of the authors. This permitted some analysis of differences in the fictions based upon gender and period. Comparisons were made within fact and fiction as well as between fact and fiction. There were instances where such comparisons were difficult due to changes in data collection in fact and fiction's detachment from fact. At times suggestions and educated guesses were the best comparisons under the circumstances. Even so, they proved of some value and application. When more sophisticated statistical efforts were possible the Chi Square test was applied.

The facts on homicide covered the two years of 1980 and 1994 as reported by the Uniform Crime Reports (UCR 1981; UCR 1995). The choice of dates is to compare periods. The addition of later periods should not effect the outcome of the study. An emergence of differences between fact and fiction is likely to take at least a decade. The fiction on homicide included 115 fictions from the mystery genre that had received accolades through prizes for authors or books and/or as best sellers. It included books published between 1912 and 1995. This established the universe from which all the books that were available from the libraries of Santa Clara and Monterey Counties were found, read and included in the sample. They were then divided into groups by gender and period – male and female authors and 1912-1985 and 1986-1995. There were 78 male authors and 37 female authors. There were 53 books from the 1912-1985 era and 62 books from the 1986-1995 era.

Fact: 1980 And 1994

When compared, these data need to be interpreted with caution and recognition that they represent two separate years and data of this nature can vary considerably over long periods of time. In 1980 there were 23,044 homicides, 10.2 per 100,000. In 1994 there were 23,305 homicides, 9.0 per 100,000. Although there was an increase in numbers of about 1.15 percent, there was a decrease in rate per population of about 1 percent. The 1980 report noted that 77 percent of the victims were males, 23 percent females; 53 percent were white, 42 percent black, with 4 percent "others." The same variables for 1994 were 79 percent male victims and 21 percent female victims; 47 percent were white, 51 percent black, and 2 percent "others." The gender distribution was similar but there was clearly an increase of black victims and a decrease of white ones. In 1980, 77.3 percent of the offenders were males and 22.7 percent were females; 51 percent were white, 48 percent were black, 1 percent "others;" 35 percent were between the ages of 18-24, 45 percent were under the age 25, and 9 percent were 17 or younger. In 1994 91 percent of the offenders were male, 9 percent were female; 56 percent were black, 42 percent were white with 2 percent "others;" 84 percent were 18 or older, 69 percent were 17-34. There was an increase in male offenders, but of particular interest was the decrease in female offenders. There were fewer whites and more blacks in 1994 than in 1980 which could be interpreted as an increase in homicides by blacks and a decrease in homicides by whites – or some kind of adjustment in the Administration of Justice system. In 1980 the FBI reported 12,310 arrests for murder and nonnegligent manslaughter; the number in 1994 was 16,156 for similar offenses. This represents an increase of about 31 percent. Crimes are often cyclical and this difference could be a result of the two years compared. It would not be difficult to select years to show a decrease in homicide.

Continuing the period comparisons, the weapons used in the homicides were examined. In 1980, firearms were used in 62 percent of the cases, 19 percent involved cutting or stabbing instruments, 13 percent included other dangerous weapons such as blunt instruments, poison, and explosives, while 6 percent were attributed to personal weapons such as hands, fists, and feet. The 1994 distribution was 70 percent firearms, 13 percent cutting and stabbing instruments, 12 percent other dangerous or unknown weapons, and 5 percent personal weapons. This period presented an increase in the use of firearms at the expense of the other types of lethal weapons. One might hypothesize that this period reflected the increase in the availability of firearms many of which were automatic, and their expanded use by juvenile gangs.

The relationship between the victim and the offender is of considerable interest in understanding crime in general. In 1980, 51 percent of the homicide offenders were relatives, friends, or acquaintances of the victims, 13.3 percent were strangers, and the rest were "unknown." In the 1994 reports, 45.7 percent were relatives, friends, or aquaintances, 13 percent were strangers, and the rest were "unknown." The differences are small, however, the tendency for the victim to know his/her killer is a consistent feature of homicide. Perhaps the axiom here is to escape victimization, it is better to lock oneself out of the house rather than in the house. The enemy is known and is not a marauding stranger.

Under the rubric of circumstances, the Uniform Crime Report assesses situations for homicides. They are grouped under arguments, felonious activity, suspected felonies, "others," and unknown. In 1980, arguments accounted for 45 percent of all homicides, 18 percent were a result of a felony, 7 percent a suspected felony, and the rest were unknown (15 percent) and "others" 16 percent. In 1994, 28 percent involved arguments, 19 percent felonious activity or suspicions of same, and 5 percent were gang killings. The rest were unknown or "other." Some of the "other" circumstances were romantic triangles, narcotic or alcoholic brawls, and gangland killings. Arguments are loosely defined and may account for the differences in that category. The felony involvements were similar. The difference of some significance is the inclusion of juvenile gang killings, a factor of growing concern.

When a felon is arrested the case is considered cleared by the police. When thrust into the rest of the justice system many things can happen ranging from release because of innocence, lack of evidence, or not guilty in a trial, or conviction, prison, or probation. For the major crimes homicide has the highest rate of clearance. In 1980 72 percent of the homicides were cleared by arrest; in 1994 it was 64 percent cleared by arrest. In general, most of the homicides are tended to and solved by the police – without Sherlock Holmes or Nero Wolfe or other fictional amateur or professional adventurous, intrepid, cavalier protagonists.

Fiction: Gender And Period

A series of variables was studied for all 115 novels and then for those written by male authors in an early and later period and then duplicated for a similar split for the female authors. Males constituted 68 percent of the authors and females 32 percent. The early period (1912-1985) contained 46 percent of the books and the latter period (1986-1995) 54 percent. The gender distribution depended on the availability of the books. The same was true of the distribution over time.

There were 529 victims in the books, 4.6 per volume. Male authors depicted a total of 366 victims or 69 percent while the female authors portrayed 31 percent (163 victims). There were 345 male victims (65 percent) 184 female victims (35 percent). Assessing author gender and victim gender, male authors killed 54 percent of the male victims and 16 percent of the female victims. The female authors slew 11 percent of the male victims and 19 percent of the female ones. It would seem that the tales were rather bloody with the male authors creating multiple victims and the female authors content with fewer bodies per tale. However, of some interest is that the female authors delineated a higher proportion of female victims while the male authors killed a greater proportion of their own gender. The male authors treated the female victims with greater delicacy than the female authors did. Some of that may have been cultural and/or political correctness.

The 529 victims were not distributed equally over time. The early period killed 36 percent of the victims (190) while the later period piled up 64 percent of the bodies (339). One can only guess at the explanation for this difference. It might be that the reading public of that genre had become inured to body counts and required more victims for interest and sales. The genre also changed from a more subtle and genteel tale paralleling the changes in society at large. Dialogue became more open, street language more prevalent, and the search for alleged "realism" more pronounced.

Fiction: The Victim

Data were collected on several facets of the victim to wit: class, offense severity, weapon, relation to offender, culpability, place offense occurred, background of violence, and motive. Each variable was examined first for all the books, then for author gender and the period of publication.

Class. – When possible, using the usual identifying factors with the focus on occupation, four classes were identified: upper, middle, working, lower. There were 456 class designations made. Sixteen percent were in the upper class, 37 percent in the middle class, 18 percent in the working class, and 29 percent in the lower class. Middle and upper class victims were in the majority, truly fictional for homicide victims.

The difference in the class of victims is meaningful for the gender of the authors. The female authors chose upper class victims 30 percent of the time while the males chose them 12 percent of the time; the female authors chose middle class victims 40 percent of the time, while the males chose them 35 percent of the time. The female chose the working class 18 percent of time and the male also chose them 18 percent of the time; at the lower class level, the female selected victims 12 percent of the time and the male selected them 35 percent of the time. The female authors had high regard for their victims choosing upper and middle class ones 70 percent of the time opposed to 47 percent of the time for the male authors. The male authors selected the two lower classes 53 percent of the time while the female authors selected them only 30 percent of the time. Again the female authors seem to be more inclined to deal with mannerly characters possibly because they are from the same classes and write about people with whom they are more familiar. The male authors also tend in that direction for the same reason, but at a lower rate. Of course, factual homicide tends to occur more often in the working and lower classes; however, the more sensational media coverage follows the rich and the famous.

The two periods from which the books were selected were also assessed for class distribution differences among the victims. The results were: in the 1912-1985 period, upper class occurred 24 percent of the time, middle class 45 percent, working class 13 percent, and lower class 18 percent. For the period 1986-1995 the results were upper class 12 percent, middle class 31 percent, working class 21 percent, and lower class 36 percent. It is clear that the earlier period victims were focused in the middle and upper classes and the later period the victims shifted to the working and lower classes. This lends credence to the notion that the later period began to try a more relalistic approach, but without being realistic. The realism picked certain areas but did not complete the picutre.

Offense severity. – Four degrees of the severity of the crime were established from very, to moderate, to little, to none. They were defined in terms of the weapons used, the presence of torture or mutilation, or (perhaps callously) a clean kill – one shot and instant death. The most severe circumstances occurred 38 percent of the time, moderate 29 percent, little 26 percent, and none 9 percent. Combining severe and moderate indicates some very nasty experiences for two-thirds of the victims.

Gender and period were determined for severity differences. The male writers inflicted severe circumstances on 40% of the victims, moderate on 28%, little on 27%, and none on 5%. The female authors inflicted severe circumstances on 33% of the victims, moderate on 33%, little on 22% and none on 12%. The female authors were somewhat more lenient in their lethal outcomes than the male authors.

In the earlier period of publication (1912-1985), the severity of the attacks upon the victims were less than in the later period. The assessment indicated that the severe circumstances went from 34 percent to 41 percent, moderate from 27 percent to 31 percent, little from 32 percent to 21 percent, and none remained the same at 7 percent. The same trend for less genteel treatment of the victims took place. This change occurred for both the male and female authors. But the female authors balanced the increase in severity with an increase in the circumstances where there were no severe inflictions on the victims.

Weapons. – The Uniform Crime Reports classify weapons as: firearms, knives or cutting instruments, personal weapons (eg. Hands, fists, feet), and unknown or other dangerous weapons (eg. Blunt instruments, poison, fire, explosives, and others). As close as possible, data on the weapons used in fiction were developed so as to mimic that which is used in fact. The lethal instruments were divided into: firearms, cutting instruments, blunt objects, personal weapons, and "others." The distribution of weapons for the entire sample was 36 percent firearms, 22 percent cutting instruments, 12 percent blunt objects, 15 percent personal weapons, and 15 percent "others." As anticipated, firearms were used most often. The "other" category was interesting in terms of the creative way the author was able to do away with the victim. Things like x-ray machines, steel rods, a crushing crowd, and others were probably intended to create interest and/or shock for the reader.

There was much similarity in choice of weapons for gender and period. The minor exceptions were the use of a few more guns and cutting equipment by the female authors and more blunt objects by the males. The later period indicated a few more guns while the earlier period showed a few more personal weapons.

Relationship. – The UCR and criminological literature makes many references to the impression that the victim of a homicide has some kind of affiliation with the killer. It is so in fact and is so noted in fiction as well. The fictional relationships were divided into friend and lover, relative, acquaintance, and stranger. The results showed that 16 percent were friends, 16 percent lovers, 41 percent acquaintances, and 27 percent strangers. There was the overwhelming presence of some kind of relationship between the victim and murderer. The attacking stranger was least apt to do the killing.

Comparing the distribution of relationships of the male and female authors showed some differences consistent with a kinship focus of the female author. They might find it more difficult to handle situations with an aggresive stranger. There were no significant changes in the distribution of the relationship from the earlier to the later period.

Culpability. – An effort was made to assess the amount of culpability the victim had in his own demise. Culpability was divided into some and none. Although there were no statistical differences, the results indicated that in a slight majority of the cases there was no culpability; however, the percentage of culpability was high (41 percent). This kind of difference was similar for gender and period comparisons. It could be reflective of the relationships that dominated the killer-victim contacts. Intimacy may reap passion; passion invites violence.

Crime setting. – Information was gathered from the fictions on the place where the crime was committed. Four categories were established: home, job, street, and "other." The latter category included transportation (eg car, boat), water, park. The plurality of homicides occurred at the victim's home (39 percent), followed by the "other" category (34 percent), then the job and street were about the same (14 percent & 13 percent). In the case of real homicides, this information is not collected for the UCR. However, it is possible that in reality many of the homicides do occur in the home, especially since so many of the participants are related in some way. There has probably been an increase in real homicides at the job sight and the streets fostered by disgruntled employees and students and juvenile gangs.

The gender comparison produced some significant differences. The female authors created more homicides in the home and less in the street and on the job than the male authors. Here again there is the tendency for the female author to feel more comfortable dealing with the home setting than the street or job one. Although the male authors also prefer the home, they do give significant coverage to the street and job. Both genders do exercise their creative talents by placing the event in the "other" category (about one-third for both).

As for the periods, there was a significant shift from the early period to the later one. The older novels centered on the home followed by the "other," then the street and job. The later novels were less centered on the home and the "other" than the former ones and more focused on the job and street.

This change probably followed that which occurred in reality reflecting changing times, especially with the tougher approach.

Background circumstances. – When possible, the background circumstances of the offender, including the milieu in which he/her operated, was examined. Three categories were established: violence, manners, and madness. Violence involved people entangled in crime, drugs, and in general, a street interactionist. Manners were people who were in a nonviolent environment and were brought up in middle or upper class circumstances. The madness category covered those who were described in psychiatric terms such as multiple personalities, paranoid, and psychopath. The offenders described in the fictions were placed in a violent cultural context 46 percent of the time, in manners 43 percent, and madness 11 percent of the time. Since these classifications are not readily available in fact, one can only guess that these may approximate the reality.

There was a significant difference in the distribution of these backgrounds between the works of the male and female authors. As one might anticipate from the previous findings, the male authors pictured the killers from a violent environment (58 percent) while the female authors pictured them from an environment of manners 71 percent of the time. The males had manners 30% of the time and females had violence only 18 percent of the time. The madness category was very similar. As for the different periods, the changes were insignificant with similar distributions.

Motive. – Motive is a crucial aspect of homicide. Of course, the motive belongs to the killer, but the victim is the consequence. Five examples of motive were identified: revenge, passion, profit, cover-up and "other." Passion referred to murder committed due to a strong emotion such as anger and jealousy: profit involved killings for money or other financial rewards; cover-up was the silencing of someone to cover the killers crimes; revenge concerned the infliction of punishment to avenge a real or perceived act against the killer. The "other" category dealt with more exotic reasons for the homicide such as a professional hit, to protect someone, and "a taste for blood." The fictional distribution was revenge 15 percent, passion 19 percent profit 26 percent, cover-up 17 percent, and "other" 23 percent. The only surprise here is the number of cover-up killings. It seems that in fiction, if someone knows what you are doing, you kill him.

Comparing the author's gender relative to the distribution of motives resulted in insignificant differences. The same was true in the selection of motive type between the earlier and later periods. Apparently motives for homicide are far from infinite and are fairly stable over several millenniums.

Fiction: The Offender

Class. – The offender class distinctions were similar to the victim class distinctions: upper, middle, working, and lower. The total allotment was 16 percent upper class, 31 percent middle class, 14 percent working class, and 39 percent lower class. Combining the upper and middle class showed 47 percent of the offenders. Middle and upper class homicide offenders in fiction are almost half the killers – a fiction unlikely to be true in fact. Again the fiction writers select an orderly ambience to weave their tales – a milieu decorated with elites.

The male author's choice of class was significantly different than the choice of the female. The latter selected more upper and lower class killers and less working and lower class killers. This is consistent with the previous indications of a more refined touch by the female writers. The period differences were nonsignificant. The same kind of class distributions *in toto* and between genders remained from the early period of the genre to the later period.

Record. – Whenever possible, information was collected on the criminal background of the offender. This was simply categorized as Yes or No. Specific information was rarely dealt with in the fictions. The outcome was 31 percent Yes and 69 percent No. This is a result consistent with the class structure of the villains. The scenarios dealt largely with people who were unlikely to have a criminal background. Even though dealing with homicides, it is likely that in fact there would be more offenders with a criminal background than in fiction, even though the crimes might not be homicides.

The female writers had significantly less offenders with a criminal background than the male writers. This was in accord with the greater female general avoidance of violence and savagery. The difference in the periods were also consistent with the later period's shift toward more down-to-earth plots. These differences were statistically significant with an increase in the Yes response and decrease in the No response.

Final resolution. – It is probable that the homicide clearance rate is among the highest of the major crimes. One of the primary reasons is the greater number of resources applied to the cases. Therefore a good number are arrested. The fictional outcomes are somewhat different. The resolution of the cases were divided into: killed, arrested, suicide, and escape. The results were: 43 percent killed, 35 percent arrested, 7 percent suicide, and 15 percent escape. Fiction's bottom line is sales, fact's is closure. Therefore, fiction needs stimulation, elan, vigor, interest, excitement, and intrigue. Fact offers prosaic, boring, somber, colorless, and uninteresting processes. Consequently, fiction vigorously pursues alternates to the simple arrest with chases, fights, and bizarre outcomes. This imperative apparently is universal among the authors and has no distinction between periods as the statistical differences in author gender and period is nonsignificant.

Gender. – The literature was surveyed for a gender identity of the offender. All the killers were simply assessed for their gender. The findings presented 77 percent males and 23 percent females as perpetrators of the homicides. Comparing the authors, they presented about the same proportion of male and female murderers. The period comparison was significantly different. The later period showed an increase of male killers and a decline in the female killers.

Protagonist. – In the processing of real homicides, the most active agency is the police. This is not so in fiction. Anybody can and does solve the crime. Three categories were established: police, private investigator, and lay person. In the assessment of the fictions, only 34 percent were solved by the police, then 5 percent were solved by a private detective and the bulk, 61 percent were solved by the authors choice of a protagonist – thief, Indian Chief, psychiatrist, housewife, drug dealer, in short, the butcher, baker and candlestick maker. The allotment of the choices were very similar between the author genders and periods – there were no statistical differences. There are occasional novels involving what is referred to as the processing stories. This includes the plodding footwork that goes into the solution of homicides by the police. The tendency is to search for more excitement and elan with some person outside of the police occupation.

Age. – With the rising involvement of juveniles in the commission of homicides, one might expect a good number of fictional juvenile offenders. The writers seem to possess more familiarity and understanding of the adult. The fictions in the survey selected adult slayers 96 percent of the time. In fact, 11 percent were under 18 and 27 percent were under 22 in 1980; 9 percent were under 18 and 45 percent were under 25 in 1994. Again, the lack of differences continued between the genders and periods of the authors.

Fact vs. Fiction

When the data for fact and fiction were available comparisons were made using the chi square statistic. There were a number of such tests possible. It was difficult to make such comparisons because of the different definitions of circumstances. Nevertheless, on the face of it, there were differences as well as statistically significant ones.

Gender of victim. – Assessments were made comparing the distribution of the victims' gender between facts as displayed in the 1994 UCR and all of the fictions; the 1980 UCR and all of the fictions; 1980 UCR and the fictions covering the period 1912-1985; 1994 UCR and the fictions covering the period 1986-1995. Each evaluation was statistically significant. They all indicated that fiction slew more females than actually occurred in the real world. Apparently drama is better served with a melange of plots that evince more corpses appealing to a wider audience than the humdrum killings in the streets.

Weapons. – In this category comparisons were made between the UCR's of 1980, 1994 and the fiction periods of 1912-1985, 1986-1995. The weapons compared were firearm, cutting, blunt, personal, and "other." Statistically significant differences occurred. In the factual use of weapons, there was an increase in the use of the firearm between 1980 and 1994, from 62 percent to 70 percent. In the fiction use of weapons there was no difference between the early and later period (for firearms it was 33 percent for the early period and 38 percent for the later period); however, there was a decided difference in the use of weapons between the real and the fictional events. The fictional weapon use was much more diverse than the factual use. Although firearms still dominated, the other weapons were not too far behind.

Contrasting the 1980 fact period with the 1912-1985 fiction period affirmed that the former used firearms twice as much as the latter. The fiction period used more blunt, personal, and "other" weapons than the fact period. This may have been due to the literary need to inveigle the reader by shifting from the more pedestrian use of guns to more interesting situations with more bizarre weaponry. Similar results happened when the 1994 fact period was compared with the 1986-1995 fiction period – much less use of firearms in the fiction period and a greater dispersal of weaponry.

Connecting the UCR fact data on weapons and the fiction author gender saw similar patterns of weapon use as above. As far as gender is concerned there was little difference in the weapon use by gender for the fiction authors, but less use of firearms and more of other weapons by both genders.

Relationship. – The three categories of related, acquaintance, and stranger were appraised within the two fact and two fiction periods. The results were statistically significant. The UCR data indicated fewer strangers and more acquaintances for the 1994 UCR than the 1980 UCR. The fiction period indicated more related and fewer acquaintances for the 1986-1995 period than the 1912-1985 period. The fiction period of 1912-1985 showed less related and more acquaintances than the UCR 1980 period. The later two periods of fact and fiction drew closer together, but the significant differences remained. The fiction period showed less acquaintances and more strangers than the fact period. The idea that many victims of homicide are known to the killer is well known in criminology and in fiction. Yet the increased use of strangers in fiction may be a response to the incorrect notion that many killers are sinister interlopers.

Offender gender. – The two fact periods and fiction periods were examined relative to the gender of the offender. The differences were significant. The 1980 UCR asserted that 84 percent of the offenders were male but increased that to 91 percent in the 1994 UCR. The female offenders constituted 16 and 9 percent respectively. In fiction, the 1912-1985 period claimed 70 percent were male offenders and this grew to 80 percent in the 1986-1995 period. The female offenders in fiction were 30 and 18 percent respectively. There was a change in both fact and fiction periods to more male offenders and fewer female ones. However, in fiction there were considerably more female offenders in both periods than in fact. Again fiction endeavored to increase the range of drama by using more female offenders as well as victims than occurs in fact.

Fiction with violence and homicide is a genre that captures a large audience of readers. For the vast majority of readers it is accepted as entertainment and not a blueprint for mayhem and murder. It is more creative and imaginative and perhaps even bizarre than fact. There may be some interchange where something is borrowed by fact from fiction, but not the need to kill. In its turn, fiction borrows from fact but, unless it is biographical, it is more likely to be distorted, modified, or even perverted in order to entertain and to sell – in reverse order.

CHAPTER ELEVEN

CONCLUSION AND COMMENTS

In the oft noted concern with the mass media role in violence, there is thought to be a connection. Violence in media breeds violence in fact. This book is not a direct test of that notion but the differences between media and reality can be assessed. This does not belie the possible occasional use of an isolated case where a real person copies a fictional one. The number of processes, motives, weapons, and other aspects of homicide are not infinite. Therefore it is very likely that an isolated case seems to mimic fiction. It is more liable to be a coincidence as fiction is more likely to mimic reality. Whatever we are and do, to some extent, comes from our own history, and this includes our violence and its consequences.

The history of homicide and its annals in America were explored. To examine the relationship between the fact and fiction of homicide, two years from the Uniform Crime Reports were assessed and compared with two periods of fiction in the mystery genre which included the two UCR periods. The selection of fiction was restricted to prized books from American authors. In an attempt to establish some historical influences on homicide in America, the legacies of myth, bible, and immigration were examined. Then the comparison of fact and fiction in homicide was effected.

A History of Homicide

Hunting and gathering dominated the lives of hominids for two million years. Hunting was shared as the results were shared. Gathering was done individually and its fruits probably were not shared. Any scarcity of food and mates increased the prospect for disputes. Early conflicts were between individuals, not groups – homicides, not wars. As weapons developed to kill game, they were quickly applied to kill each other. Why man misbehaves remains poorly understood. However, it occurs. It happened in the past, it happens in the present. It occurs in animals, it occurs in men.

The first known murder trial was recorded in Sumer in ancient Mesopotamia in 1850 B.C. Three men were sentenced for slaying a temple servant. Even earlier there was evidence of brigands and pirates. Rome, for all its glory, became notable for the frequency of its assassinations, sex perversions, murders, and massacres. Whether or not they deserved it, the Vikings are known to us principally for their pillage, plunder, rape, and hit and run raids. Genghis Khan over ran much of Asia and parts of Europe, killing hundreds of thousands in his conquests. The renaissance taught that man, not God, was the measure of all things. It also taught those concerned how to murder and dispose of one's opponents. In the twentieth century some 38 million deaths occurred from genocide.

By 1765, one hundred and sixty offenses were punishable by death in England on the supposition that the gallows was the only serious deterrent to crime and the only way for the elite to protect themselves from the "mob". However, the list of capital offenses was soon shortened when it was decided that hanging had no deterrent effect and that there were alternatives – some being fines, whippings, imprisonment, and transportation. Yet in 18th century London, casual violence was widespread and life was cheap. Pickpocketing, drunkenness house storming, assaults, smuggling, debased coinage, high treason, murder, and all other behaviors in the lexicon of crime continued unabated.

For centuries, crime control was largely a private effort. Gradually this shifted as official government police agancies were established between the 17th century on the continent and the 19th century in England. America in the 18th century was relatively law abiding. The so-called Puritan ethic was dominant and was perhaps an effective preventive or deterrent to crime along with lack of opportunity. One conspicuous exception was Samuel Green, America's first mass murderer.

As with England, America feared the potential for oppression from a centralized police force. Americans then as, to a large extent, even now, preferred to believe that crime was a local matter for local authority to solve. The office of sheriff was imported from England but in most jurisdictions he was an elected official whose term was limited to one or two years. He could not succeed himself and his powers stopped at the county line. A number of local constables and U.S. Marshals achieved enough fame to color the legends of the Old West but so did a number of renegades and outlaws.

For the most part, patterns of crime and justice surfaced in Western societies following industrialization, urbanization, the expansion of state resources, and the actual diminishing of the kind and degree of violence that marked medieval times. Whether these components of modernization have made for more or less crime is a moot question. Hand guns are associated with more crime and are more readily available now than in the recent past. However, homicides are now more visible and are more frequently reported and recorded, whereas they were under reported in the 19th century and recorded, if at all, by variable and unreliable systems. For these reasons it is risky to speculate how much crime modernization has brought.

A recital of deadly deeds from past to present reminds the reader how copiously men have spilled one another's blood and still do. There is Beane, a Scotsman, who murdered travellers in the 15th century and ate parts of some of them. Bluebeard was a 15th century French aristocrat who tortured and killed a hundred children. Dracula was a Romanian nobleman who impaled hundreds of victims on stakes, also in that bloody 15th century, before he was killled in battle with the Turks. Elizabeth Battory, the "Bloody Countess of the Middle Ages," burned her captives genitals and bathed in the blood of her servants. Jack the Ripper disemboweled five prostitutes in 19th century London and thereby frightened the whole nation for years long after the killings stopped. He was never positively identified, although there is some evidence that he was Frank Tumblety, an American quack doctor who hated women. He died in 1903. Loeb and Leopold tried to commit the perfect crime in the 1920's with the killing of a high school friend. They failed as they were apprehended, tried, convicted, and imprisoned. Loeb was killed by fellow-inmates in Joliet prison. Nathan Leopold was paroled in the 1960's and died in Puerto Rico. During his forty years in confinement he made significant contributions to the science of criminal statistics.

Gruesome homicides continue. Even the rates show repetition by occurring in cycles. But there is some solace in the fact that the vast majority of people do not kill.

The Genre

Mystery and detective tales have deep roots as far back as the Bible, and in all literate cultures. Poe created Auguste Dupin in *Murders in the Rue*

Morgue, which is believed to be the first of the genre and became the forerunner of a host of sleuths like Sherlock Holmes, Hercule Poirot, Philo Vance, and Nero Wolfe. In England Wilkie Collins introduced the first police detective, Naigo Marsh, a New Zealander, presented Inspector Roderick Alleyn in some thirty books, Ethel White inspired at least two famous movies, Edgar Wallace produced over 170 books, short stories, and scripts, including King Kong, in a twenty-seven year career.

Detective fiction became fashionable in France after World War I. Care was taken with the language and descriptions of the French people. Yet some imported a tough-guy writing style from American authors. The American detective fiction has been highly successful and inventive. One of the highly acclaimed writers was Ellery Queen, actually a pseudonym for two cousins. Dashiell Hammett and Raymond Chandler, with their mastery of street smarts and the slanguage that goes with it were exceptionally popular.

The style used in writing detective stories evidenced several changes. Early stories were simply a puzzle solved by patience and persistence. Later novels introduced ethnic differences. Mysteries became complex. The private eye appeared and commanded wide popularity with such heroes as the Saint, Mike Hammer, and James Bond. The gothic or romantic-suspense style started in the 18th century and still maintains its special appeal. The 1930's gave us the hard-boiled novels of Hammett, Chandler, and Ross MacDonald. This was the realistic school of crime fiction packed with violence, action, and earthy language. Genre style changed again after World War II in both England and America. The hard working humane police detective appeared, plodding through his routine methods solving crimes after many frustrations and much danger. This style might have reflected the rapid professionalization of the police at that time and the wide-spread disenchantment with corrupt politics. Laurence Treat, Sue Grafton, Ed McBain, J. J. Marric, Evan Hunter, and Joseph Wambaugh were among the prominent masters of this style.

Detective fiction is packed with notable characters who solve crimes. The most memorable is Sherlock Holmes. Other prominent ones include Hercule Poirot and Miss Marple, products of Agatha Christie, Van Dine's Philo Vance, Gardner's Perry Mason, Stout's Nero Wolfe, Spillane's Mike Hammer, and Chandler's Philip Marlowe. Some of the famous assistants include Dr. Watson for Holmes, Della Street for Mason, and Nora Charles for husband Nick.

Women mystery writers outnumber men three to one. The number could be higher but many have been unwilling to disclose their gender until recently. The list contains the first to write detective fiction, the American Anna Katherine Green. Others include Agatha Christie, Dorothy Sayers, Mary Roberts Rinehart, Naigo Marsh, and P. D. James. As previously noted, Christie introduced Poirot and one of the many female sleuths, Miss Marple. In England, the tradition of the woman operative dates from 1861 with Mrs. Paschal by W. S. Hayward. After World War I, female detective fiction in the United States moved from the genteel to the gutsy crime fighting stories of action, independence, and professional competence that differed from the private eye only in gender.

At present, it may be that the most important contemporary writers in this genre are Ross MacDonald, John D. MacDonald, and Dick Frances. Ross MacDonald introduced us to Lew Archer. John MacDonald created Travis McGee. Dick Francis of England is well known for his suspense novels within the horse racing milieu. Sharing current prominence are such writers as Brian Garfield, Robert Parker, Isaac Asimov, Peter Lovesey, Frederick Forsyth, and Tony Hillerman, all adding color to the genre of mystery, crime, and detective literature.

Myth

Culture includes myths of the past. Today many are weakened in influence by science and by reason in place of faith. Many others survive. They are told and re-told. Some are believed, some are questioned but not disbelieved because they suggest answers to persistent problems that science does not solve convincingly – where did we come from, where are we going, how will we know when we get there. Some influence us in ways that do not question because we are not consciously aware of how they shape us and because they can be identified only by scholars.

Webster defines the word myth to be "....a usually traditional story of ostensibly historical events that serves to unfold part of the world view of a people or explain a practice, belief, or natural phenomenon." Briefly, a myth is an embellished account of a thing, person, or event that probably never existed, but is accepted anyway in whole or in part. Myth differs from legend in that legend is based on something or some one that actually did exist but is thickly embellished as is the myth. The legend is probable; the myth is improbable. Both become parts of a people's belief system. Nature plays a significant role, especially in myths – an untamed nature requiring explanation and control. Even the stars, moon, sun, rainbow, waterfalls, particular rocks, trees, mountains, and rivers have an animate life. Myths are timeless either in their original or their modified form.

Greek myths are "....familiar to non-Greeks, so much so that Americans have been described as the intellectual descendants of the early Greeks, (Hamilton, 1940: 16)" "In Greece man first realized what mankind was, (Hamilton, 1940: 16)" and that realization included all aspects of man himself – the social and the anti-social, the peaceful and the aggressive, the forgiving and the punitive. For example, Theano, a mortal woman, was seduced by the god Poseidon by whom she had two sons, Aeolus and Boetus. She pretended that Metapontus, her earthly husband, was their father. Later she bore two other sons by Metapontus. He favored them over the first two. This enraged Theano. She plotted to have the second pair kill Aeolus and Boetus but this scheme went awry. Aeolus and Boetus killed their half-brothers. Overcome by grief and shame. Theano killed herself with a hunting knife, (Graves, 1972: 158-159).

Tereus, a powerful mortal king, married Procne. Their son was Itys. Later, Tereus fell in love with Philomela, Procne's sister. Tereus cut out Procne's tongue, locked her up, pretended she had died, and married Philomela. But the two sisters found each other. Procne killed her son Itys, boiled him, and served him to Tereus as part of a meal. When Tereus learned what he had eaten, he tried to kill the two sisters, but the gods intervened and changed all three into birds – Procne into a swallow, Philomela into a nightingale, and Tereus into a Hoopoe, (Graves, 1972: 165).

Ares, a god who loved killing in battle, was accused by his fellow-deities with murdering Halirrothius. He justified the murder on the grounds that Halirrothius had raped his daughter. The court acquitted him. This is the first judgment ever pronounced at a murder trial, the site being the Arieopagus, meaning the hill of Ariea, one of Athene's names, (Graves, 1972: 73-74).

Athene is the goddess of Athens. She possesses all peace time assets, although she is also the goddess of war. "....Her mercy is great; when the judges' votes are equal in a critical trial at the Arieopagus, she always gives the casting vote to liberate the accused." As with all their gods and myth-heroes, the Greeks developed several versions of Athene's origin:

19. She was born in the water of a lake. She accidentally killed her playmate Pallas and set his name before her own as penitence – Pallas Athene.

20. Pallas was her father. She killed him when he tried to rape her, flayed him, and made her aegis out of his skin.

21. Itonus was her father, and Iodama her sister. Athene killed Iodama for trespassing in a sacred precinct and turned her into a block of stone.

22. Poseidon was her father but she disowned him and successfully prevailed upon Zeus to adopt her.

23. Zeus made love to Metis and swallowed her. This gave him a raging headache. Either Hermes or Prometheus split Zeus's head open to relieve his agony and out sprang Athene fully armed and with a mighty shout, (Graves, 1972: 44).

There are dozens of Greek myths like these. They vary by time and by narrator. They include such epics as Homer's Iliad and The Odyssey, chronicling the Trojan War and acquainting us with myth-heroes like Agamemnon, Achilles, Hector, Odysseus, Telemachus, Penelope, Helen, Menaleus, Iphegenia, Casandra, and many fabled locales. Other myths tell us of Apollo, Pegasus, Hermes, Orpheus, Eurydice, Dionysus, Oedipus, Antigone, Aphrodite, Diana – all of whose deeds are sometimes heroic and beneficent, sometimes vengeful and murderous, sometimes limited to Olympian heights, sometimes visited upon mortal men.

This vast body of literature on Greek and Roman mythology provides a clear thread through the American tapestry. Less apparent but by no means obscure, are the myths of other cultures that are also part of the American ethos. There are the Norse gods who are by-words for our persistence in the face of defeat. They were constantly in danger and fated to be doomed. Their choice was to go down fighting heroically. The day would come when they would be destroyed and the fate of the gods would be the fate of mortals. Mortals knew they could not save themselves but they would die resisting and die bravely – and thus enter Valhalla.

The chief Norse god was Odin whose main concern was to postpone the day of reckoning when both heaven and earth would be destroyed. His attendants were the Valkyrie who carried those who died bravely to Odin.

Evil entered the circle of Norse gods through Loki who killed Odin's son Balder by having one of the lesser gods strike Balder with a branch of mistletoe. For this deed, Loki was executed by serpent venom, yet the gods go on, warring to the very end against the doom that descends upon their twilight.

While the pantheon of Egypt is not central to American culture, it survived as its principle deities took on new identities through Greek, Roman, Germanic and Scandinavian tales while preserving some of their original character but modified by time and diffusion.

Myths have become part of American culture. Their effect on character cannot be precisely demonstrated, but they do make suffering and illicit death and heroics part of normal life. Joseph Campbell has said that myths are the symbols that support the moral order. He cautions that science demolishes or modifies myths logically. This unsettles the society and leads to social disorganization. Many myths remain unassailed by these processes. Many more have been diminished. Where this has happened, their legacy is violence and death, particularly where they stress that one increases life through killing, (Campbell, 1973: 9, 31, 177, 181).

The Bible

The Bible has been pored over for two millenia. While it exercises great moral influence, it is also teeming with violence. Is this a legacy that encourages heinous behavior when so interpreted?

What is widely accepted as the first murder occurred when Cain killed Abel. But it is a hazy story with different versions of the Bible using different terms. One says Cain slew Abel, another that he killed Abel, and a third that he murdered Abel. Slaying is ambiguous. Killing could have been by accident or in self-defense. Murder requires intent and malice. No where does Cain admit to any of these. He is accused and condemned by circumstance, not evidence. God put a mark on Cain so no one would kill him. What was this mark? How did it work? We do not know. All we do know is that God withheld his wrath from Cain for whatever happened to Abel and allowed Cain to leave the area just as he allowed Adam and Eve to leave the Garden of Eden.

This suggests a God who tempers justice with mercy. It stands in marked contrast with later accounts where killing and murder are prominent in biblical history. One concordance lists 597 entries for killing and 81 for murder or murderers. Violent death is repeatedly featured in both the Old and New Testaments. The motives for homicide in fact or imagery in those ancient days ring a contemporary note and fall into several groups such as these:

Revenge – A man kills those who killed his brother, his father, his servants; pariahs; hated foreigners.

Breach of Mores – Sexual misconduct; misdirected hostilities; heretics; foul talk; blasphemies; groundless animosities.

Mercy Killing – Helping a man to die who was mortally wounded and in great pain.

Superior Orders – Obedience to God; evasion; threat of death.

War – Tribal war in response to a rape; thousands killed on both sides; many other wars for other causes, all with high casualties.

Jealousy – Lust for another's wife; sibling rivalries.

Limitations – Sanctuary following an accidental death; number of witnesses required; innocence of a victim of rape.

It is sobering to read what the Bible reports on violence *en masse*. Exodus 32 contains the account where the Levites killed 3,000 Israelites on orders from Moses for worshipping a golden calf. The Book of Judges tells us that 90,000 men were killed in wars between the Israelites and the Benjamites. In I and II Samuel and I Kings, the Israelites lost 34,000 men to the Philistines before David appeared, slew Goliath, and later killed 49,000 Philistines, Moabites, Rheobites, and Arameans. When his son Absalom rose against him, David triumphed after killing both Absalom and 20,000 of his troops.

How accurate are these body counts? How accurate are the sanctions for killing offenders who commit a host of lesser offenses than Cain's, such as theft, possession of too many wives or slaves, gambling, poor trade practices, and others like these? We do not know. In most instances, it appears likely that fact, myth, and legend have been woven together to instruct or frighten the faithful to insure conformity to the codes of a developing society. The number of dead at the foot of Mount Sinai, the 90,000 killed in the war between the Israelites and the Benjamites, the slaughters as massive as those credited to David added to so many more which the Bible chronicles elsewhere would have eliminated Palastine, Israel, and Judah from history. These reports of what happened and these threats of what might happen to the disobedient seem mythical and legendary. If they occurred as they were recorded, there would have been no surviving culture, for there would have been too few to witness these events and no one to write about them.

Yet some readers take it all quite literally. Where this is so, is the bible being interpreted as approving homicide? Is homicide an unrecognized legacy of the bible under these circumstances?

Immigration

When masses of people voluntarily migrate or are forcibly moved from one region to another, the cultures of both the migrant and the receiving populations are effected. Since it is universal, this includes homicide. However, as with all other culture traits and practices, diffusion is at work. It is not clear what specific values and practices in homicide are borrowed and what are imposed – guns for knives, gang slayings for single killings, generational feuds for flash murder, vendettas for law enforcement, the garotte for the cudgel, poison for strangling. What is clear is the process of cultural exchange.

The culture of the arriving immigrant may not have included a propensity toward violence. But, there could be traits that in a collision with America produce a response that includes violence. The person could come from a culture that respected social distance which clashes with American openness. This might lead to stress and loss of control. Perhaps one can come from a culture that rewards controlled aggression which is forsaken in America and responded to with disrespect leading to a violent reaction. Thus, the culture of lethal violence in a region of the Kentucky-Tennessee border is traceable to the way early British colonists handled disputes three centuries ago. The James boys of the American west are the cultural descendents of the legendary Robin Hood. The secret and criminal Triad Society of Hong Kong adopted new crime patterns as the Chinese moved to the United States. Australian settlers developed strong protective measures designed to control convicts transported there in the late 18th and 19th centuries. Some of them helped build the new dominion. Others contributed to its criminal subculture, including its homicides.

The last part of this century is duplicating the first half of this century in one respect and different in another respect. Immigration came back with a bang. However, the immigrants of the new wave are different and diverse. They differ in social class and national identity. America too is different in the many aspects of a complex society. The early experience was one of assimilation; the new experience might be quite distinct. The twenty-five million new people are more likely to become fragmented and their children will be challenged as a new group in an altered America (Portes 1996). These circumstances will develop a legacy for the future – a legacy that along with the best of outcomes will be more unfavorable ones. One such effect will be crime including homicide.

It is highly unlikely that a causal relationship can be made between the contributions to homicide from the country of origin to the host country. Some associations might be possible but the process is extremely complex. At one time it was widely believed in the United States that its high crime rates were chiefly due to immigration. Later, careful studies indicated that high rates varied from one immigrant group and from one immigrant generation to another.

Organized crime. – It is within organized crime that a measure of importation of the homicide process can be traced. Yet the expression "organized crime" is itself ambiguous, sometimes referring to casual street gangs or any crime involving more than one person. Strictly considered, the term may best be defined in America as groups of people, highly organized and exclusive, who deal in illicit goods and services involving large sums of money, who kill when deemed necessary, who act with a great deal of impunity, and remain relatively immune from apprehension and prosecution for substantial periods.

The Mafia in the United States fits these criteria. It controls its members through a code of conduct similar to that of the Sicilian Mafia which is not a formalized written document, but effectively demands loyalty, honor, silence, obedience, dependability, and courage. While other criminal groups with like values appeared in American cities in the immigrant waves of the 19th and 20th centuries, the Mafia rose to power and dominance over its rivals during the Prohibition era.

In its early days, the victims of the Mafia were other Italian immigrants from whom it extorted payments for a variety of so-called services. In time it expanded to control the production and distribution of liquor, at that time outlawed. Soon it had spread into prostitution, gambling, stevedoring, trucking, and many other activities, finally penetrating conventional businesses, maintaining its control by violence including homicide and gang warfare when opposed.

While the FBI places the Mafia at the apex of criminal organizations, it is followed by other groups which reflect the cultural pluralism of the United States. Thus, there are the Irish, Syrian, Mexican, Russian, Puerto Rican, and Afro-American mobs found in many of America's urban centers. Each group has brought its distinctive way of life to the country, many beneficent, some nefarious. All have contributed to a cultural whole which in turn has influenced each ethnic enclave by diffusion over time. Acculturation is a two-way process and this includes all aspects of life including violence and homicide and its several aspects.

It is clear that the legacy of myth, the bible, and immigration is overwhelmingly positive. This study simply focused on the possibility of a negative contribution in one area – violence and homicide.

Fact vs. Fiction

Viewing violence from an historical perspective, from prehistory to the present, it would seem to be prolific. One is struck by the banality of violence and its too often consequence of homicide. Yet mystery stories can become tales beyond carnage when compared to the reality of homicide. The eras effected the content. Wartime showed less prejudice and the technology (cars, bugs, weapons), were linked to the events. The earlier mysteries had fewer victims and the characters, including the killers, seemed more courteous and sensitive. The depth of evil has increased in the newer tales of homicide. There tends to be more bodies, more viciousness, less understandable motives, and characters with less integrity. Even the protagonist has shifted from the dignity, grace, and erudition of Holmes to the plebeian and violent Mickey Spillane – a veritable moral eunuch. Literature and fact use different processes in the solution of a homicide. The former often use civilians caught up in the chase while the latter use the police process. Many contemporary stories in the genre claim realism, but they are either outright fantasies or real emotions juxtaposed with a rainbow of fantasies.

Based on the Uniform Crime Reports, the facts indicated that the rates of homicides per 100,000 general population were 10.2 in 1980 and 9.0 in 1994. The volume of homicides ranged between 23,000 and 23,300. Further facts about homicide are shown by percent distribution for the two key years in Table XI.1.

When the 115 crime novels are reviewed (see chapter on the comparisons), some of the results are these:

24. There were 529 victims, 4.6 per volume.
25. Sixty-five percent of the victims were males.
26. Female authors killed a higher percentage of females than the males.
27. Firearms were the most often used weapons.
28. Almost half of the offenders were from the upper and middle classes.
29. Thirty-four percent of the homicides were solved by the police, five percent by a private detective, and the rest by everyone else.

In comparing fact with fiction, some of the results were:

1. Fiction killed more females than did fact.
2. Fiction used a more diverse selection of weapons than fact.
3. Fiction used more strangers as killers than did fact.
4. In fact, the more usual motive was arguments, while in fiction it was profit.

Homicide in fact does not seem to echo homicide in fiction. The fact is prosaic, the fiction creative. In either case, homicide is an ancient act and part of all cultures at all times with differences in propensity and prodigality. As often or as little as it occurs, for most people it remains abhorrent.

TABLE11.1

SELECTED FACTS OF HOMICIDE, 1980 AND 1994, BY PERCENT

TRAITS	1980	1994
Victims		
male	77	79
female	23	21
white	53	47
black	42	51
other	4	2
Offenders		
male	77	91
female	23	9
white	51	42
black	48	56
other	1	2
Weapons		
guns	62	70
cutting	19	13
personal	6	5
other	13	12
Victim-Offender Relationships		
friends, rels.,	51	46
strangers	13	13
unknown	36	41
Circumstances		
argument	45	28
felony	25	19
gang	—	5
unknown, etc.	30	48
Cleared	72	64

APPENDIX A

THE 115 NOVELS REVIEWED FOR THIS STUDY

Andreae, Christine. 1992. *Trail of Murder*. New York: St. Martin's Press.

Armstrong, Charlotte. 1967. *Lemon in the Basket*. New York: Coward-McCann, Inc.

Ball, John. 1965. *In the Heat of the Night*. New York: Carroll & Graf Publishers Inc.

Banks, Oliver. 1980. *The Rembrandt Panel*. Thorndike, Maine: Thorndike Press.

Beinhart, Larry. 1986. *No One Rides For Free*. New York: William Morrow & Company, Inc.

Bennett, Mary Lou. 1988. *Murder Once Done*. Menlo Park, California: Perseverance Press.

Bentley, E. C. 1953. *Trent's Last Case*. New York: Alfred A. Knopf. Originally published in 1913.

Biggers, Earl Derr. 1926. *Fifty Candles*. New York: Buccaneer Books.

Blain, W. Edward. 1990. *Passion Play*. New York: G. P. Putnam's Sons.

Blauner, Peter. 1991. *Slow Motion Riot*. New York: William Morrow & Company, Inc.

Block, Lawrence. 1991. *A Dance at the Slaughterhouse*. New York: William Morrow & Company, Inc.

Boyer, Rick. 1982. *Billiingsgate Shoat*. Boston: Houghton Mifflin Company.

Brandon, Jay. 1991. *Fade the Heat*. New York: Pocket Books.

Brown, Fredric. 1979. *The Fabulous Clipjoint*. Boston: Gregg Press.

Buchanan, Edna. 1990. *Nobody Lives Forever*. New York: Random House.

Burke, James Lee. 1989. *Black Cherry Blues*. Boston: Little, Brown & Company.

Burns, Rex. 1975. *The Alvarez Journal*. New York: Harper & Row.

Cain, James M. 1934. *The Postman Always Rings Twice*. New York: Alfred Knopf.

Chandler, Raymond. 1976. *The Lady in the Lake*. New York: Garland Publishing, Inc. Originally published in 1946.

Chehak, Susan Taylor. 1989. *The Story of Annie D.* Boston: Houghton Mifflin Company.

Coburn, Andrew. 1989. *Goldilocks.* New York: Charles Scribner's Sons.
Connelly, Michael. 1992. *The Black Echo.* Boston: Little, Brown & Company.
Constantine, K. C. 1973. *The Man Who Liked to Look at Himself.* Boston: G. K. Hall & Company.
Cook, Thomas H. 1988. *Sacrificial Ground.* New York: Putnam's Sons.
Cornwell, Patricia Daniels. 1990. *Post Mortem.* New York: Charles Scribner's Sons.
Crais, Robert. 1993. *Free Fall.* New York: Bantam Books.
Cross, Amanda. 1964. *In the Last Analysis.* New York: MacMillan Company.
Daly, Elizabeth. 1950. *Death and Letters.* New York: Rinehart & Company, Inc.
Davis, Dorothy Salisbury. 1987. *The Habit of Fear.* New York: Charles Scribner's Sons.
DeAndrea, William L. 1978. *Killed in the Ratings.* New York: Harcourt Brace Jovanovich.
Devon, Gary. 1987. *Lost.* Boston: G. K. Hall & Company.
Eberhart, Mignon G. 1983. *The Patient in Cabin C.* New York: Random House.
Ellin, Stanley. 1985. *Very Old Money.* New York: Arbor House.
Estleman, Loren. 1990. *Whiskey River.* New York: Bantam Books.
Eustis, Helen. 1946. *The Horizontal Man.* New York: Penguin Books.
Evanovich, Janet. 1994. *One for the Money.* New York: Scribner's.
Faherty, Terence. 1991. *Deadstick.* New York: St. Martin's Press.
Fearing, Kenneth. 1946. *The Big Clock.* New York: Garland Publishing, Inc.
Feldmeyer, Dean. 1994. *Viper Quarry.* New York: Pocket Books.
Fenwick, Elizabeth. 1963. *The Make-Believe Man.* New York: Harper & Row Publishers.
Fine, Peter Heath. 1959. *Night Train.* New York: J. B. Lippincott.
Furst, Alan. 1976. *Your Day in the Barrel.* New York: Atheneum.
Gardner, Erle Stanley. 1944. *The Case of the Crooked Candle.* New York: Garland Publishing, Inc.
Gifford, Thomas. 1976. *The Cavanaugh Quest.* New York: G. P. Putnam's Sons.
Goodrum, Charles A. 1977. *Dewey Decimated.* New York: Crown Publishers, Inc.
Gores, Joe. 1986. *Come Morning.* New York: Mysterious Press.
Goulart, Ron. 1977. *After Things Fell Apart.* Boston: Gregg Press. Originally published in 1970.

Green, George Dawes. 1994. *The Caveman's Valentine.* New York: Warner Books.

Guterson, David. 1994. *Snow Falling on Cedars.* New York: Harcourt Brace & Company.

Haddam, Jane. 1990. *Not a Creature Was Stirring.* New York: Bantam Books.

Handler, David. 1990. *The Man Who Would Be F. Scott Fitzgerald.* New York: Bantam Books.

Harriss, Will. 1983. *The Bay Psalm Book Murder.* New York: Walker & Company.

Hart, Carolyn G. 1995. *Mint Julip Murder.* New York: Bantam Books.

Hillerman, Tony. 1988. *A Thief of Time.* New York: Harper & Row.

Hintze, Naomi. 1969. *You'll Like My Mother.* New York: G. P. Putnam's Sons.

Hitchcock, Jane Stanton. 1992. *Trick of the Eye.* New York: Dutton.

Hornig, Doug. 1984. *Foul Shot.* New York: Charles Scribner's Sons.

Howe, Melodie Johnson. 1989. *The Mother Shadow.* New York: Viking.

Hudson, Jeffrey. 1968. *A Case of Need.* Hungham, Massachusetts: Wheeler Publishing, Inc.

Izzi, Eugene. 1989. *The Booster.* New York: St. Martin's Press.

Jones, Craig. 1978. *Blood Secrets.* New York: Harper & Row Publishers.

Kellerman, Jonathan. 1985. *When the Bough Breaks.* New York: Signet.

King, Laurie. 1993. *A Grave Talent.* New York: St. Martin's Press.

Klavan, Andrew. 1991. *Don't Say a Word.* New York: Pocket Books.

Laiken, Deidre S. 1987. *Death Among Strangers.* New York: MacMillan Publishing Company.

Langton, Jane. 1955. *Emily Dickinson is Dead.* New York: St. Martin's Press.

Larson, Charles. 1973. *Someone's Death.* New York: J. B. Lippincott Company.

Lathen, Emma. 1988. *Something in the Air.* New York: Simon & Schuster.

Law, Janice. 1975. *The Big Pay-Off.* Boston: Houghton-Mifflin.

Leonard, Elmore. 1983. *La Brava.* New York: Arbor House.

Levin, Ira. 1967. *Rosemary's Baby.* New York: Random House.

Lindsey, David L. 1988. *In the Lake of the Moon.* New York: Atheneum.

Littell, Robert. 1981. *The Amateur.* New York: Simon & Schuster.

Lochte, Dick. 1985. *Sleeping Dog.* New York: Arbor House.

Lupica, Mike. 1986. *Dead Air.* New York: Villard Books.

MacDonald, John D. 1981. *Free Fall in Crimson.* New York: Harper & Row, Publishers.

MacDonald, Ross. 1977. *Lew Archer, Private Investigator.* New York: Mysterious Press. Originally called *Find the Woman*, a short story published in 1946.

MacLeod, Charlotte. 1987. *The Corpse in Oozak's Pond.* New York: The Mysterious Press.

Maling, Arthur. 1979. *The Rheingold Route.* New York: Harper & Row, Publishers.

Margolin, Philip. 1978. *Heartstone.* New York: Bantam Books.

Maron, Margaret. 1992. *Bootlegger's Daughter.* New York: The Mysterious Press.

Matera, Lea. 1988. *A Radical Departure.* New York: Ballantine.

McBain, Ed. 1989. *Cop Hater.* Cambridge: University Press. Originally published in 1956. McBain's real name is Evan Hunter.

McCrumb, Sharyn. 1988. *Bimbos of the Death Sun.* New York: TSR Books.

Millar, Margaret. 1970. *Beyond This Point Are Monsters.* New York: Random House.

Mosley, Walter. 1990. *Devil in a Blue Dress.* New York: W. W. Norton & Co.

Muller, Marcia. 1993. *Wolf in the Shadows.* New York: Warner Brothers.

Naha, Ed. 1991. *Cracking Up.* New York: Pocket Books.

Newman, Christopher. 1991. *Midtown North.* New York: Fawcett Books.

North, Darian. 1993. *Criminal Seduction.* New York: Dutton Book, Penguin Group.

Nunn, Ken. 1992. *Pomona Queen.* New York: Pocket Books.

O'Connell, Carol. 1994. *Mallory's Oracle.* New York: G. P. Putnam's Sons.

Papazoglou, Orania. 1984. *Sweet, Savage Death.* Garden City, New York: Doubleday & Company.

Parker, Barbara. 1994. *Suspicion of Innocence.* New York: Signet.

Parker, Robert B. 1990. *Stardust.* New York: G. P. Putnam's Sons.

Pearson, William. 1984. *Chessplayer.* New York: The Viking Press.

Philips, Judson. (AKA Hugh Pentercost). 1988. *Murder Goes Round and Round.* New York: Dodd Mead & Company.

Queen, Ellery. 1963. *The Player on the Other Side.* New York: Random House.

Rosenbaum, David. 1993. *Zaddik.* New York: Mysterious Press.

Sanders, Lawrence. 1970. *The Anderson Tapes.* New York: Putnam's Sons.

Sheldon, Sidney. 1970. *The Naked Face*. New York: William Morrow & Company, Inc.

Smith, Craig. 1992. *Ladystinger*. New York: Crown Publishers, Inc.

Smith, Julie. 1990. *New Orleans Mourning*. New York: St. Martin's Press.

Smith, Martin. 1972. *Canto for a Gypsy*. New York: Putnam's Sons.

Spillane, Micky. 1989. *The Killing Man*. New York: E. P. Dutton.

Stein, Aaron Marc. 1979. *The Rolling Heads*. New York: Doubleday & Company, Inc.

Stout, Rex. 1983. *Too Many Cooks*. New York: Bantam Books. Originally published in 1938.

Thomas, Ross. 1984. *Briar Patch*. New York: Simon & Schuster.

Traver, Robert. 1981. *People Versus Kirk*. New York: St. Martin's Press.

Walker, Mary Willis. 1994. *The Red Scream*. New York: Doubleday.

Wambaugh, Joseph. 1993. *Finnegan's Week*. New York: William Morrow & Company, Inc.

West, Chassie. 1994. *Sunrise*. New York: Harper Paperbacks.

Whitney, Phyliss A. 1992. *The Ebony Swan*. New York: Doubleday.

Wolfe, Susan. 1989. *The Last Billable Hour*. New York: St. Martin's Press.

Woods, Stuart. 1991. *Palindrome*. New York: Harper Collins, Publishers.

APPENDIX B

EXAMPLES OF BOOK REPORTS

G-22-M
McBain, Ed. 1989. *Cop Hater*. Cambridge: University Press. Originally published in 1956. McBain's real name is Evan Hunter.

This is the first of the 87th precinct novels. The protagonist is a conglomerate of heroes – the cops in the precinct. The setting is a mythical city like New York. It is an early example of procedural police stories influenced by Dragnet.

Officer Reardon is shot and killed in the street on the way to work. Two bullets are in the back of his skull. The 87th is assigned the case; Carella and Bush are dispatched. Reardon's partner Foster also is shot while walking home. He is killed by four bullets in the chest. Ballistics show the same gun killed both. A rookie cop is shot in the shoulder with a zip gun coming out of a bar, by a juvenile gang. He was mistaken for a reporter Savage who had interviewed a gang member trying to connect the murders to the gang. They want to scare him off. On the way home from work Bush is ambushed. He manages to pull out his gun and shoot the attacker in the shoulder at the same time he is hit four times. He charges the attacker and manages to grab his hair and some flesh before succumbing. This helps identify a description of the murderer.

Savage interviews Carella, off the record. Then he puts it in the paper and mentions Carella's girl friend and her neighborhood. The killer goes to her address looking for Carella fearing he may know too much. Carella figures that this might happen and rushes to her place. He pushes through the door and manages to shoot the killer twice wounding him. The killer is the lover of Alice, wife of Bush. She hated her husband and schemed to have her lover kill a couple of cops then Bush to make it look like a cop hater motive. Alice and killer are tried and sentenced to death.

B-110-M
Klavan, Andrew. 1991. *Don't Say A Word*. New York: Pocket Books.

Sport, ex-corrections officer and the brains, and Maxwell, sex fiend and the muscles, con their way into an old lady's apartment. Maxwell sexually assaults her, viciously cuts her throat and kills her. They need her apartment to spy on Dr. Conrad for their caper.

Conrad, a psychiatrist, agrees to assess an 18 year old patient Elizabeth who allegedly cut a man to pieces. Conrad gets her to talk. She had a "secret" friend who allegedly killed her mother. She also allegedly killed a Dutch sailor. Conrad's daughter Jennifer is kidnapped by Sport and Maxwell. They want Conrad to get a "number" from Elizabeth. They claim any attempt to notify police would lead to the death of the child.

Aggie, Conrad's wife, manages to notify a neighbor to contact police. Sport comes to the apartment posing as a plumber and claiming to be a cop. Maxwell kills the neighbor in his usual way before he can get to police. Conrad gets the "number" from Elizabeth and leaves the hospital with her. Conrad gives Sport the number. Aggie contacts another neighbor and a real cop D'Annunzio shows up.

Investigation reveals that the killings allegedly by Elizabeth were done by Maxwell. The caper involved diamonds buried in her mother's coffin. The number identified her grave. Sport recovers the diamonds. Police get the information from Elizabeth and they find Sport and arrest him. Conrad figures out where Jennifer is being held. Maxwell had been told by Sport to kill the child as he had the diamonds. Conrad finds a broken broom stick, enters the hiding place and manages to kill Maxwell by stabbing him in the kidney with the stick. D'Annunzio manages to force Sport to reveal the hiding place and the police get there and find Conrad hurt, the girl safe, and Maxwell dead.

D-43-F
Haddam, Jane. 1990. *Not A Creature Was Stirring*. New York: Bantam Books.

The Hannaford's are a wealthy and dysfunctional family from Bryn Mawr. The children are scattered. Left at home are Robert Hannaford the father, hateful invalid Cordelia the mother, and Anne Marie their daughter a 40 year old spinster taking care of the house and mother. There are three other daughters: Bennis, a successful novelist; Myra, married to a wealthy man and stealing from him in hopes of garnering enough money to divorce him; and Emma, the youngest just getting started on her own. There are three sons: Chris, a radio disc jockey and compulsive gambler heavy in debt to mobsters; Teddy, English Professor in trouble for plagiary and sexual involvement with his students; and Bobby, embezzling money from the Hannaford finance company. They all hate the father. Myra insists they all get together at the family home for the Christmas week because of concern about the family. The Mother was dying, Anne Marie was about to have a breakdown, and the father was on the warpath. Gregor Demarkian, a retired and famous former FBI agent is invited to dinner by the father. He offers $100,000 to an Armenian priest if Gregor would do something for him. Thus the invitation to dinner.

Bennis discovers Robert dead on the floor his head bashed in with a bust of Aristotle. Then Emma is found dead from an overdose of Demerol in her tea. Myra is the next victim found in the TV room killed with a silver candlestick. Her face is battered into gore.

Gregor figures it out. It was Anne Marie. If the father was dead the mother would inherit a 2 million dollar insurance policy. Anne Marie could end up with nothing – no money, no skill, no home. So she killed her father, and then was trying to kill alll the sisters so that she would inherit the money after her mother died.

C-131-F

Papazoglou, Orania. 1984. *Sweet, Savage Death.* Garden City, New York: Doubleday & Company.

Patience (Pay) Campbell McKenna is a writer of romance novels to subsidize more serious literary efforts. She attends the funeral of her mentor who was murdered in the park by repeated stabbing. Returning to her apartment, she discovers her literary agent's body. He also was stabbed to death. Pay is a suspect.

Attending a literary conference, Pay discovers the body of Mary Allard an editor. Patience again is a suspect. She discusses the events with a colleague and they agree that the murders were the consequence of financial shenanigans. While searching for falsified financial documents, Pay is attacked by the murderer with a knife. Pay's colleague saves her life by hitting the attacker over the head with a blunt instrument.

The murderer is arrested by the authorities. She was cooking the books to make it appear that her work was successfully bringing money into the company. Otherwise, she feared she would lose her job. The victims were killed to keep them from exposing her.

APPENDIX C

DATA SHEET FRAMEWORK

A. VICTIM

1. Demographics: gender, adult or juvenile, occupation, class.
2. Culpability: involved in crime, blackmailed, contributed, none.
3. Relationship to Offender: relative, friend, acquaintance, stranger.

B. CIRCUMSTANCES

1. Context of Milieu: violence, manners, madness.
2. Crime Scene: home, job, street, other.
3. Protagonist: chief cause of final outcome; police, private. Investigator, other (lay person).

C. OFFENDER

1. Demographics: gender, adult or juvenile, occupation, class.
2. Motive: passion, profit, revenge, others.
3. Heinousness of Offense: very, moderate, little, none.
4. Weapon: firearm, cutting device, blunt instrument, others.
5. Criminal Record: yes or no.
6. Final Disposition: killed, arrested, suicide, escape.

APPENDIX D

DATA COLLECTION SHEETS

VICTIM	TITLE
DEMOGRAPHICS	
RELATIONSHIP	
CULPABILITY	
OFFENDER	
DEMOGRAPHICS	
MOTIVE	
WEAPON	
OFFENDER	
HEINOUSNESS	
CRIMINAL RECORD	
FINAL DISPOSITION	
CIRCUMSTANCES	
CONTEXT OF MILIEU	
CRIME SCENE	
PROTAGONIST	

REFERENCES

Ackroyd, Peter. 1994. *The Trial of Elizabeth Cree.* New York: Doubleday.

Aeschylus. 1961. *The Oresteia.* New York: The Heritage Press. Originally performed in Athens 458 B.C. The trilogy includes the plays: Agamemnon, The Libation-Bearers, The Furies.

Ardrey, Robert. 1961. *African Genesis.* New York: Atheneum.

Auel, Jean M. 1980. *The Clan of the Cave Bear.* New York: Crown Publishers, Inc.

Babbie, Earl. 1979. *The Practice of Social Research.* Second Edition. Belmont, California: Wadsworth Publishing Company, Inc., Chapt. 9.

Ball, John. 1976. "Murder at Large." In John Ball, Ed. *The Mystery Story.* Del Mar, California: University Extension, University of California at San Diego.

Ball, John. Editor. 1976. *The Mystery Story.* San Diego: University Extension University of California.

Ball–Rokeach, Sandra J. 1973. "Values and Violence: A Test of the Subculture of Violence Thesis." *American Sociological Review*, 38: 736-749.

Banay, R. 1952. "Study in Murder." *The Annals*, 284: (Novermber).

Barzun, Jacques & Wendell Hertig Taylor. Editors. 1976. *Fifty Classics of Crime Fiction, 1900-1950.* New York: Garland Publishing.

Bell, Daniel. 1962. *The End of Ideology.* New York: Free Press.

Bensing, Robert C. & Oliver Schroeder, Jr. 1960. *Homicide in an Urban Community.* Springfield, Illinois: Charles C. Thomas.

Benvenuti, Stefano & Gianni Rizzoni. 1979. *The Whodunit.* Translated by Anthony Eyre. New York: MacMillan Publishing Co., Inc.

Berelson, Bernard & Patricia Salter. 1946. "Majority and Minority Americans: An Analysis of Magazine Fiction." *Public Opinion Quarterly*, 10: 168-190.

Berelson, B. 1952. *Content Analysis in Communication Research.* New York: Free Press.

Blau, Judith R. & Peter M. Blau. 1982. "The Cost of Inequality: Metropolitan Structure and Violent Crime." *American Sociological Review*, 47: 114-29.

Bloch, H. & G. Geis. 1970. *Man, Crime, and Society.* New York: Random House.

Blumberg, Abraham S. & Arthur Niederhoffer. 1973. "The Police in Social and Historical Perspective." In Arthur Niederhoffer & Abraham S. Blumberg. *The Ambivalent Force: Perspective on the Police*. San Francisco: Rinehart Press.

Bohannan, Paul, (Ed.). 1960. *African Homicide and Suicide*. Princeton: Princeton University Press.

Booth, Alan. 1995. *Looking For the Law*. New York: Kodansha International.

Brown, Richard Maxwell. 1969. "Historical Patterns of Violence in America." In Hugh Davis Graham and Ted Robert Gurr, *The History of Violence in America*. New York: Bantam Books, 45-84.

Browne, A. & K. R. Williams. 1987. "Resource Availability for Women at Risk: Its Relationship to Rates of Female-Perpetrated Partner Homicide." Paper Presented at the Annual Meeting of the American Society of Criminology, Montreal, November 11-14.

Brunswick, Ann F. 1970. "What Generation Gap? A Comparison of Some Generational Differences Among Blacks and Whites." *Social Problems*, 17: 358-371.

Bullock, Henry A. 1955. "Urban Homicide in Theory and Fact." *Journal of Criminal Law, Criminology, and Police Science*, 45: 565-575.

Calhoun, John B. 1983. *Environment and Population; Problems of Adaptation*. New York: Praeger.

Campbell, Joseph. 1973. *Myths to Live By*. New York: Bantam Books.

Chaiken, Jan M. & Marcia R. Chaiken. 1982. *Varieties of Criminal Behavior*. Santa Monica, California: Rand Corporation.

Clark, Ronald J. & Phillip V. Tobias. 1995. "Sterkfontein Member 2 Foot Bones of the Oldest South African Hominid." *Science*, 269: 521-24.

Craig, Patricia & Mary Cadogan. 1981. *The Lady Investigates*. New York: St. Martin's Press.

Cressey, Donald R. 1969. *Theft of the Nation: The Structure and Operations of Organized Crime in America*. New York: Harper and Row.

Cressey, Donald R. 1972. *Criminal Organizations*. London: Heinemann.

Cressy, Donald R. 1968. "Culture Conflict, Differential Association, and Normative Conflict." In Wolfgang, Marvin E., (Ed.). *Crime and Culture*. New York: John Wiley & Sons, Inc., 54-55.

Crutchfield, Robert D. 1995. "Ethnicity, Labor Markets, and Crime." In Hawkins, D. F. Editor, *Ethnicity, Race, and Crime: Perspectives Across Time and Place*, Albany, NY: State University of New York Press, 194-211.

Culotta, Elizabeth. 1995. "New Finds Rekindle Debate Over Anthropoid Origins." *Science*, 268: 1851.

Daly, Martin & Margo Wilson. 1988. *Homicide*. New York: Aldine De Gruyter.

Davis, David Brion. 1957. *Homicide in American Fiction, 1798-1860: A Study in Social Values*. Ithaca, New York: Cornell University Press.

Davis, David Brion. 1970. "Violence in American Literature." In Hartogs, Dr. Renatus & Eric Artzt, *Violence: Causes and Solutions*. New York: Dell Publishing Co., Inc.

Devine, Philip E. 1978. *The Ethics of Homicide*. Ithaca: Cornell University Press.

Doerner, William G. 1975. "A Regional Analysis of Homicide Rates in the United States." *Criminology*, 13: 90-101.

Driver, Edwin D. 1961. "Interaction and Criminal Homicide in India." *Social Forces*, 40: 153-158.

Duncan, Jane Watson & Glen M. Duncan. 1971. "Murder in the Family: A Study of Some Homicidal Adolescents." *American Journal of Psychiatry*, 120: 125-130.

Durant, Will. 1950. *The Age of Faith*. New York: Simon & Schuster.

Durkheim, Emile. 1951. *Suicide*. Translated by John A. Spaulding & George Simpson. New York: The Free Press of Glencoe.

Durkheim, Emile. 1964. 8th Edition. *The Rules of Sociological Method*. Glencoe, Illinois: The Free Press.

Ellis, Albert & John Gullo. 1971. *Murder and Assassination*. New York: Lyle Stuart, Inc.

Emsley, Clive & Louis A. Knafla, Eds. 1996. *Crime History and Histories of Crime*. Westport, Connecticut: Greenwood Press.

Euripides. 1953. *Medea, Hippolytus, The Bacchae*. New York: The Heritage Press. Written in the second half of the fifth century B.C.

Everitt, David. 1993. *Human Monsters*. Chicago: Contemporary Books.

F. Tennyson, Jesse. 1952. *Murder and Its Motives*. Revised Edition. London: Harrap.

Falk, Gerhard. 1990. *Murder*. Jefferson, North Carolina: McFarland & Company, Inc., Publishers.

Farley, R. 1980. "Homicide Trends in the United States." *Demography*, 17: 177–88.

Federal Bureau of Investigation, U.S. Department of Justice. 1981. *Uniform Crime Reports, Crime in the United States, 1980*. Washington, D.C.: Government Printing Office.

Federal Bureau of Investigation, U.S. Department of Justice. 1995. *Uniform Crime Reports, Crime in the United States, 1994.* Washington, D.C.: Government Printing Office.

Federal Bureau of Investigation, U.S. Department of Justice. 1998. *Uniform Crime Reports, Crime in the United States, 1997.* Washington, D.C.: Government Printing Office.

Ferracuti, Franco. 1968. "European Migration & Crime." In Wolfgang, Marvin E., (Ed.). *Crime and Culture.* New York: John Wiley & Sons, Inc., 189-219.

Ferrell, Jeff & Clinton R. Sanders. 1995. *Cultural Criminology.* Boston: Northeastern University Press.

Fisher, Joseph S. 1976. "Homicide in Detroit." *Criminology,* 14: 3.

Frazer, Sir James George. 1970. *The Golden Bough.* New York: The Limited Editions Club, Volumes I & II. Originally published in 1890 and expanded and reissued at several other times.

Garfinkle, Harold. 1941. "Research Notes on Inter and Intra Racial Homicides." *Social Forces,* 27: 369-81.

Garton, Stephen. 1996. "The Convict Taint: Australia and New Zealand." In Clyde Emsley & Louis A. Knafia, (Eds.). *Crime History and Histories of Crime.* Westport, Connecticut: Greenwood Press.

Gastil, Raymond D. 1971. "Homicide and a Regional Culture of Violence." *American Sociological Review,* 36: 412-427.

Gelles, R. J. 1974. *The Violent Home: A Study of Physical Aggression Between Husbands and Wives.* Beverly Hills, California: Sage.

Gelles, R. J. 1979. *Family Violence.* Beverly Hills, California: Sage.

Gelles, R. J. & M. A. Straus. 1989. *Intimate Violence: The Causes & Consequences of Abuse in the American Family.* New York: Simon & Schuster.

Gibbons, Ann. 1996. "Homo Erectus in Java: A 250,000 Year Anachronism." *Science,* 274: 1841-1842.

Gilbert, Martin. 1979. *The Holocaust.* New York: Hill & Wang.

Gillin, John L. 1946. *The Wisconsin Prisoner.* Madison: University of Wisconsin Press.

Glaser, Daniel, Donald Kenefick, and Vincent O'Leary. 1966. *The Violent Offender.* Washington, D.C.: Government Printing Office.

Gluckman, Max. 1968. *Politics, Law, and Ritual in Tribal Society.* New York: Mentor Books.

Goetting, A. 1989. "Patterns of Marital Homicide: A Comparison of Husbands and Wives." *Journal of Comparative Family Studies,* 2: 341-354.

Graham, Hugh Davis & Ted Robert Gurr. 1969. *The History of Violence in America*. New York: Bantam Books.

Graves, Robert. 1960. *The Greek Myths*, Volume I. Revised Edition. London: Penguin Books.

Graves, Robert. 1972. *The Greek Myths*. Volume I. Revised Edition. London: Penguin Books.

Graves, Robert. 1988. *The Greek Myths*. Mt. Kisco, New York: Moyer.

Grimshaw, Allan. 1999. "Genocide and Democide." In *Encyclopedia of Violence, Peace, and Conflict*. Edited by Les Kurtz and Jennifer Turpin. San Diego: Academic Press.

Gurr, Ted Robert. 1980. "Development and Decay: Their Impact on Public Order in Western History." In James A. Inciardi & Charles E. Faupel. *History and Crime*. Beverly Hills, California: Sage Publications.

Guttmacher, Manfred S. 1960. *The Mind of the Murderer*. New York: Farrar, Strauss, and Cudahy.

Gurrmacher, Manfred S., Editor. 1967. *Studies in Murder*. New York: Harper & Row.

Hackney, Sheldon. 1969. "Southern Violence." In Hugh Davis Graham & Ted Robert Gurr, *The History of Violence in America*. New York: Bantam Books, 505-527.

Halttumen, Karen. 1998. *Murder Most Foul*. Washington, DC: Howard University Press.

Hamilton, Edith. 1940. *Mythology*. New York: The New American Library.

Hansen, M. & M. Harway, (Eds.). 1993. *Battering & Family Therapy: A Feminist Perspective*. Newbury Park, California: Sage.

Harris, Nigel. 1995. *The New Untouchables*. New York: I. B. Tauris Publishers.

Hartman, Mary S. 1977. *Victorian Murderesses*. New York: Shocken Books.

Haskell, Martin & Lewis Yablonsky. 1974. *Crime and Delinquency*. Second Edition. Chicago: Rand McNally College Publishing Company.

Hawkins, Darnell F. 1987. "Devalued Lives and Racial Stereotypes: Ideological Barriers to the Prevention of Family Violence among Blacks." In R. L. Hampton, Editor, *Violence in the Black Family*. Lexington, MA: Heath, Lexington Books.

Henry, Andrew F. and James F. Short, Jr. 1954. *Suicide and Homicide*. New York: Free Press.

Hepburn, John R. 1971. "Subcultures, Violence, and the Subculture of Violence." *Criminology*, 9: 87-98.

Hillerman, Tony & Rosemary Herbert. Editors. 1996. *The Oxford Book of American Detective Stories*. New York: Oxford University Press.

Hoebel, E. Adamson & Thomas Weaver. 1979. *Anthropology and the Human Experience*. New York: McGraw-Hill Book Co.

Holmes, R. M. & J. DeBurger. 1985. "Profiles in Terror: The Serial Murderer." *Federal Probation*, 53: 53-59.

Holmes, R. M. & J. De Burger. 1988. *Serial Murder*. Newbury Park, California: Sage.

Holmes, Ronald & Stephen T. Holmes. 1994. *Murder In America*. Thousand Oaks, California: Sage Publications.

Hughes, Steven C. 1966. "Brigands, Mafiosi, and Others: Italy." In Clyde Emsley & Louis A. Knafia, (Eds.). *Crime History and Histories of Crime*. Westport, Connecticut: Greenwood Press.

Ianni, Francis A. J. 1973. *Ethic Succession in Organized Crime, Summary Report*. National Institute of Law Enforcement and Criminal Justice. Washington, D.C.: Government Printing Office.

Ianni, Francis A. J., with Elizabeth Reuss Ianni. 1972. *A Family Business: Kinship and Social Control in Organized Crime*. New York: Russell Sage Foundation.

Ianni, Francis A. J. 1978. "The New Mafia." In Savitz, Leonard D. and Norman Johnston. *Crime in Society*. New York: John Wiley & Sons.

Inciardi, James A. 1975. *Careers in Crime*. Chicago: Rand McNally College Publishing Company.

Inciardi, James A. & Charles E. Faupel. 1980. *History and Crime*. Beverly Hills, California: Sage Publications.

Johanson, Donald, Lenora Johanson, & Blake Edgar. 1994. *Ancestors*. New York: Villard Books.

Johnson, Elmer H. 1974. *Crime, Correction, and Society*. Third Edition. Homewood, Illinois: The Dorsey Press.

Johnson, Guy B. 1941. "The Negro and Crime." *The Annals*, 277: 93-104.

Jones, Ann. 1980. *Women Who Kill*. New York: Fawcett Columbine Books.

Jones, Richard Glyn, Editor. 1989. *The Mammoth Book of Murder*. New York: Carroll & Graf Publishers.

Kelleher, Michael D. & C. L. Kelleher. 1997. *Murder Most Rare: The Female Serial Killer*. New York: Praeger.

Kirkham, James F., Sheldon G. Lerry, & William J. Crotty, (Eds.). 1969. *Assassination and Political Violence*. Staff Report Submitted to the National Committee on the Causes and Prevention of Violence. Washington, D.C.: Government Printing Office.

Klein, Malcolm. 1995. *The American Street Gang: Its Nature, Prevalence, and Control.* New York: Oxford University Press.

Kohlenberger, John R. III. 1991. *The New Revised Standard Concordance, Unabridged.* Grand Rapids, Michigan: Zondervan Publishing House.

Kratcoski, P. 1987. "Families Who Kill." *Marriage & Family Review*, 12: 47-70.

Kugel, James L. 1997. *The Bible As It Was.* Cambridge: Harvard University Press.

Land, Kenneth C., Patricia L. McCall, and Lawrence E. Cohen. 1990. "Structural Covariated of Homicide Rates: Are There Any Invariances Across Time and Space?" *American Journal of Sociology*, 95: 922-63.

Lane, Roger. 1980. "Urban Homicide in the Nineteenth Century." In James A. Inciardi & Charles E. Faupel. *History and Crime.* Beverly Hills, California: Sage Publications.

Leakey, Richard E. & Roger Lewin. 1978. *People of the Lake.* Garden City: Anchor Press/Doubleday.

Levine, Felice & Katherine J. Rosich. 1996. *Social Causes of Violence.* Washington, D.C.: American Sociological Association.

Loftin, Colin & Robert H. Hill. 1974. "Regional Subculture and Homicide: An Examination of the Gastil-Hackney Thesis." *American Sociological Review*, 39: 714-724.

Loftin, Colin, David McDowall, and James Boudouris. 1989. "Economic Change and Homicide in Detroit, 1926-1979." In *Violence in America: The History of Crime*, vol. 1, edited by T. R. Gurr. Newbury Park, California: Sage Publications.

Lombroso, Cesare & William Ferrero. 1915. *The Female Offender.* Translated by W. D. Morrison. New York: D. Appleton & Co.

Lorenz, Konrad. 1966. *On Aggression.* New York: Harcourt Brace.

Lowenthal, L. 1961. *Literature, Popular Culture and Society.* Palo Alto, California: Pacific Books, Publishers.

Lyon, Jeff. 1985. *Playing God in the Nursery.* New York: W. W. Norton & Company.

McLynn, Frank. 1989. *Crime and Punishment in Eighteenth-Century England.* London: Routledge.

Menninger, Karl. 1938. *Man Against Himself.* New York: Harcourt, Brace.

Mercy, J. & L. Saltzman. 1989. "Fatal Violence Among Spouses in the United States." *American Journal of Public Health*, 79: 595-99.

Montell, William Lynwood. 1986. *Folk Justice in the Upper South.* Lexington, Kentucky: University Press of Kentucky.

Moore, Kelly & Dan Reed. 1988. *Deadly Medicine.* New York: St. Martin's Press.

Morris, Terence & Louis Blom-Cooper. 1964. *A Calendar of Murder: Criminal Homicide in England Since 1957.* London: Joseph.

National Commission on the Causes and Prevention of Violence. 1969. *To Establish Justice, To Insure Domestic Tranquility: The Final Report of the National Commission on the Causes and Prevention of Violence.* Washington, D.C.: Government Printing Office. The Task Force reports submitted to the Commission included: James F. Kirkman, Sheldon G. Levy, & William J. Crotty. 1969. *Assassination and Political Violence.* Washington, D.C.: Government Printing Office; George D. Newton & Frank E. Zimring. 1969. *Firearms and Violence in American Life.* Washington, D.C.: Government Printing Office; Jerome Skolnick. 1969. *The Politics of Protest: Violent Aspects of Protest and Confrontation.* Washington, D.C.: Government Printing Office; The report by the Task Force on historical and comparative perspectives on violence in America can be found unabridged in, Graham, Hugh Davis & Ted Robert Gurr. 1969. *The History of Violence in America.* New York: Bantam Books; The Final Report was also privately published by Praeger in 1970.

National Commission on the Causes and Prevention of Violence. 1969. *Crimes of Violence.* Washington, D.C.: Government Printing Office.

Nettler, Gynn. 1982. *Killing One Another.* Cinncinnati: Anderson Publishing Co.

Nicholas Biddle, Editor. 1962. *The Journals of the Expedition under Capt's Lewis and Clark.* Volume I. New York: The Heritage Press.

Oliver, Douglas L. 1995. *A Solomon Island Society.* Boston: Beacon Press.

Oswalt, Wendell H. 1966. *This Land Was Theirs.* New York: John Wiley & Sons, Inc.

Palmer, Stuart. 1960. *A Study of Murder.* New York: Thomas Y. Crowell.

Pearson, Patricia. 1997. *When She Was Bad: Violent Women and the Myth of Innocence.* New York: Viking.

Peterson, Richard A., David J. Pittman, & Patricia O'Neal. 1962. "Stabilities in Deviance: A Study of Assaultive and Non-Assaultive Offenders." *Journal of Criminal Law, Criminology, and Police Science*, 53; 462-470.

Phillips, Jim. 1966. "Crime and Punishment in the Dominion of the North Canada from New France to the Present." In Clyde Emsley & Louis A.

Knafia, (Eds.). *Crime History and Histories of Crime.* Westport, Connecticut: Greenwood Press.

Piers, Maria W. 1978. *Infanticide Past and Present.* New York: Norton & Company, Inc.

Pokorny, Alex D. 1965. "A Comparison of Homicides in Two Cities." *Journal of Criminal Law, Criminology, and Police Science*, 56: 479-487.

Pollak, Otto. 1950. *The Criminality of Women.* Philadelphia: University of Pennsylvania Press.

Portes, Alejandro, Editor. 1996. *The New Second Generation.* New York: Russell Sage.

President's Commission on Law Enforcement and Administration of Justice. 1967A. *The Challenge of Crime in a Free Society*, Washington, D.C.: Government Printing Office.

President's Commission on Law Enforcement and Administration of Justice. 1967B. *Task Force Report: Organized Crime.* Washington, D.C.: Government Printing Office.

Quinney, Richard. 1965. "Suicide, Homicide, and Economic Development." *Social Forces*, 43: 401-406.

Reiss, Albert J., Jr. & Jeffrey A. Roth, Editors. 1994. *Understanding and Preventing Violence.* Washington, D.C.: National Academy Press.

Riedel, Marc. 1993. *Stranger Violence.* New York: Garland Publishing, Inc.

Rolo, Charles J. 1957. "The Metaphysics of Murder for the Millions." In Bernard Rosenberg & David Manning White, Editors. *Mass Culture.* Glencoe, Illinois: 165-175.

Roth, Jeffrey A. 1994. "Understanding and Preventing Violence." *National Institute of Justice, Research in Brief.* Washington, D.C.: U.S. Department of Justice, National Institute of Justice.

Rousseaux, Xavier. 1996. "From Medieval Cities to National States, 1350-1850: The Historiography of Crime and Criminal."

Rudoff, Alvin. 1971. "The Incarcerated Mexican-American Delinquent." *The Journal of Criminal Law, Criminology and Police Science*, 62: 224-238.

Rudoff, Alvin. 1971. "The Soaring Crime Rate: An Etiological View." *The Journal of Criminal Law, Criminology and Police Science*, 62: 543-547.

Rudoff, Alvin. 1991. *The Paths to Social Deviance and Conformity.* Lewiston, New York: Edwin Mellen Press.

Rumbaut, Ruben & Charles F. Hohm, Editors. 1997. "Immigration and Incorporation." Special Issue. *Sociological Perspectives*, 40, #3.

Sayers, Dorothy L. & Jill Paton Walsh. 1998. *Thrones, Dominations*. New York: St. Martin's Press.

Schultz, Leroy G. 1962. "Why the Negro Carries Weapons." *Journal of Criminal Law, Criminology, and Police Science*, 53: 476-483.

Shackley, Myra. 1980. *Neanderthal Man*. Hamden, Conn.: Archon Books.

Shannnon, Lyle. 1969. "The Economic Absorption and Cultural Integration of Immigrant Workers." *American Behavioral Scientist*, 13: 36-56.

Sheppard, Colin. 1971. "The Violent Offender: Let's Examine the Taboo." *Federal Probation*, 35: 12-19.

Skogan, Wesley G. 1989. "Social Change and the Future of Violent Crime." In *Violence in America: The History of Crime*. Vol. 1, revised edition, edited by T. R. Gurr. Beverly Hills, California: Sage Publications.

Smith, Dwight. 1975. *The Mafia Mystique*. New York: Basic Books.

Solecki, Ralph S. 1972. *Shanidar*. London: Allen Lane The Penguin Press.

Spencer, Carol. 1966. *A Typology of Violent Offenders*. Sacramento, California: Research Division, California Department of Corrections. Research Report No. 23, September. The types were originally identified by John P. Conrad and then the first four were validated in the study.

Spencer, Herbert. 1897. *Principles of Sociology*. New York: D. Appleton. Three volumes, volume I: 439; volume II: 24-34, 220-226.

Stark, Rodney and James McEvoy, III. 1972. *Change: Readings in Society and Human Behavior*. Del Mar, California: CRM Publications.

Stein, Marc Aaron. 1976. "The Mystery Story in Cultural Perspective." In John Ball, *The Mystery Story*, Del Mar, California: University Extension, University of California at San Diego.

Stevenson, Robert Louis. 1952. *Strange Case of Dr. Jekyle and Mr. Hyde*. New York: Heritage Press. Originally published in 1886.

Stohl, M., Editor. 1988. *The Politics of Terrorism*. Third Edition, Revised. New York: Marcel Dekker.

Stordeur, R. A. & R. Stille. 1989. *Ending Men's Violence Against Their Partners: One Road to Peace*. Newbury Park, California: Sage.

Stringer, Christopher & Clive Gamble. 1993. *In Search of the Neanderthals*. New York: Thames & Hudson.

Sutherland, Edwin H. 1937. *The Professional Thief*. Chicago: University of Chicago Press.

Sutherland, Edwin H. & Donald R. Cressey. 1978. *Criminology*. Tenth Edition. New York: J. B. Lippincott Company.

Svalastoga, kaare. 1956. "Homicide and Social Contact in Denmark." *American Journal of Sociology*, 62: 37-41.

Swigert, Victoria Lynn. 1977. "Normal Homicides and the Law." *American Sociological Review*, 42: 16-32.

Swisher, C. C. III, W. J. Rink, S. C. Antón, H. P. Schwarcz, G. H. Curtis, A. Suprijo, Widias Moro. 1996. "Latest Homo Erectus of Java: Potential Contemporaneity with Homo Sapiens in Southeast Asia." *Science*, 274: 1870-1874.

Talking About Genesis. 1996. Public Affairs Television, Introduction by Bill Moyers. Edwin Friedman, pp. 54-55. Christopher Leighton, pp. 50-53. New York: Doubleday.

Tanay, Emanuel. 1976. *The Murderers*. Indianapolis: Bobbs Merrill Co., Inc.

The Editors. 1992. *The European Challenge*. Alexandria, Virginia: Time-Life Books.

The New English Bible. 1971. New York: Cambridge University Press.

Thernstrom, Stephan, (Ed.). 1980. *Harvard Encyclopedia of American Ethnic Groups*. Cambridge, Massachusetts: Harvard University Press.

Thomas, W. I. & F. Znaniecki. 1927. *The Polish Peasant in Europe and America*. New York: Knopf.

Thomas, W. I. 1923. *The Unadjusted Girl*. Boston: Little, Brown.

Thrasher, Frederic M. 1927. *The Gang: A Study of 1313 Gangs in Chicago*. Chicago, Illinois: University of Chicago Press.

Toch, Hans. 1969. *Violent Men: An Inquiry Into the Psychology of Violence*. Chicago: Aldine.

Tonry, Michael, Editor. 1997. *Ethnicity, Crime, and Immigration*. Chicago: University of Chicago Press.

Trinkaus, Erik & Pat Shipman. 1992. *The Neanderthals*. New York: Alfred A. Knopf.

Tyler, Gus, Editor. 1962. *Organized Crime in America*. Ann Arbor: University of Michigan Press.

Tylor, Sir Edward Burnett. 1958. *The Origins of Culture*. New York: Harper Torchbooks. Originally published in 1871 as *Primitive Culture*.

U.S. Department of Justice, Bureau of Justice Statistics. 1991. *Sourcebook of Criminal Justice Statistics*. Washington, D.C.: Government Printing Office.

U.S. Department of Justice, Federal Bureau of Investigation. 1994. *Crime in the United States*. Washington, D.C.: U.S. Government Printing Office.

Unnithan, N. Prabha, Lin Huff-Corzine, Jay Corzine, & Hugh P. Whitt. 1994. *The Currents of Lethal Violence*. Albany, New York: State University of New York Press.

Van Gennep, Arnold. 1960. *Rites of Passage*. Translated by M. K. Vizedom and G. L. Caffee. Chicago: University of Chicago Press. Originally published in 1908.

Vecoli, Rudolph J. 1995. *Gale Encyclopedia of Multicultural America*. Volume I. New York: Gale Research Inc.

Vetter, Harold J. & Ira J. Silverman. 1986. *Criminology and Crime*. New York: Harper & Row.

Von Hentig, Hans. 1948. *The Criminal and His Victim*. New Haven: Yale University Press.

Voss, Harwin L. & John R. Hepburn. 1968. "Patterns in Criminal Homicide in Chicago." *Journal of Criminal Law, Criminology, and Police Science*, 59: 499-508.

Waldo, Gordon P. 1970. "The 'Criminality Level' of Incarcerated Murderers and Non-Murderers." *Journal of Criminal Law, Criminology, and Police Science*, 61: 60-70.

Wells, H. G. 1967. *The Invisible Man*. New York: The Heritage Press. (Originally published in 1897.)

White, J. 1991. *Terrorism: An Introduction*. Belmont, California: Brooks Kole.

Whitney, Phyllis A. 1976. "Gothic Mysteries." In John Ball, *The Mystery Story*, Del Mar California: University Extension, University of California at San Diego.

Wilson, Colin & Donald Seaman. 1983. *Encyclopedia of Modern Murder, 1962-1982*. New York: Putman.

Wilson, Colin. 1972. *Order of Assassins*. London: Rupert Hart-Davis.

Wilson, Colin. 1984. *A Criminal History of Mankind*. New York: G. P. Putman's Sons.

Wolfgang, Marvin E. 1957. "Victim-Precipitated Criminal Homicide." *Journal of Criminal Law, Criminology, and Police Science*, 48: 1-11.

Wolfgang, Marvin E. 1958. *Patterns in Criminal Homicide*. Philadelphia: University of Pennsylvania Press.

Wolfgang, Marvin E. & Franco Farracuti. 1967. *The Subculture of Violence: Towards an Integrated Theory of Criminology*. London: Tavistock.

Wolfgang, Marvin E. 1970. *Crime and Race*. New York: Institute of Human Relations Press.

Wolfgang, Marvin, E. & M. Zahn. 1984. "Homicide: Behavioral Aspects." In S. Kadish, Editor. *Encyclopedia of Crime and Justice*, New York: Free Press.

Yarvis, Richard M. 1991. *Homicide*. Massachusetts: Lexington Books.

Zahn, Margaret A. and Mark Bencivengo. 1974. "Violent Death: A Comparison Between Drug Users and Nondrug Users." *Addictive Diseases: An International Journal*, September: 283-96.

Zahn, Margaret A. 1980. "Homicide in the Twentieth Century United States." In James A. Inciardi & Charles E. Faupel. *History and Crime*, Beverly Hills, California: Sage Publications.

ABOUT THE AUTHORS

Thomas Conway Esselstyn

Esselstyn graduated from Hobart College in 1934 with honors in history and spent six years as social work with juvenile delinquents and felons in New York City. In 1940 he was inducted into the army and served in the South West Pacific, the Philippines, Japan, and the United States, discharged as a Lieutenant Colonel. He received an MA in 1947 and Ph.D. in 1952 in sociology and area studies from New York University. Esselstyn served as an assistant professor of sociology at the University of Illinois and staff director of the United States Board of Parole in Washington, D.C. He accepted a professorship of sociology at San Jose State University retiring as emeritus. He authored twenty articles in criminology and corrections.

Alvin Rudoff

Rudoff served with the Marines in World War II and the Korean War. He graduated from the University of Southern California with a B.A. in Psychology *cum laude* and an M.A. in Social Studies. He married in 1949. He served as Parole Agent and in a state prison for the California Department of Corrections. He received the Ph.D. in Sociology from University of California, Berkeley. He taught at San Jose State University and served as Department Chairman. He is presently an Emeritus Faculty. He also taught at Berkeley, Chinese University of Hong Kong, and University of Maryland overseas campus. He obtained a research associate at the Advanced Planning section at NASA during a sabbatical. Rudoff has published several books, monographs, journal articles, and government reports.

INDEX

A

B

C

G

H

I

J

K

L

M

N

O

P

R

S

T

U

W

Y

Z